To Toni's
BARBER SHOP

From
"The Poet"
Thomas Kruger

The Poet
On the Wings of the Wind

by

Thomas Kruger

PITTSBURGH, PENNSYLVANIA 15222

ISBN: 978-1-4349-9761-6
Printed in the United States of America

First Printing

For more information or to order additional books, please contact:
RoseDog Books
701 Smithfield Street
Pittsburgh, Pennsylvania 15222
U.S.A.
1-800-834-1803
www.rosedogbookstore.com

To God be the glory.

Silly Sally

Silly Sally
Sat upon a sycamore stump,
Right into some sycamore
Yucky, sticky, gooey, oozy gunk

Like super glue it held her there
As it clung to the backside of her lap,
Then suddenly she realized
There was more there than sycamore sap

For Silly Sally
When sitting upon that sycamore stump,
Got a sycamore sliver
In her rump

And up Silly Sally did jump
Up from that old sycamore stump
And pulled that sycamore splinter
From her rump

Sill Sally's setter
Was sore,
And upon that sycamore stump
Silly Sally sat no more

The Rock

The bible, the written word of God
Is alive within the folds of it's pages,
Unfailing promises, indelibly inscribed
Tested and proven down thru the ages

It is our guide book for living
It is the most fantastic amazingly true story,
About the creation and the creator
Our most Holy Lord God of glory

The Rock
It is the foundation on which we build faith,
It is the map, the guide book that shows us the way
To our savior, Lord God of grace

O' For a thousand tongues
To sing and shout his praises,
O' To be enfolded into his everlasting arms
For all the trials that face us

O' For the faith that moves the mountains
O' For faith as that of a mustard seed,
O' For the faith that the God of grace
Will meet our every need

You have not because you ask not
God says: ask and you shall receive,
All things, god says all things
Are possible to those who believe

He is the Rock
On which we've built our faith,
Steady, unmoveable, and unshakeable
The Holy Lord God of grace

Half a Pair

I've lost a sock
I know not where,
All I know is
I've only half a pair

I've looked high
And I've looked low,
I know not where
My sock did go

I know that when I put on socks
I put on two,
It doesn't make any sense to wear just one
Two's just right and one's to few

I don't go around with one sock on
And one foot bare,
Now what could have happened
To half of my pair?

I've looked in the washer and the dryer
And in my sock drawer too,
I've looked and I've looked
Where it's at I have no clue

Where O' Where
Has my little sock gone?,
Hey I think that would make a good title
For a song

I believe on a milk carton
I'll put my sock's picture,
I may have lost my marbles too
Of that, I'm not to sure

High on Life

The days of living off the land are in the past
Of setting a mile stretch of victor traps in muskrat runs,
Of hunting pheasants and quail over a good bird dog
Of owning several old reliable guns

The old trusty 97 Winchester
Was the all around best of the lot,
A 12 gauge with modified choke, slide action, and exposed
hammer
I couldn't begin to account for all the game it's got

Then there's the bolt action single shot Winchester
410 model 41,
That's taken more squirrels
Than any other gun

And there is the great times of hunting waterfowl
Over a couple dozen bluebill decoys,
Huddled up in a cattail blind
With a couple other good ole boys

And ice fishing
Setting on an old wooden box,
Spudding a 7" hole
And wearing heavy clothes and 3 pair of soxs

Mushroon'n and frog'n
And dry fly fishing with a fiberglass wonderrod,
Surrounded by virgin woods and open fields
And the uncluttered beauty created by God

This was my boyhood of wonder and excitement
Growing up in a time of living off the land,
We were low on money but High on Life
In a time when life was O' So grand

God's Best

To walk out on ice crystal clear
And hear it's thunderous roar,
As freezing ear splitting cracks
Unravel and travel from shore to shore

Falling symetric shapes
God's white diamonds of shimmering light,
Moonbeams and stardust
Set ablaze these sparkles of sheer delight

Giant puffs of fluffy white clouds
Floating lazily across Robin Egg Blue Skys,
Shimmering blue pools
Reflecting mirror images back to awestruck eyes

Hot summer days
Warm refreshing showers,
Strawberries and rassberries
And rainbow colored flowers

The beauty of autumn leaves
Transluscent rainbows,
Hiking, camping, and fishing
And canoeing winding river flows

Fireflies moon us
With blinking butt lights,
Treefrogs and bull frogs
Peep and rumble throughout the hot summer nights

Going for a swim, getting a tan
Being outside for any excuse or reason
Just enjoying life to the fullest
God's Best of every season

The Blood on the Lintel

Upon the midnight hour
The death angel passed throughout Egypt land,
Searching out and destroying the first born
Of every beast and man

The only escape
From this rider of the pale horse, was the blood of the lamb
On the lintels
And on the side posts of the doors

There is another day coming
A great and wonderful day,
A day when the saints of god through out the world
Will be suddenly whisked away

This time he is not coming for the first born
But for all who have been born again,
For all the faithful throughout the world
Who have claimed him as Savior, Lord, and God, and friend

He is coming with clouds
Clouds of loved ones who have gone on before,
Our passover
The Blood on the Lintel of heaven's door

A Sense of Humor

I believe that a sense of humor is vital to life
And that there is at least a smidgen in each of us,
And that a warm friendly smile will melt the coldest heart
And that laughter is contageous

If it tickles your fancy
Let out a giggle,
Loosen up the old funny bone
And chuckle a little

Come on
If it strikes you funny let it roar,
Don't hold back, let it go
Laugh till you can laugh no more

Get a new lease on life
Give a few ho-ho's,
Let that belly jiggle
And forget your woes

A Sense of Humor is a lot of fun
Come on and give it a try,
Laugh until your belly hurts
Laugh until you cry

Best Friend

Jim and barb have been our friends
For almost fifty years,
Barb has asked me to write something
As Jim's time with us drew near

Barb you didn't have to ask
Jims been on my mind since we learned of the cancer,
And I wanted to write my feelings down
As we all prayed for this cancer's cure

Jim and I worked together for many years
And over that time we became not only good friends,
But best friends

We hunted and fished together
And spent many and most of our new years eves with one another,
We camped, we played cards
Jim was a friend that was closer than a brother

These last two years we planned and took our vacations together
Friendship that lasts that long has got to be true,
Jim you were my best friend
And I'm going to be lost without you

Best friends are hard to come by
And they cannot be measured in years alone,
I know it was so hard for family and friends to let Jim go
As the angels came to take him home

I know for sure, for God has promised
We will see Jim again,
Our love goes with you beyond heaven's gate
So long for now my friend

Written for the best friend I ever had

Put your Hand in His

Why have we fallen in love with stuff
That rots, corodes, and rusts?,
The world's treasures
And it's many enticing lusts?

Our lord offers us eternal rewards
Of everlasting love,
Treasures that fade not away
In his kingdom up above

If we spend each day
Filling our own selfish desires,
How then shall we escape
Hell's unquenchable damnation fires?

Jesus is reaching out
His desire is that none be lost,
Reach for heaven's gold
And forsake this world's dross

Joy and peace and love
Are the greatest of all treasures,
These all await the repentant soul
Who chooses Jesus over worldly pleasures

His hand is reaching out today
Won't you Put your Hand in His?,
Follow where he leads
And be a reflection of all that he is?

There is no greater treasure
Than that which god has to give,
Put your hand in his
And live

The Miracle of Springtime

The land is a-thirst
The doves coo for rain,
God responds and opens the heavens
And gives us the miracle of spring

Woodducks spook from every pond and puddle
Turtles line half submerged logs,
Dragonflies flit through the air
Snatching mosquitos from the stagnant bogs

The forest's floor becomes a carpet of flaming colors
The redbuds and the dogwoods blossom and bloom,
Mayapples open their giant umbrellas
The jack in the pulpit appears and up pops the mushroom

Pussy willows and crabapples
Add their vibrant colors to this beautiful scene,
As the miracles of springtime
Turns winter's drab world into glorious shades of green

The earth breaks forth in abundance of life
Beautiful butterflies emerge from cocoons,
The ponds respond with the chirping of frogs
And the wrens add their gay little tunes

The earth is being sumptiously arrayed
As only God could adorn,
For through him her fertile womb is opened
And his Miracle of Springtime is born

The Springtime of Everlasting Life

Springtime is like a breath of fresh air
As it brings new life upon the land,
It's almost like being born again
And being touched by Jesus's hand

Summeritme brings the earth to it's full strength
As a man who is rooted and grounded in the words of god's book,
As a tree whose roots go down deeper and deeper
Nourished to life by an undergound brook

The frost brings beautiful changes to the trees
In the colorful transforming of their leaves,
So does old age bring beauty to the golden years
Of the soul who trusts and believes

Silver lines the hair
As frost upon the ground,
As we look upon the outward aging beauty
Of the souls that are heaven bound

As the trees shed their beautiful leaves
And all is buried in crystals of snow that glistens in the light,
So shall we put off our outer covering
To be clothed in robes of white

As springtime brings upon this earth
The breath of new life,
So the inner man is renewed daily
In all who trust in Christ

We anticipate with all joy
Of Christ's coming to take us home,
Home to a place where we shall stand in awesome wonder
Of the beauty spread out before god's throne

Home to a city
Whose maker and creator is Jesus Christ,
A place where we shall forever dwell
In the springtime of everlasting life

Millenium

Death descended upon the earth and walked the streets of Egypt
Killing the first born within every abode whose doorways were
Not marked by the blood of the lamb,
Thus displaying both the wrath and the mercy
Of the great and only God "I am"

God who is not a respector of persons
Smote with death the firstborn of the slave to the firstborn
Of the hard hearted pharoah,
Only those who had placed their trust in the blood of the lamb
Were able to escape that terrible woe

There is another time coming
And we shall rejoice in that hour,
When God shall once again
Display his awesome power

The Angel of the Lord will descend from heaven
And bind Satan with a great chain,
Casting him into the bottomless pit and setting a seal upon him
And thus shall be the begining of Christ's Millenial reign

There will be no remembrance of sin, nor sickness, nor sorrow
Retained within the hearts of man,
Satan will not be loosed for a thousand years
And peace shall predominate and permiate the land

Love will descend upon the earth
It will be so heavy and so strong you'll be able to see it
And smell it, and feel it,
It will penetrate every living thing
Warmth of peace and vibrance of joy shall be the fruits of it

The trees will sing and the hills will jump for joy
And the rocks shall cry Hossanna's to the King,
As all of mankind rejoices
In the glorys of Christ and his Millenial reign

Home

Indiana is where I roam
North Webster is where I call my home,
Out back, on top of plowed ground
Indian arrowheads are still to be found

Tri. Co. Game reserve is near by
Where there are clear waters to reflect the sky,
Quiet and peaceful, with green hills and calm lakes
Also deer and pheasant and rattlesnakes

A place to gather mushrooms in the spring
And apples in the fall
And nuts, and puffballs, and that's not all

You can fish and hunt and hike
And travel them dusty dirt roads on a bike
And even rest and loaf if you like

The rest of the state is beautiful too
There's rivers, beaches, and lakes for you,
Also Brown Co., spring mill, and turkey run
And a lot of other places to camp and have fun

So keep this in mind
That you will never find,
No matter where in the world you roam
Any place quite like home

A Summer Nightmare

Things that go bump in the night
And keeps you awake in a terrible-fright,
Deer flies buzz and bite and drive you insane
The mud and mess that comes with the rain

Whiskers a grow'n all over your mug
You open your mouth and swallow a bug,
The weather's so hot your backside gets galded
You spill your tea water and get yourself scalded

In the dark spot in the cool of shade
You step in the mess your buddy has made,
Poison ivy, poison oak, poison sumak too
The nettles you wiped on because the leaves were to few

Clouds of mosquitos looking for something to chew
And the only thing available that's chewable is you

When the last of daylight begins to fade
And the mosquitos from the swamp begin to invade,
And you remember you forgot your can of raid

You itch and you scratch and are in such pain,
You can hardly wait until next year for vacation again

Old Black Joe

An endangerd species
The crows fly high and free,
They roost in groves of tall pine trees
And post lookouts called sentrys

Crows are real smart, I'll give em that
As memories of hunting them all comes back,
I used to talk to them, and them to me
When they were considered pests, all across the country

They would move in just before spring
And I would grab my shotgun, and do my thing,
They would see me coming from a-far
I think they even recognized my car

For me they had great respect
When they seen me coming, they'd hit the deck,
And go off screaming in trembling fear
And tell their brothers that I was here

With decoys and a call, I could bring them down
An old black Joe would hit the ground.
Then I would call the others in close
And pull up old ninety seven and give'm another dose

Sometimes they would fly in without a sound,
So you got to be alert, and keep looking around

Then I would call, and they'd come in
They'd look down where the sound had been,
A think'n I'm one of their kin
And I'd give em hell all over again

Sometimes one will come in quiet and low
And I move my gun up kind of slow,
And chalk up one more wily crow

Then one would fly over just above a tree
And he would look down and see me,
And old ninety seven's big black eye
Pointed in his direction, towards the sky

He would flap his wings and squawk and fuss
And them old black feathers would turn to dust,
As I recall with fond memories
Of hunting that ole black cuss

Bluegill Grandad

With an eagle eye
I flipped that fly
Where I figured they was hid,
Them bluegill grandads
Right up a-mid
Two big lilly pads

There was a small swirl
And my line began to curl,
As he sucked that bug
And started to tug

The line sang across the water
It sounded like a bullet,
Then he really began to fight
As he started to pull it

Lord this is a big one
I've got no doubt,
As I stood up in the boat
And began to shout

He started to churn up the lake,
As I swung around
And looked at his wake

A bluegill it was
As big as could be,
And a whole lot of line
Between him and me

I fought him for an hour
Or maybe it was two,
He finally gave in
But I did too

Lord what a fight we had
Me and that old bluegill grandad

I removed him from the hook
And thanked him for the fight,
As I put him back in the water
And watched him swim out of sight

Little but Mighty

With the strength of faith
And the determination to be free,
This small but mighty nation
Has gone down in history

To be the strongest in the world they say
America, the good old U.S. of A.
Freedom and religion are the greatest things in life
To able to worship in our own way, God's son Jesus Christ

People moved to America
In their great search to be free,
They fought and bled and died
To defend our little country

For what they have done here
We have the right to shout,
For their belief in God
Is what it's all about

If we lose our faith
In our Lord Jesus Christ,
We also lose our freedom, our strength.
And our way of life

The Good Old Days

I love to hear the old timer, tell'n of the old ways
Recollect'n them with fond memories as the good old days
The days of corn liquor in corked up jugs
And out houses and thunder mugs

The old victrola runn'n down
Making a weird and funny sound,
Tin lizzys and high button shoes
And crank telephones to spread the news

Boot leg whiskey, and smoke'n corn silk
And a horse drawn wagon deliver'n the milk,
Everyone sitt'n around the radio
Listen'n to all them storys they loved so

Ice boxs in every home
Elliot ness and al capone,
Silent movies ran supreme
Along with hot dogs, crackerjack, and home made ice cream

Penny candy and jelly beans
And Orville and Wilber and their flying machine,
Al Jolson and Rudy Valley
Black bottom and tin pan alley

Bussels and Corsetts and Bloomers
And the local pub spread'n all the rumors,
And steam engines smoke'n down the track
And on and on
As yesterdays memories all come back

Big Ole Bucket Mouth Hog

I got up this morning about half awake
And jumped in the boat and went out on the lake,
Then I got one big surprise
As I looked down in the water, I just couldn't believe my eyes

There was an old bucket mouth hog
Lazily laying under a half sunken log,
That was the biggest bass that I had ever seen
I rubbed my eyes, I thought it was a dream

I throwed a bait at that big so and so
And he picked it up and started to go,
I pulled, and yanked, and set the hook
And he came out of the water and wallowed and shook

Then he went to the bottom and back to the top
And I was begining to wonder if I could land him or not,
Lilly pads were being cut off by my fast moving line
As it ran across the water with a zinging whine

I fought and tugged and began to sweat
And he came out of the water and got me all wet,
Then he came along side and I thought he was done
The fight was over, and I thought I had won

I grabbed for the net, and as I turned back around
That big ole bass was no where to be found,
Just when I thought he was finally mine
He really started pulling out line

This was his last chance for freedom
He had to shake that hook,
Then I horsed him to hard
And that's all that it took

The line snapped and the bass was free
And a good warm feeling came over me,
I was kind of glad that he had got away
That big ole bass that I hooked that day

It was the biggest bass that I ever saw yet
And he gave me excitement that I'll never forget,
That big ole bass that got away from me
Swims again, wild and free

Cherished Moments

In a wilderness camp rests a contented man.
As spring spreads it's beauty all across the land

Hot bisquits, butter, and strawberry jam,
And filleted fish frying in the pan

Sky blue lakes and green meadows,
And the warm west wind gently blows

Drinking cold water from a natural spring,
And listening to the little birdies sing

Gazing upwards towards the sky,
Watching white puffy clouds float by

Nothings complicated, it's just the way you like it,
Everythings peaceful, beautiful, and quiet

Picking wild strawberries from amongst the flowers,
Daydreaming and loafing for hours and hours

Sleeping next to the fading firelight,
Occasionally waking up and listening to the sounds of the night

What a beautiful feeling you get out here.
Where God draws you O' So near

It makes you feel like part of the land,
Endless and timeless as the shifting sand

Like God has given you this place and time,
And you stand there in the breeze like a lonesome pine

Enjoying life and all that it'll give,
Cherishing these moments as long as you live

To Save a Buck

Unhappy, bored, and all alone
The little women set to home,
Rabbit season widows, neglected sportsman's honeys
While the beagles are a beller'n after bounce'n bunnies

This is our winter sport, our outdoor fun
A watch'n them old rabbits run,
Constantly on the go
A track'n them bunnies through the snow

A tromp'n through the briar patch
A look'n for a rabbit to catch,
Then the big brave hunter returns, dead on his feet
A carry'n a couple of shot up bunnies to eat

He figures with any luck, that he saved a buck
But he ain't a figure'n the gas and shells and guns and gear,
And the wear and tear on his truck

The little woman done some figering
And she said,
This has got to cease
Them bunnies cost us forty bucks a piece

For that much money we should have a feast
You could have at least,
Shot us a cow
Or some other big beast

The Light

A lost soul
Wandering in the night,
Searching, searching
But never finding light

There are no dark spots
Or shadows where you can hide,
For no matter where you are
Jesus is by your side

Why do you keep on walking
In the shadows of the night?,
Give your life to Jesus
And step out into the light

Give your life a goal,
Search for Jesus
And he will cleanse your soul

Jesus is the light,
Give your life to him
And end your search tonight

Today

Give me strength for the day O' Lord
To do your will in all things,
For who knows what sorrows or joys
Your tommorow brings

I Seek a Place of Peace

When I think of freezing rain
Or sickness, or pain,
Or heartaches and sorrows
And many other things

I think of heaven
And what it will be like there,
Peace and contentment
With no more troubles to bare

This thought alone
Would make me change my life,
To inherit a spot in heaven
And be with Jesus Christ

For this cruel world
Is full of pain and tears,
And I seek a place of peace
For all my eternal years

Jesus is my comfort
As I walk this earth today,
And he does ease my burdens
When I take them to him and pray

For the rest of my life
My happy heart will sing,
For the peace and joy that is to come
With Jesus Christ the King

When My Little Girl Crys

My childs broken heart
When her little dog dies,
And those big ennocent tears
That pour out of her eyes

It hurts me so
Oh God what can I say?,
Give me the words
Or show me the way

Oh lord she needs comfort
And so do I,
For it pulls at my heart
To hear my little girl cry

You have not always promised
Sunshine and blue skys,
But I pray to you now Lord
As my little girl crys

Please stop this pain
And give her comfort to endure,
For she loves you dear Jesus
And I know you love her

When my little girl crys
A part of me dies,
And I pray once again
For those beautiful blue skys

Give us the comfort
Of a brighter tomorrow,
To ease the pain
Of this heartbreaking sorrow

Dear father I pray
Let her smile Again,
Open her heart
And let the son shine in

Of Days Long Gone By

I Remember of days long past
Walking down a country lane,
And feeling those big warm drops
Of a gentle summer rain

O' Those beautiful days of summer
Of Days Long Gone by,
Of running through green meadows
Beneath a bright blue sky

Summer and outdoor fun
Seemed to go had in hand,
As I went chasing after rainbows
And walked barefooted in the sand

Going fishing
Using a string and a bent pin
And a tree limb for a pole,
And those lazy days of skinny dipp'n
Down at the ole swimm'n hole

I keep thinking back
As I walk that memorable country lane,
Of childhood days
And of playing in the rain

Those were the days
My youthful days that I loved so,
Precious beautiful memories
Of days of long ago

Me and My Tree

The rain and the sun
Which God gives free,
We both need
Me and my tree

When the sun gets hot
I've got it made,
As I lay there
In my big tree's shade

We grew up together
I grew and inch and it grew a limb,
And my big tree protected me
From the sun and the wind

In the fall of the year
It's leaves turn red,
And it starts to sleep
As though it were dead

My big tree's beauty
Spreads across the sky,
As it's beautiful red leaves
Go floating by

People are going to think
I'm really out of my tree,
Writing this kind
Of weird poetry

But you had better not tease me and my tree
Because my tree is ready to fight,
But just between you and me
It's dark is worse than it's bite

Very strange poetry
This is true,
But don't you secretly wish
You had a tree to

A Special Place to Pray

I climbed a hill in the wilderness
And stood on a grassy spot amongst the trees,
Surrounded by unspoiled beauty amoungst the birds and the
flowers

A place of tranquil peace

A beautiful spot, a beautiful day,
I had found my sanctuary
My special place in which to pray

What undescribable beauty
This spot, this day, this moment
That God has given to me,
A time to think, a place to pray
Alone, just God and me

To Alice - My Valentine

You're probably expecting
A perty paper valentine,
And fancy loving words
In a mushy rhyming line

Or a big expensive present
Or some poetic goo,
But I will be giving
None of these to you

Sweets would rot your teeth
And cars cost to much,
And I would have to break your leg
To present you with a crutch

I would give you the moon and stars
But these belong to God,
So I wonder if you would settle
For a broken fishing rod

I have one thing left
This little heart of mine,
Would you accept this gift
For a proper valentine

I will throw in all my love
And my fishing pole too,
For these are all my treasures
And I will give them all to you

If I was a knight in shining armour
I would give you a palace,
And I would battle dragons for you
My dear sweet Alice

But all I've got to give is my love
(The fishing pole is just a loan),
But I also give to you
This crazy goofy poem

      With Love
        From your Hubby

The Terror of the Night

He rides on the wings of the night
Death is beneath his shadow,
Murder is in his flight
As terror spreads below

He glides without a sound
Seeking out his victim,
His eyes searching along the ground
As he lights upon a limb

The great horned owl
The king of the sky in the night,
He kills for the love of killing
And puts all that's in the woods afright

With eight mighty talons
He pierces his victim through,
Splattering their blood
In the grass and the morning dew

Dying screams
Shatter the stillness of the night,
As another victim falls
To that terror on a deadly flight

Who Am I?

You created the world
And all of the life there in,
What is man Lord
That you are mindful of him

Lord, how great thou art
Thou, in thy holy trinity,
The creator of the heavens
Which stretch forth far into infinity

You created the mountains
And the endless sea,
Who am I Lord
That you are mindful of me?

Through thy spirit thy glory can be felt
Deep down in one's heart,
And by the heaven's and earth thy glory can be seen
O' Father, how great thou art

You spoke
And the world came to be,
You spoke again
And great mountains raised up out of the sea

O' Lord
Who am I,
That you are mindful of me?

Death is Not the Answer

You say you've tried it all
And your ready to die,
Well don't give up yet brother
Until you've given God a try

He will wash away your sin
That's rotting within,
And give you a clean slate
So you can start life again

He will never leave thee
Nor forsake thee
You shall never again be alone,
He will guide you through your valley
Your deepest darkest valley
Into the glorious light of his throne

For his life giving word
You will hunger and thirst,
And you will eat and drink
Until you think you will burst

And you will go to church
Craving even more,
And one after the other
God will open each door

He answers your prayers
And gives you blessings each day,
Now I tell you dear brother
There is no better way

And he will dwell with you and in you
All of your days,
And heaven's treasures will be yours
If you would but follow in his ways

There is no love greater
Than what God has to give,
So reach out dear brother
And live

The Only Way

If the human mind
Could but grasp the thought,
Of the price
For which his freedom was bought

And that life on earth
Is but a passing moment,
And eternity will be spent in the bliss of heaven
Or hell's everlasting torment

Jesus died
This is true,
But what you've got to know and believe
Is that he died for you

And God raised him from the dead
And he lives today,
And through him is salvation
And there is no other way

Mother Mary, Blessed By God

There was one Mother
That was a Mother extraordinary
The beloved Mother of Christ
The blessed Virgin Mary

Among women
Mary was pure,
And God in every phase of his glory
Honored her

The Father favored her
The holy ghost overshadowed her and filled her with child,
And that child was Jesus Christ,
No other woman was blessed like Mary
Nor ever will be again
Throughout the existance of life

She was a Mother extraordinary
Her heart was pure with faith,
She was the blessed virgin
To whom God gave his favor and grace

She brought to flesh upon this earth
The creator of all things,
For there was born to her "The Messiah"
The eternal King of Kings

He Is

He is the awesome power
That holds the heavens in place,
He is the loving savior
Who gives us life through grace

He is the helping hand
That reaches down to help you out,
When you start to sink in the murky depths
Of worldly fear and doubt

Through the darkest cloud
He comes shining through,
For he is the light of heaven
And he is also the light in you

Uncondemned Pride

Let your light so shine before you
In the presence of all men,
For to be proud of the gifts that God has given
Is not the pride of sin

God given talents
Are a glory to behold,
Through music, song, and poem
His life giving word may be told

What God has given to you
Do not try to hide,
Let your light shine out
In uncondemned pride

A candle you are
In a dark world, burning bright,
Shining out to others
Reflecting God's life giving light

Be proud of your talent
For this is not the pride of sin,
What God has given to you, be proud to use
To honor and glorify him

The House of the Lord

There is no place so dear to me
There is no place I would rather be,
Except for heaven's beautiful eternity
Than in the Lord's house of prayer

To be with the members of the body of Christ
As the minister rightly divides
The word's of life
In the Lord's house of prayer

The blessings of worshiping with others
To be with the faithful
Sisters and brothers
In the beautiful house of prayer

Trials are easier to bare
When you are with people that really care,
In the Lord's
House of prayer

With all of our liberty
In this land of the free,
There is no place on earth that I would rather be
Than in the Lord's beautiful house to prayer

Concerning Spiritual Gifts

My brother does err from the truth
Misleading many into the paths of destruction,
I pray that God will open his eyes
To a brother's love and righteous instruction

Do not wrestle with the scriptures
But grow in the grace and knowledge of Christ,
Dig into the meat of the truth
Into the perfect wisdom of the words of life

Take nothing out of context, add nothing to
And do not take anything away from, God' printed word's of life,
There are no contradictions
There is but one truth, one baptism
For there is but one Christ

This is God's word
The word of life,
This is the word that was made flesh and dwelt among us
And is known to the world as the Christ

Love, cherish, and obey God's word
And learn of it's truth through the guidance of the holy spirit,
And rejoice and praise God for this glorious wisdom
That you receive when you read it and hear it

My hand is stretched out to my brother in Christ
I beseech you dear brother, reach back and put your hand in
Mine,
For we are all members of the body of Christ
And we were made lights that his glory may shine

Your gift is the tongue
Mine is the hand,
As we have received from the holy spirit
Of the different gifts he gives unto man

I write poems with pen and ink
Glorious praises to his name,
You raise your voice in a heavenly tongue
Praising him and his power, and glory, and fame,
Our gifts differ
But I beseech you dear brother to know
That our giver is the same

God's Church

Ye body of Christ, and members in particular
Respect the sabbaths and unite in truth and love,
Forsake not the assembling of yourselves together
To exalt the light and glory from above

You have been born into Christ and given new life
Through the son and the father who have made their abode
Withyou,
With the holy ghost you have been sealed
So be ye holy in all that you say and do

Be guided along life's path
Through the power of the holy spirit,
And let him guide you into all truths
Through his word as you read and hear it

Take no man's word for anything
Unless scripture proves it true,
And let these words be the guide for your life
In all that you say and do

The church is not a building
It is the members of the body of Christ,
It is those who live in spirit and truth
And have been sealed into eternal life

Jesus said: where two or more are gathered in my name
I am there,
You are the church, you are the body
You are the Lord's house of prayer

I do not dwell in buildings
Made by human hands,
I dwell in holy temples
Inside the hearts of man

Be firm in the faith
Let no man decieve you,
Try the spirits
And prove all things- whether they be true

There is one faith, one truth, and one baptism
And one Jesus Christ in whom we love and live,
And as we have received freely of him
Let us go forth and freely give

For we are God's church
We are Christ's light upon this earth,
Shining out his timeless message
Of salvation and new birth

Fire Up

Are you faithfully watching
By day and by night,
Anticipating Christ's return
In joyful delight

Or is your lamp flickering dim,
From your low flame within

Are you keeping your lamp full
And burning bright,
Filled with the oil
Of God's words of light

Or is it damaged by worldly fear and doubt,
Well if it is
Then I want to call your remembrance to the five virgins
Whose fires went out

They thought
There is yet time,
But the bridegroom came and went
And they were left behind

Fire up get hot,
For Christ comes
In a time you know not

Let him be the light out of your life
Let his flame within you burn,
As you anticipate with all joy
His glorious return

The Conversation

Hey buddy! you want some stuff to get high on?
"What have you got?"
You name it I've got it
"Have you got something I can stay high on all the time
Day and night?"
There ain't no such thing
"Oh yah! well I've got it"
Hey I want some of that, what's it called?
"It's called Jesus Christ"
Your putting me on
"No I'm not, with him I can face each day
And I can face eternity without fear"
They say you Christians have to give your lives to Christ
"Christ gave his life for us"
You've got all the answers haven't you?
"All of the answers are in God's book"
You mean the Bible?
"That's the place to look"
Ah! But Christ wouldn't have me
"Any that come unto him he will in no wise cast out"
But my sins are to many
"If there was one sin left unatoned for
Christ would still be in the tomb"
You mean he will forgive all of my sins?
"Though they be as scarlet, they shall be as wool"
I want your God to be my God
"Repent and be baptised calling on the name of the Lord
And your sins shall be washed in Christ's blood
And behold all things shall become new"
Hallelujah- praise the Lord, I've opened my heart
To let the son shine in

Outer Darkness

If it is the lust of the eyes and the pride of life
And worldly lusts that you choose,
Well brother, let me tell you now, tho you gain the world
Your soul you shall lose

Hell is a place where the maggot crawls
Constantly eating at the flesh,
Where the fire penetrates to the center of the soul
With a pain that's worse than death

Without Christ
You cannot escape it,
Your soul shall wallow forever
In Satan's slimy pit

In a darkness that is so deep
In penetrates the marrow and the bone,
A very crowded place
And yet you shall be desperately alone

There shall be weeping and gnashing of teeth
Hell's soul shall not find peace,
And there shall be pain beyond endurance
With never a moments relief

Lusts and cravings that can never be fullfilled
Constantly plagueing the mind,
Where moments have no beginings and no endings
In eternity's circle of time

There is no friendship nor love in hell
It is a place that is filled with hate,
And when you close your eyes in death without Christ
You have chosen this eternal fate

Witness

When Christ comes to gather his elect
From sea to shining sea,
Lukewarmness is a state of being
In which we must not be

Let us be found watching
With our fires burning bright,
Looking to the clouds with joy
Awaiting heaven's light

Let us be found witnessing
Showing others the way,
That none be lost
Because of what we did not say

Do you want to be responsible
For a soul burning in hell,
Because of the salvation message
That you did not tell

Take the opportunities as they come
And witness of him,
For each passing moment is precious
And cannot be called back again

The blood of my savior is just as powerful today
As it was two thousand years ago,
And the undying faith in my risen Lord
Is the only power that will save a soul

He has not promised us a tomorrow
But he has given us this day,
Let us witness of the light that burns within
That others might find the way

Sing O' Saints, Sing

Forordained by the trinity of God
The redemption plans were laid,
And the horrors of the cross
Was part of those plans that they made

Cod incarnate
Born of a virgin womb,
Bore the cross for our offences
And for our justification was raised from the tomb

It is because Christ died
That we are justified,
And it is because he lives
That one day we shall be glorified

It is by the gift of grace
That we have an inheritance into eternal life,
Through the shed righteous blood
Of our Lord and Savior Jesus Christ

We cannot earn it
It is received by faith alone,
Faith in a risen savior
Who is coming one day soon to take us home

His love for us
Is the reason that he came,
And his second coming shall be joy
To all who trust his name

God so loved the world
That he gave his only begotten son,
That through him
The victory might be won

Sing O' Saints, sing
Of the glory due the name,
Of the lamb of God
Who to this dying world came

Awesome Wonder

A drab and dirty image appears
When winter's snow melts from off the scene,
But God quickly takes his miraculous touch
And paints a covering of cleansing green

The breath of spring
Awakens all that's in wintery sleep,
And penetrates the frost
To reach the slumbering seeds of the deep

All of life that had enjoyed this rest
Of winter's long long slumber,
Bursts through the ground to reach the light
In beautiful awesome wonder

God's beauty of spring is rolled out like a carpet
Before the astonished amazement of man,
Springing forth in abundance of life
In a spectacular display upon the land

Tree's buds brake forth into leaves
And birds open up for joy and sing,
And everywhere the flowers appear In
God's awesome wonder of spring

We faced the harshness if winter
With our hearts filled with the hope each day,
Knowing that the God of all creation
Would soon send spring our way

If Only

The Robins appear
And the little wrens sing,
Of the wonderous joys of spring

The ground opens up and adds it's beauty
Pushing forth flowers of yellow and blue,
While the green returns to the willow
And the frost to the morning dew

O' What beauty God has given to thee
O' Earth that is filled with sin,
O' But the beauty that could have been yours
Is more than I can comprehend

If Adam had not have fallen
O' What a poem this thought has inspired,
Of a perfect world in perfect peace
And in perfect beauty attired

A garden of Eden forever
Of peace and joy and love,
Receiving unending blessing
From the maker and creator above

The place where God walked in the cool of the day
O' Eden my thoughts go back to what you could have been,
And the springtimes that man could have experienced there
If only Adam had not of sinned

That Moment

The clouds came rolling in an I thought it was a storm
Then in their midst appeared something white,
It looked like as unto the son of man
A glorious angel of light

I felt weightless
As my feet left the ground,
I was moving through the air to meet the Lord
At the trumpet's triumphant sound

The Lord's arms were stretched out before me
He said" I have come to take you home,
Goose bumps formed all over me
As if ice water ran through my bones

The joys of that moment
Will be cherished throughout eternity,
Of that great reunion with those who had gone on before
Waiting in the clouds for me

Yes! There is a Hell

A certain rich man
So the bible does tell,
Died
And opened up his eyes in hell

Do not try to fool yourself
For there is such a place my friend,
And the gates thereof are opened wide
To receive all who foolishly enter therein

I am the way, the truth, and the life
This is what the God of love said,
But this same God of love is the God of wrath
Who small judge the quick and the dead

God has the books of judgement
And he has also the book of life,
To be found in the books is to inherit the lake of fire
But to be found in the book is to live forever with Christ

God made hell for Satan and the fallen angels
But it is also a place for all who choose to live in sin,
But thanks be to God through Jesus Christ we have eternal life
If we choose to follow him

Your will is your own, you have a choice
You must choose with whom you want to be,
But remember that the choice you make
Is for all of eternity

To those who choose God
He is the God of love,
But to all others
Comes only the wrath from above

Satan gives you the lust of the eyes
The lust of the flesh, and the pride of life,
But the doorway to heaven
Is Jesus Christ

Christ died on the cross for you
He paid the price for your sin,
He has opened the doors to heaven
But it is up to you to enter therein

The Work

Praise the God that parted the waters
Praise the God that made the seas,
Praise the God that created the mountains
For his redeeming work on Calvary

O' Holy God of heaven
O' How you must have loved us from on high,
To have given us your most cherished only son
To suffer the agony of the cross and die

He took our place
Those three nails were ours,
Crimson blood flowed from the hands
Of the creator of the earth and stars

It was for our sins
That he hung there,
It was for his love for us
He took our sins to bare

O' God of heaven, God of love
We thank you for our Lord and savior Jesus Christ
In that he drank of the cup and suffered the shame
That opened the door of life

I Shall Not Fear

The angel of the Lord encampeth around about those
Who fear and trust in him,
My trust is not in the arm of the flesh
But in my Lord who dwells within

His love has entered my soul
My Lord is ever near,
His perfect love
Casteth out all fear

My Lord is only a prayer away
He is closer than a brother
He is my strength
I will place my trust in no other

He is my light and my salvation
A very present help in time of need,
He is the strength of my life
Through whom my soul was freed

He has legions of angels and firey chariots
And all the powers from above,
I shall not fear what man can do
For I abide in my savior's love

The King

Make a joyful noise unto the Lord
Exalt his glorious name,
Tell the world of the wonderous works
Of Jesus Christ the King

He is heaven's glory
His name stands above all others,
And we who claim his name
In God's love are sisters and brothers

My soul in joy shall sing
Of the glory of the king,
My lips shall unceaseingly proclaim
The praises due his name

In him is salvation
His priesthood shall never cease,
Let us make a joyful noise
Unto the glorious prince of peace

Of his magnificent glory
In the great congregation let us continually shout,
Let all of God's children lift up their voices
As they leave their joy within ring out

The lamb of God is worthy
Let this be the song that we sing,
As we praise and give due honor
To Jesus Christ the King

The Increase

My thoughts are to youward Lord
All my day my heart is stayed on thee,
As I continually shed the tears of joy
For thy grace that set me free

You have called me by your word
And you have drawn me by your love,
You have taken my eyes off the treasures of this world
And have set my sights on things above

I shall not lean upon mine own understanding
I will trust in thee with all mine heart,
I will cease from my own wisdom
And I will not let thy words from- my soul depart

I will commit my works unto thee O' Lord
I will acknowledge thee in all my ways,
Looking to you to direct my paths
Resting my hope in thee all my days

My soul shall lean upon thy promises
I shall meditate upon thy word day and night,
And I shall faithfully bring to those that dwell in darkness
Your marvelous words of light

We plant dear Lord and water
But it is you that giveth the increase,
And of all the pleasures that are in the world
We know that it is only through you that a soul finds true peace

Place hungry souls across my path dear Lord
That I may take of thy words and witness of thee,
That my joy may be full in serving you
And of seeing your increase of souls set free

The Separation

As the just live among the unjust
So does the sheep with the goats,
And the tare grows amongst the wheat
But one day there shall be a great separation
When man appears before the judgement seat

All of man's going forths shall be made bare before God
There shall be nothing whatsoever hid,
That which was done in secret shall be declared from the
Housetops
Of all of the deeds that ever he did

The just from the unjust
God shall separate them as the day from the night,
The one he shall cast into outer darkness
And the other shall dwell in Christ's light

The dead shall be judged acording to their works
But no condemnation shall come to those in Christ,
And as the dead's inheritance is the lake of fire
So shall heaven be the inheritance for those found written in
The book of life

The tares shall be gathered, bundled, and burned
And the goats shall be separated from the sheep,
And whatsoever man has sown upon the earth
In that day he shall reap

All of time is fast coming to a close
As the great white throne judgement draws near,
But those that are sealed with the spirit of Christ
Of that time and judgement they need not fear

Some men's sins follow after them
And some go on before,
But we who have been washed in the blood of Christ
Are Christ's forever more

Make a Joyful Noise

The Lord loves the voice of the crow
As well as the sweet songs of the nightengales,
And his rewards are in direct proportions to our efforts
And not in whether we succeed of fail

I was glad when they said unto me
Let us go into the house of the Lord,
For together in the congregational assembly
We shall make a joyful noise unto the Lord

It does not matter whether our voice is that of the nightengales
Or that of the crows,
For it is the innermost intents of the heart that counts
And in this, only you and the God of heaven knows

So do your part
And God will do his,
As you cherish and use of the gifts
That he gives

Rejoice and make a joyful noise unto the Lord
With the voice of an angel sing unto our savior divine,
And if you do not have the voice of an angel, sing anyway
Even if you got a voice like mine

My Prayer

Fill me Lord with thy ever prescence
Reveal to me the deep shadows of thy word,
Take me to the very depths
Of the understanding of all that is heard

Damnable heresies are polluting thy truths
Satan is at work everywhere,
Give me the power to wipe out his lies
This father is my fervent prayer

In vain they worship you father
Teaching for doctrines the commandments of men,
For those that have been called and washed in Christ's blood
I pray that they be not yoked into bondage again

Dear father reveal to me thy truths
That by your living waters within,
I can bring them unto the wandering brothers
And in love lead them back again

The Christian Life

Have you repented and put your trust in the Lord
Do you bring honor to the Christian name?,
Do you witness of him to others
Declaring him as your savior and your king

Do you live by his commandments?
Do you study upon his word?,
Do you go to the holy book
To find the truths of what is heard?

Do you believe that he died for you?
And that he is risen and lives today?,
Do you acknowledge him in all of your ways
Do you daily kneel and pray?

Do you love thy Lord with all thine heart
Do you share this love with others?,
Are you treating god's children
As your sisters and your brothers?

In times of trouble
Do you truly trust in him?.
Do you believe that Christ's blood
Has washed away your sin?

Do you really care
What happens to your fellow man?.
When your neighbor is in trouble
Do you reach out a helping hand?

Are you rejoicing every day
For all that god has given?,
If so dear brothers keep it up
For this is the Christian life your live'n

The Fruit of the Spirit

Souls are in need of being saved
Shall they see Christians that bicker and fight?,
Or shall they see the joy and peace and love
Of United Christians reflecting Christ's light?

Christ is coming soon
And the fields are ripe to the harvest,
Let us labor together in the Lord of Love
That many more souls may enter into god's rest

Love thy neighbor as thyself
Expound to him of the prince of peace,
And trust God to the saving of the soul
As he adds the increase

Let Satan not have his way
For it is he that would have us divided,
But rather let us unite in truth through the Holy Spirit's guidance
By God's perfect way that he has provided

When you are truly born again you shall live for him
And you shall rejoice in his joys every day,
Being filled with the fruit of the spirit
And the light of heaven to guide your way

T. L. C.

A Mother is T. L. C.
That is Tender Loving Care,
And today throughout the churchs across the land
She is being honored in song and prayer

She is the one who patchs the wounds
Of skinned elbows and knees,
Of the little ones who run and fall
And tumble out of trees

My mother taught me my night prayers
Of now I lay me down to sleep,
She taught me that if I should die befor I wake
That my Lord would take my soul to keep

Mothers are wonderful
They give their very best to us,
And in return we give to them
Our devoted love and trust

She teachs us right from wrong
And that a spanking hurts her worse than it does us,
She fixs our meals and washs and irons our cloths
And does it all without a fuss

She sets a fine example
Of which we should follow every day,
Of doing things for others
Without expecting reward or pay

What is a mother
Of this I'm sure we'll all agree,
A mother is tender loving care
She is T. L. C.

Millenium

Death descended upon the earth and walked the streets of Egypt
Killing the first born within every abode whose doorways were
Not marked by the blood of the lamb,
Thus displaying both the wrath and the mercy
Of the great and only god " I Am"

God who is not a respector of persons
Smote with death the firstborn of the slave to the firstborn
Of the hard hearted pharoah,
Only those who had place their trust in the blood of the lamb
Were able to escape that terrible woe

There is another time coming
And we shall rejoice in that hour,
When God shall once again
Display his awesome power

The angel of the Lord will descend from heaven
And bind Satan with a great chain,
Casting him into the bottomless pit and setting a seal upon him
And thus shall be the begining of Christ's millenial reign

There will be no remembrance of sin, nor sickness, nor sorrow
Retained within the hearts of man,
Satan will not be loosed for a thousand years
And peace shall predominate and permiate the land

Love will descend upon the earth
It will be so heavy and so strong you'll be able to see it
And smell it, and feel it,
It will penetrate every living thing
Warmth of peace and vibrance of joy shall be the fruits of it

The trees will sing and the hills will jump for joy
And the rocks shall cry hossanna's to the king,
As all of mankind rejoices
In the glorys of Christ and his millenial reign

Thy Delight

Make studying upon God's word
Thy soul's delight,
And meditate thereon
Day and night

Study to show thyself approved unto God
A workman that needeth not to be ashamed,
Rightly dividing the words of truth
Proud to wear the christian name

Acknowledge him in all thy ways
Trust in him with all thine heart,
Fill thy soul with his words of light
And from thy remembrance let them not depart

Strive for perfection
Believe not all that is heard,
But through prayer and the Holy Spirit's guidance
Rightly divide God's word

Sleep upon it and awake to it
And give of it to others,
And trust in it's saving power
To gain you new sisters and brothers

Lean not upon thine own understanding
Cease from thine own wisdom,
And he shall entrust to you
The mysteries of his glorious kingdom

Change of Kings

Hey world I use to love you
But listen now, can't you hear my happy heart sing
I've been born again
I've become a child of the risen king

The glory of heaven now dwells in me
I forsake you world and all your ways,
My joy is now in the Lord of Lords
To him alone I give my praise

The ways of the world are the ways unto death
But I have found the way unto life,
I have found salvation by the grace of God
Through the blood of Jesus Christ

In peace I lay me down
In joy I awake and rise,
I forsake you world and your king
That deceiving father of lies

I am in you world
But you have no part in me,
For my Lord who dwells within
Has wonderously set me free

One day Christ shall set up his millennial reign
And that great deceiver shall be cast down and bound,
One day O' Dying world
Your king shall lose his crown

Hey world I use to love you
But no more, for now you see,
The light that shines in heaven
Now shines in me

God's Rest

The rapture is over
And the seven year tribulation has passed
And it is the beginning of Christ's millennial reign,
Satan has been bound
And there is no more cursing sound
As Christ dwells upon earth as her king

The hills jump for joy
The trees clap their hands
As the brook runs singing through the meadow,
Christ has restored the land as in the days of eden
And the thorn and the weed cease to grow

The lamb and the lion lay side by side
No more carnally stirred by the prince of the power of the air,
"Praise the Lord"
For his peace and joy that is everywhere

The mountains bow down and the valleys stand up
And the rocks cry hosannas to the king,
As all of creation sings out for the glory
Of Christ and his millennial reign

O'Rebelious Soul

Get in!, Get in!, Get in!
And do it soon my friend,
For that day is coming all to soon
When the day of grace shall end

Satan says: You've got plenty of time
Of that day and hour no man can tell,
Are you going to trust a murderer and a liar
Who would see your soul in hell

When the leaves begin to turn
You say that winter is neigh,
Well heed the signs of the times
Ye discerners of the sky

They scoffed to in Noah's day
As Noah poured out his soul to them,
So shall it be in these last days
That few shall enter in

Some shall say in that day
Wait!, Wait! Don't yet close the door,
For I will yet let you save my soul
After I've sinned just a little more

And God will say: you had your day
And now that day is done,
With all my love I reached out to you
I gave you my only son

When you rejected him you rejected me
O' Lost rebellious soul,
Now you shall be cast into the outer darkness
Of hell's eternal hole

The Bible Speaks

To the deaf I bring hearing
And to the blind I bring sight,
To those that are engulfed in darkness
I am the penetrating light

Lying scribed across my pages
And centered around Jesus Christ,
Enthroned within the walls of my covers
Lies the words of everlasting life

I am the truth
I am not to be added to nor taken away from,
Genesis is my begining
And with the completion of revelation I am done

I am the way
Follow me,
My words are the words of life
That were written to set men free

Yes the gospel of life is written across my pages
I am the never changing word of God
Standing firm down through the ages

They who feed their souls upon me
Shall hunger and thirst no more,
For I am the written word of God
I am the gateway to heaven's door

Feed upon me O' Hungry soul
And I shall satisfy thy longing heart's appetite,
For with the council of almighty God
I shall fill thy soul with light

Salvation is in my chambers
God's wisdom, knowledge, and understanding are within my fold,
I have hidden treasures
More precious than diamonds, rubies, and gold

In me is peace and joy
I dispel and wipe away all fear,
If you have doubts then open me up
For all doubts end here

The True Riches

In the eyes of the world a man is deemed poor
If he lacks earthly material possessions,
But I tell you that the man who has Jesus Christ does not lack
But is rich in God's promises and blessings

The rich man who trusts in his riches
Is the one who is really poor,
But the man who places his trust in Jesus Christ
Has found true riches door

For a rich man whose joy is in his riches
Cannot for all of his material wealth,
Buy salvation's joy, nor eternal life
Nor perpetual youth and health

But with God all things are possible
For he gives the more abundant life, not only hereafter but
Here and now,
But the rich man who trusts in his riches
Shall one day weep and howl

Where are your priorities
Are they in this world my friend?,
Look back to what God says of trusting in riches
And of that man's ultimate terrible end

If you want the true riches
Then herein is what you must do,
Seek you first the kingdom of God
And all these things shall be added unto you

Herein is where the true riches are
And therein is where you must go,
To the Lord and Savior Jesus Christ
Through whom all blessings flow

Let Your Light So Shine

Stand up for Jesus Christ
Let the world, through you, see his light,
Adorn the full armour, be a good soldier
Fight the good fight

Become a channel
Through which the love of Jesus flows,
Speak the words of comfort
That will lift the spirits of weary souls

Grow in grace and truth
And penetrate the darkness with Christ's light,
Bring to the dead and lost of this world
The eternal words of life

Satan may be the power of darkness
But into the light of Jesus he cannot enter in,
Satan connot enter the soul
Where Christ dwells within

Satan sends mighty tempests
To drown the souls of men,
But they whose trust is in the Lord
Shall ride out the storms with the calm of Jesus within

Let not Satan and his demons who are as the rocks and the waves
Shipwreck souls along your borders any more,
Like a beacon in the night let your light so shine
To guide souls towards the safe haven of heaven's peaceful shore

Agape Love

No one who receives it can hold it in
No human vessel could contain the fullness thereof,
For it is a river flowing with mercy and grace
It is the fountain of God's Agape love

Yes! Herein is God's love
Not that we loved him, but that he loved us,
For he gave us the most precious gift of all
When he gave us Jesus

O' A love so beautiful, so wonderful
And O' So grand,
That God would send his only begotten son
In the form of corruptible flesh likened as unto sinful man

These plans were perfect and complete
Nothing was left undone,
And the heaven's opened
And God through the Virgin Mary made manifest to the world
His only begotten son

The lamb of God would be the perfect sacrifice
An offering once and for all for all of sin for all of time,
Without blemish, without spot, without sin
He would take the wrath of God for all of mankind

God's love for us brought Christ to earth
Christ's love took him to the cross,
He came to a dying world
To save that which was lost

All of the punishments he suffered were ours
The shame, the thorns, the stripes, and the nails,
He and he alone could satisfy the wrath of God
Our Jesus never fails

For all who reject God's son
For all who miss the blessed hope of Christ's return,
God's grace and love shall turn to wrath
And the earth and all that is therein shall burn

Accept God's love
Escape the wrath which is to come,
Reach out now in trust and faith
And accept God's son

On The Wings of the Wind

The heavens and the earth are his
And all that is therein,
The clouds are his chariot
He rides on the wings of the wind

He has spread the stars as a curtain
He is wrapped in garments of light,
He has founded the foundations of the earth
He has set the boundarys for the day and the night

His eyes look to and fro upon the earth
He observes the goings forth of the children of men,
Before him is a consuming fire, his wrath is kindled
Woe to the inhabitors of the earth that are continueing on in their sin

The moon shall be turned black as sackcloth
And the sun shall fail to reveal her light,
The stars of heaven shall fall to the earth
And there shall be pestilence, plague, and blight

But before this great tribulation
God's glory shall be revealed in the sky,
All ye partakers of the blessed hope, rejoice and look up
For your redemtion draweth neigh

The resurection, the rapture, the blessed hope
The shout of the arch angel's triumphant cry,
For those whose hope is in Christ, they shall be lifted up unto Christ
In the twinkling of an eye

He is coming for all that are his
He is coming for all those that belong to him,
He is coming with clouds
Riding on the wings of the wind

The Resurrection Story

The stone rolled away before the door of the tomb
And upon it sat an angel of light,
And the guards became as dead men
For fear of this terrible sight

It was very early
Being yet before the dawn of the day,
When Mary came to the empty tomb
Wherein only the burial linens lay

The grave was bare
Christ was not there,
Where have they taken him?
Mary Magdalene cried out in anguishing despair

Then there appeared two angels
And this testimony to Mary they gave,
Look not amongst the dead for the living
For Christ has risen from the grave

Christ lives!
Death could not hold him,
He died for our sins
And then rose to life again

Our savior sets upon his throne
At the right hand of the father in glory,
And this is the bible's glorious account
Of the resurrection story

Circle of light

Make Jesus the joy of your life
And studying upon his testimonies thy soul's delight,
And as you grow in grace and in the knowledge of our lord
You shall walk in an ever widening circle of light

Apply God's revealed light into your life
And that circle's circumference will continually grow,
And rejoicing, plant it into the hearts of others
For these are god's precious seeds that you sow

Be not wise in thine own eyes
And depart from every evil way,
And the parables and the dark sayings in the depths of God's word
Shall be revealed as the light of the day

If you step out of this circle of light
You are no longer in the light, but in the dark,
For you are only wise in that revealed light
Which the holy ghost has placed within your heart

We must walk in that circle of light which we have
Ever increasing it's widening rim,
Ever shining out to others
Of everlasting life through him

If thine eye be single
And if it is fixed upon him,
Then you shall have an everwidening circle without
As you are filled with his light within

Your circle shall grow larger day by day
As in god's testimonies you continually delight,
And you shall rejoice in the blessings
Of an ever abundance of light

Walk in the Light

If your work and your pattern of living
Seems humdrum, boring, and drab
And life seems to be yielding very little reward,
What you need to do, is do all that you do
As though you are doing it unto the Lord

You will find joy and peace in this pattern for life
Which is described in detail in God's holy book,
Wherein are all of the answers to all of life's questions
For all who would open it up and look

You are to do all that you do, heartily as unto the Lord
This is what God's word tells you to do,
You are to obey God's word and enjoy his blessings
And in so doing, his peace and joy he gives unto you

Open up God's book of the word's of life
And let it's light be a lamp unto thy feet,
And let it guide you along life's path
And in the treating of all along the way that you meet

Walk in the light as he is in the light
In him is no darkness at all
And if you stand firmly anchored in him
You shall never fall

Live the Christian's life of victory
By faith and not by sight,
Live the holy life
By walking in the light

Midnight

Knowledge has increased
Man has walked upon the moon,
The chariots are jossling in the streets
Christ is coming soon

The book of truth
Foretold of these signs,
Which would be in the latter days
Of the end times

Put on the helmet of salvation
Gird thyself about with mercy and truth
Walk in the light,
Watch, work, and pray, for the day is far spent
And we are in that last minute approaching midnight

Fix your eyes upon Jesus
For all that are his need not fear,
Of the impending doom
Which is drawing near

The elects days upon earth shall be shortened
We that are Christ's shall not be left behind to face that midnight
hour,
For he shall come in the clouds and catch us away
And change and perfect us according to the working
Of his almighty power

Halleluah to the lamb of god
Who is worthy of all praise,
Who for the elects sake
Has shortened those days

Let us be vigilant
As we await Christ's return,
Filled with his light
And letting our lights burn

The night comes when no man can work
Let us reach the world of the lost while it is yet day,
Let us take the gospel of Jesus Christ
And show others the way

If you are yet in darkness
Stand up and step out for Jesus Christ and be filled
With his light,
For the time is fast running out
As the prophetical clock races towards midnight

Shine Forth His Glory

You are a light, you are a lamp unto the world
You are a part of the bright and morning star,
You are a ray of sunshine in the lives of others
You are a candle upon a candle stick, this is what you are

You shine forth with joy
With his joy, peace, and love,
As you are filled with the glory
Of the light from heaven above

You stand out unto the world
Your hands hold forth the words of life,
And as you bring joy unto others
You bring joy unto Christ

It is the God of love
Who has placed that sparkle in your eye,
This is the love that overcomes the world
This is the love that money can't buy

Jesus has made you all that you are
He has made you wondrfully grand,
An uncut diamond taking shape
Sparkling in the master's hand

Jesus Love

They talk of the tribulation
The false prophet, the dragon, and the beast,
But I have Jesus joy
And I have Jesus peace

They say : look down, the pits of hell are about to be opened
But I said : nay-but I shall look up, for my help cometh from above,
And I have that Jesus joy
And I have that Jesus love

They said: man ain't you scared
Isn't there anything that you're afraid of,
And I said: God alone do I fear
And whom I fear I love

I am saved from the wrath of god
Through the blood of Jesus Christ,
I who once abode in death
Now abide in life

I look unto the clouds
From whence my help shall come,
Anticipating the blessed hope
Of the appearing of god's son

I fear not the things coming upon the earth
My help cometh from above,
And I have that Jesus peace
And I have that Jesus love

The Eternal Question

Would you have your children to dwell forever
In hell's horrible abode,
All because the salvation story
Never to them was told?

Would you have your loved ones
To burn in the eternal flame,
All because they were denied the gospel
Of salvation through Christ's name?

Now the question that I ask is
Where will you spend eternity?,
Now make your decision wise,
Will you spend it with the God of love
Or in the lake of fire with the father of lies?

Would you choose hatred, hell, and pain
Which eternally shall never cease?,
Or will you choose to walk those golden streets
In joy, love and peace?

Only a fool chooses death
The wise man chooses life,
And that eternal joy can today be yours
Through the atoneing blood of Christ

Forsake your pride, forsake your lusts
And forsake all your worldly ways,
Accept the Lord, be born again
And give god the glory and praise

Christ's offer is eternal life
O' Lost soul why do you wait?,
Open your heart and let him in
Before it is eternally to late

God's salvation
Is not in righteous works which you have done,
But his eternal question shall be
What have you done with my son?"

Power of Powers

Satan, by reason of vanity, fell to the sin of pride,
And he was cast out of heaven down to the earth
And a third of the angels followed by his side

The powers of darkness are the powers that rule this world
Spiritual powers which are beyond all human comprehension,
But there is a power which is the power of powers
Which became manifest in the flesh for the suffering of death
Followed by the miracle of the resurrection and the ascention

No flesh can stand against Satan and his powers
In the spiritual warfare of darkness and light,
But the soul which is born again, adorning the full armour
Has the power within to put Satan and all the fallen angels
To flight

When you are adorned with the helmet of salvation
The power of powers makes his abode in you,
Your darkness then turns to light
And all things become new

This is the change
The transformation called the new birth,
The fullfilling of the scripture
Greater is he that is in you, than he that is in the earth

Take God's word with you whereever that you go
For this is the sword of the spirit,
It's penetration gives life
To all who have ears to hear it

When Satan sends forth his firey darts
The shield of faith shall deflect them away,
When he sends forth his lies
It is God's truth which we must continually obey

One day Christ shall reign over all
And Satan's powers shall cease,
Let us add to our armour
The glorious gospel of peace

Lord of Lords, King of Kings
The only God potentate, Jesus Christ,
In his left hand is glory and power
In his right hand is life

There is a power that walks this earth
It is the power of the darkness of the night,
But there is a power that is far greater than all
It is the power of powers, "The God of Light"

Peace Be Still

Are your mountains so big
That you have taken your eyes off Jesus Christ?,
Can your problems be greater
Than the one who gave you life?

Is your heart waxed heavy?
Are your eyes growing dim?,
Then fix your heart upon the Lord
And turn your eyes upon him

The eyes of the lord are upon the righteous
His ears are open unto their cry,
In every valley he is there
And upon every mountain high

The lord shall sustain you
Through all the problems of life,
And he shall never be ashamed
Whose heart is stayed on Christ

Pray the prayer of faith
And he shall give you all that you ask,
For if you believe and do not doubt
The Lord shall bring it to pass

Though every way of this world shall fail
My Jesus never will,
So quit my troubled heart
Peace be still

My House, My Home

The roof leaks
And the pipes rust shut,
The basement seaps
And the drains plug up

The walls are chipping
And the wash machine won't go,
The windows are cracked
And the fuses blow

All these things may make up our house
But these do not make up our home,
For Jesus Christ lives within our walls
And we do not face our trials alone

Hearts filled with Jesus
Sing joy to the walls,
And praises to his glory
Echos down the halls

Jesus has blessed our home
And he meets our every need,
As we look to him in that ever growing faith
As that of a mustard seed

Thank you father for Jesus
Thank you father that we need not bare our burdens alone,
Thank you for coming to live with us
And making our house a home

The Accuser of the Brethren

Satan goes about as a roaring lion
Seeking whom he might devour,
But this same Satan also whispers in the ear
So be aware of his diversities of power

There are those going forth praising glory to the Lord
Shining forth for all to see,
Satan crys out:
Fanatics, fanatics are these, says he

And those quiet Christians
Meek, humble, Lord loving souls
Quiet witness's of the Lord's wonderous love,
Satan says these are but Luke warm
And are from beneath and not from above

Be careful how you see
Be careful how you hear,
Be careful of the dragon
Planting seeds in your ear

For there are false Christians planted among the true Christians
Tares sown among the wheat,
These shall be divided in the harvest
To the left and to the right of the judgement seat

The tares shall be gathered on the left
And they shall be cast into the lake of fire,
But those that are gathered on the right
Shall know peace and love and all the joys of their righteous
Heart's desire

Be not deceived, God is not mocked
For what so ever a man soweth that shall he also reap,
And for those whose trust is not in the Lord
Every sin shall be a witnessing heap

So when Satan whispers his lies in your ear
And comes in to plant his little seeds of doubt,
Stand firm in the strength of the Lord
And in the truth of his word
And in the name of Jesus, cast that old dragon out

Dead

Knowledge of the gospel leads to life
But knowledge without understanding is dead

And understanding without wisdom is dead
And wisdom without faith is dead

And faith without works is dead
And works without love is dead

As also the body without the spirit is dead
So is the soul without Christ "dead"

Overflowing

O' To be filled with a love so pure
That they call it Jesus love,
A love that reachs out with joy and tears
To share the light above

A love that fills the cup of the soul
To the rim and overflowing,
A love that reaches out and touches others
Radiantly everglowing

A love that plants seeds
And waters them with tears,
A love that is born inwards and shines outwards
And knows no bounds nor fears

A love that places others first
A love that connot be contained,
A love that suffers all loss
But for the love of Christ counts it gain

This love is Jesus love
Are you listening dear sisters and brothers,
This love seeks not to be rich
But to bring Christ's riches to others

Fill our cups, I pray, dear father
With the living waters above,
Good measure, shaken down,
And overflowing with Jesus love

In the Twinkling of an Eye

Be ready
Your lights burning bright,
In all joy looking upward
Anticipating that glorious appearing of heaven's light

For when that daystar on high shall suddenly appear,
From off of the face of the earth
The saints shall miraculously disappear

Oh what a wonderous sight to see
Of the lifting upwards of the children of light,
Graves being opened, bodys being changed,
The resurrection, the rapture, the blessed hope,
The catching away as a thief in the night

Yea! That trumpet shall surely sound
And those who have ears to hear shall hear,
Yea! The arch angel shall give his shout, and in the twinkling
Of an eye,
The saints of God shall disappear

For the unsaved
The searching shall go on in vain,
Looking for loved ones
In tears calling our their name

Praying
O' God, this is more than I can bare,
My friends, don't miss
That catching away in the air

For there shall be weeping and gnashing of teeth
Sorrow and anguish and pain,
Woe sayeth the angel unto the inhabitors of the earth
Who have never been washed in the blood of the King

Yea! The Lord shall come in the twinkling of an eye
I pray, don't miss
That glorious catching away in the sky

The Second Death

Her mouth is opened wide
Her belly is never full
Her inside coverings are outer darkness
Oozing with putrid stench,
Where the worm never dies
And the fire cannot be quenched

Her depths have no bottom
Her moments have no end,
As she awaits patiently, arms outstretched
To receive all who would foolishly enter therein

One day she shall cough up her slimey innards
Of rotting dead men's bones,
And her dregs shall stand resurrected
Before that great white throne

She shall cough up and spew out
Her foul remains,
And in their nakedness, before their maker
They shall stand in open shame

And there shall be weeping and gnashing of teeth
As the books are opened and the pages turned,
As each one receives
Of the wages he has earned

Page after page, spilling out each slimey thought,
Rotten deed, and dark desire,
As each one awaits his turn
To be cast into the lake of fire

Eternally regreting their procrastination of salvation which
was continually offered with each Passing breath, as they
enter into the everlasting torment
Of the eternal judgement of the second death

Joy in the Morning

*A backslidden Christian
Is a most miserable human being,
But upon repenting and returning to the lord
His heart can once again rejoce and sing*

*I made a commitment at the altar
A few Sundays ago,
There I renewed my first love
And returned to the shepherd of my soul*

*Peace flooded over me
As the burdens of the world rolled away,
Like sunshine after the rain
Christ came back into my heart to stay*

*Now my Jesus walks and talks with me
All the day long,
He has renewed unto me the joy of my salvation
And he has given me a brand new song*

*You have put a song in my soul O' Lord how great thou art,
Heaven is my goal
And joy fills my heart*

*God has clothed me
With a beautiful adorning,
Of peace in the night
And joy in the morning*

*Joy in the morning
That my name is written in the lamb's book of life,
Joy in the morning that Christ lives in me
And that I shall dwell forever in his evercleansing light*

Lumbering Giants

The brook runs laughingly through the hills and valleys
On its ever downward flow,
Past the lumbering giants on its melodious quest
To dance in the meadows below

The sun lifts its eye across the horizon
To peek over her darkened crest,
The hills stand up and the valleys bow low
To these golden beams gleaming through to the west

The dew runs and hides as the sun rises high
And the darkness flees from the light,
The stars fade in the fast disappearing shade
As the dawn replaces the night

The birds sweet songs hang in the crisp autumn air.
As dawn breaks bright and fair

The countryside flares
With splatterings of yellows, reds, and greens,
Brilliant hues bursting through
In beautiful eye pleasing scenes

The flowers turn their radiant faces toward heaven
Gleaming beauty from every stem,
Filled with the smell of the nectar of kings
A sweet smelling savour for him

Then autumn goes out in a splender of glory
In one last awe inspiring fling,
As the lumbering giants shed their many colored coats
Singing hosannas to the king

The Crumpled Rose

God's thoughts are not our thoughts
And his ways are past finding out,
We may never know the whys
Of the things he brings about

But we can know that all things work together for the good
To those who love God and are the called according to his purpose,
For this is one of the many great and precious promises
Sealed by the blood of Jesus

The rose of sharon
Became a crumpled rose in his father's hand,
When he willingly gave his all
For the likes of fallen man

Many a crumpled rose
Are pressed in the pages of the book of life,
The thief on the cross who turned to Christ
That day saw paradise

Paul the apostle had a thorn in his side
And Jesus said: my grace shall be sufficient for thee,
For though you are weak in the flesh
Your strength shall come from me

The sweetest fragrance
And the most beautiful flowers in all the land,
Cannot compare to the crumpled rose
When found in my father's hand

The most beautiful people in the world
Are born again spirit filled souls,
But the most beautifu of all is in my father's hand
It is the crumpled rose

My thoughts as I wrote this poem were of Valerie
A crumpled rose in my father's hand

The Tempter's Song

I am Satan
I am awake every minute of every hour,
I go about as a roaring lion
Seeking whom I might devour

Give me an opening
Open the door and let me in,
And I will restore unto you your old nature
And your former life of sin

Then Satan's voice lifted
To the beat of this song:,
The world is flowing in earthly pleasure
Forget your troubles and come on along

Life is short
Grab all the gusto you can,
Oh my what a song
Play it again Sam

My best old song is still
If it feels good do it,
To most of the crowd
This is still the number one hit

Put it on the turntable
Play it again Sam,
Let's turn these children of light
Into the children of the damned

O' I do a good job
I do my job very well,
Bringing down the multitudes
Into the firey pits of hell

Give me an opportunity
And I'll give you earthly pleasure,
All I ask in return
Is all your heavenly treasure

Christ says: deny thyself
And take up thy cross and follow me,
But I have no restraints
I say do whatsoever comes naturally

Now their feet are a tapp'n
And their lips are a humm'n,
To the hypnotic rythmic beat
Of old Satan's drumm'n

Ah! I got em now
I got em humm'n along,
Play it again Sam
Play em the tempter's song

A Day in the Life

At the first breaking of dawn
In the fading twilight,
The trees and the fog stand as shadowy ghosts
Haunting the last fleeting moments of the night

Out of the stillness comes a faint sound
A rustle of leaves in the tree tops,
Then a noise hits the leaf strewn ground
In a splatter of falling dew drops

Out of a leafy nest a fox squirrel scurrys
Leaping from tree to tree,
In it's hurrying search for the ripening fruit
Of the majestic shagbark hickory

His furry tail flops and with a bark he scolds
All invaders and intruders of his domain,
Adding to the enchantment of the morning watch
As dawn sweeps the sky as a flame

Chewing, grinding noises drift through the fog
As teeth shred through hickory nut shells,
Sending little shavings in downward streams
As water from artesian wells

Belly full he stretchs out on a limb
Catching the warmth of the rising sun,
Lazily snoozing through the heat of the day
Only to awake to some mischievious fun

Another squirrel has entered his tree
And around the trunk they go,
Up and down and around and around
Enjoying life in all of it's ebb and flow

Then the shadows return
As the sun disappears in the western sky,
And the squirrel curls up in the safety of his nest
Another day in the life gone by

Something Good

Jesus Christ is coming
We have this promise from on high,
From our God who does not fail
And our God who cannot lie

Listen up my Christian brothers
And Christian sisters to,
Something good is about to happen
And it's going to happen to me and you

Oh the glory of it all
No mind can fully comprehend,
Of the wonders that await beyond
In that world without end

Gates of pearl, streets of gold,
The half has not been told

With firey chariots on every side
And under angel's watchful eyes,
All the saints who have faithfully run the race
Like the dew towards heaven shall rise

Lifted up to the God of glory
Clothed and robed in white,
Glowing in that golden morn
Of the appearance of heaven's light

This is that something good
That God's trumpet is about to play,
This is the full fillment of the blessed hope
Of that long awaited day

To God be the glory

Due His Name

When his name forms upon our lips
Let it be to honor, glory, and praise,
Worshiping him in spirit and truth
As we number our earthly days

It is in fullness of joy
Of my first love that I now sing,
From a heart overflowing with halleluahs
Of the glory due his name

Halleluah to him who took our sins
Who upon the cross bore our shame,
Halleluah to the lamb of God
Glory to his name

He gave his all to free us,
Precious is the name of Jesus

In awe of the wonder of it all
I sing halleluahs to the one who gave me life, praise, glory, and honor
To the name of Jesus Christ

Here and down the golden streets of heaven
Let the halleluahs continually ring,
From hearts in fullness of joy
Of the praises due his name

Body, Soul, and Spirit

Do the imaginations of the mind
And the thoughts and intents of the heart,
Come out in words that do honor to the lord
And to the hearers joy impart?

At your work place, do you work as men pleasers
Do you honor the lord in all you say and do?,
Do you do your very best
Irregardless of man's reward to you?

Do you honor your body
As the holy temple prepared for the master's use?,
As the home of the holy spirit
Free of drugs and harmful abuse

With proper diet and exercise
Do you honor the lord in soul, spirit, and flesh?,
Giving your all to the master
Giving him your very best

Is the television tuned to the proper channels?
Are the books respectable that you read?,
Do you turn your eyes from the temptations of life? are
You keeping your heart pure and clean?

In all of life's choices
Make your decisions in the lord and stick to it,
Honoring him always with the total person
Of body, soul, and spirit

Loosed from the Bondage

Would you be loosed
From your burden of sin?
From worldly lusts
And all the bondages therein?

Of the deceitfullness of riches
And earthly treasures?,
Of the pride of life, the lust of the eyes,
And the pursuit of earthly pleasures?

Soul in bondage to the world
Their lives lived out in wanton waste,
Their only purpose
To gain this worlds riches in all haste

And then?, and then?,
And then comes the end

You need not be in bondage to this world
Jesus Christ has provided the way,
Through the blood of the cross
You can come and be cleansed today

The altar is there for all
Free for all who would come,
God's gift of eternal life
Paid for in full by the blood of his son

Praise God, praise God, praise God
The Christian has what the world cannot give,
Stand up, come up, bow down
And reach out to Jesus and live

The Amber Jug

All sin is rooted in these three things
The lust of the flesh, the lust of the eyes, and the pride of
Life,
The world, the flesh, and the devil
Are the enemys of the cross of Christ

Whiskey drags down and drowns the souls of men,
And those who are deceived thereby are enslaved in this bondage of sin

The drunkered arises early in the morning
His eyes all swollen and red,
Seeking his love in an amber jug
Inflamed, he stumbles and returns to his bed

He lies in his vomit
Bound to the enemy of his soul,
Death, hell, and the lake of fire
Patiently awaits as his final goal

Yes! like a venomous snake it will strike him at the last
And he shall fall never again to arise,
And as the rich man of the rich man and lazarus
In the torment of hell he shall lift up his eyes

Take heed there is hope
If you want to enter into life this is what you must do,
Seek the lord with all of your heart
And he will be found of you

To those who seek the fire wrapped in an amber jug
I tell you the answers to life are not there,
But there on bended knee before the cross of Christ
They can be found in the sinner's prayer

And Then Came Sunday

It was a time when the man of sorrows walked this earth
A time when miracles were taking place,
The kingdom of heaven was at hand
And God was ushering in his day of amazing grace

The religeous leaders of the day were moved to envy
And sought false witness's against this man called Christ,
They sought that they might find cause to accuse him
And take away his life

Oh yes those false witness's came
They did not know that it was for this very purpose that the
Lord had come,
To shed his atoning blood for the remission of sin
And offer it freely to everyone

He died, he was buried,
It all happened on a dark Friday just this way,
But Friday passed, and Saturday passed,
And then came Sunday

The grave was empty
The tomb was bare,
An angel rolled the stone away, and witness's looked in
Jesus wasn't there

Halleluah he is alive,
Ascended into the heavens
To which we lift our eyes

We now look for that day of the resurrection of the just
We are looking for the coming of heaven's light,
When Christ comes in the clouds for us
And our faith is gloriously transformed into sight

Yes Good Friday happened
And it happened just this way,
But Friday passed, and Saturday passed
And then came Sunday

Treasures

Man since the begining of time
Has tried to derive his joy from earthly pleasures,
But let me tell you, the lust of the flesh and the pride of life
Are the world's deceiving treasures

Satan is a murderer and a liar
The world is not what it seems,
It is a land of fading beauty
A place of broken dreams

In this failing world
There remains one hope for the human race,
It is the never failing truth of God
And his amazing grace

Reach out to Jesus
Receive him as your very own,
For he and he alone gives the joy
That surpasses any and all that you have ever known

I plead to the world, go to now
For now is the accepted time,
There is no greater treasure anywhere
That you could ever find

Reach out for God's treasures of tomorrow
Live for Christ today,
Let your light shine out
That others might find the way

Sweet and precious promises of Jesus
Are Christ's now treasures of love,
But the souls we lead to Christ
Are our forever treasures above

Morning Song

He is my morning song
He loves me,
He suffered the agony and shame ot the cross
And died to set me free

I meditate upon him in the night watches
He is my joy and my delight,
He is in my every waking thought
He is my salvation and my light

He is fullness of joy
He is amazing grace,
He is the radiant glow
On every born again Christian's face

He is my morning song
In the cool of day he walks with me,
He will never leave me nor forsake me
My friend he shall ever be

I awake in wonder
To what each new morning brings,
I awake in joy
And my heart takes flight on eagle's wings

Singing his praises in their morning songs
I awaken to the music of the birds,
Praising glory to their creator
With songs more beautiful than words

Let the morning joy overflow
Come on and sing along,
Wake up to Jesus
And make him your morning song

I Want to Write a Poem

Someday I want to write a poem
With the beauty and power of psalm twenty three,
I want the words to penetrate to the bones and marrow
And to set souls free

I want to express in simplicity
The way to eternal life,
I want to tell of the death, burial, and resurrection
That glorious victorious gospel of Jesus Christ

I want the holy spirit
To touch it with his own hand,
I want God to add his power
When I tell of the savior of man

I want souls to reach out
In full assurance of what can be theirs,
Jesus Christ, saving grace
And a lifetime of answered prayers

I want this poem to express the joy
Of the friend which sticketh closer than a brother,
I want it to expound the love of God
And the life than can be found in no other

I want it to express God's love
In giving the world his son,
And that the cross of Christ was not a loss
But the greatest victory ever won

Well I know that I may never write a poem
As beautiful or as moving as David's psalm twenty three,
But I thank God for the poems I've written, the life he's given
And all that he means to me

The Master's Brush

Adorning the world in gold and crimson
God lifts his brush to the land,
Giving the world a magical glow
An autumn original from the master's hand

The hills are alive and on fire
With beautiful eye pleasing scenes,
Dripping colors from painted trees
Of yellows, reds, and greens

Splashes here and splatterings there
God's hand is everywhere,
The never changing creator's ever changing beauty
Hanging breathlessly in the crisp autumn air

Hazy summer turning to radiant fall
In one glorious magical fling,
God's fullfilling promise of the changing of the seasons
As the birds and the leaves take wing

Yes the hills and the valleys are a living masterpiece
Painted with the creator's brush,
Beautiful beyond all imagination
A living testimony of the master's touch

Miracles

I want to tell you of the miracles
Begining with the immaculate conception of the virgin womb,
Through his life and death
And the miracle of the empty tomb

An angel visited the Virgin Mary
And said that the holy ghost would overshadow her
And that she would conceive and bare a son,
And that he would be the Messiah, the Savior of the World
The promise of the holy one to come

Flesh and bones clothed heaven's light
And for thirty three years he graced this earth,
His generation was one of miracles
Begining with the miracle of the virgin birth

He was born in a manger beneath a beautiful star
And Kings came to honor and worship him,
And an angel came down with a message of hope and peace
And joy spread throughout the Hills of Bethlehem

Jesus grew in wisdom and stature
And pleased his father above,
And the holy ghost descended upon him
Coming down from heaven like a dove

At the age of thirty his minstry began
Of the coming Kingdom of God he did preach,
Repentance and reconcilliation
Was the message that he began to teach

Miracles were at his fingertips
At the touch of his garment virtue went out from him,
Everywhere that he went miracles were taking place
Within him was the power to forgive sin

Lepers were cleansed, the dead raised to life
The lame were made to walk and the blind to see,
Miracles strawed the path
Of this man from galilee

Miracles from his miraculous birth to the glorious asscention
And the promise of his coming again,
From his infancy to the cross of calvary
And his sacrifice for the atonement for sin

Yes and he went on from there and appeared unto many
Then asscended to the father of lights,
And they that stood by looked on in awe
Gazing upwards at this wonderous sight

The angel said: why do you gaze to the heavens
For your lord will return in like manner that he went,
Yes the blessed hope will return in glory and power
In a fullfilling promise that was heaven sent

Our lord and savior is coming again
This miracle man of the virgin birth,
And at the mount of olives at the place he left
He shall set his foot back down to this earth

And as surely as he lives and breathes
His miracles will never cease,
Praise, glory, and honor
To the glorious prince of peace

Children of Innocence

Their angels do always commune
Before the glory throne above,
As their father in heaven looks down
Upon these innocent gifts of love

Children are a heritage of the lord
Little treasures with big responsibilities,
Little joys that light up our lives
To be raised to the best of our abilities

Show your children that you care
With loving parental guidance and direction,
Admonish them in the lord
And shower them with love and affection

With the children of innocence
God has wonderfully blessed our hearts,
Let us not grieve our lord
By any failings on our part

And when we discipline
These little ones
That God has entrusted to our care,
When we bring punishment upon them
Let us be honest and let us be fair

When you raise your voice or your hand to your child
Let it not be in anger or physical or mental abuse,
But let it be the loving hand,
Of correction that you choose

A willful child needs correction
But let it be correction applied with love,
Never come at them in anger
Or grieve the father above

In innocence your child gives you their love and trust
In all to them be faithful and true,
And the love that you have given to them
Will surely and wonderfully come back to you

Life without End

O' What a joy it is to know the lord and savior
As lord and savior
And to come to church and feel the excitement in his name,
Sing glory to it
And to hear it mentioned where it is not used in vain

A place where like believers come together
And worship before the lord,
One body, one mind,
With one purpose and accord

Rejoicing before their lord
Singing glory and halleluah to Jesus Christ,
Praising the holy name
By which we have received this wonderful life

Life is more abundant here and now
And eternal halleluahs in the hereafter,
Shout it to the rooftops
And let it echo from the rafters

Jesus Christ is lord he has wonderously set us free,
Let us sing and shout
Rejoicing in the victory

Inside these hallowed walls
The redeemed of Christ are found,
And the windows rattle and the rafters shake
At their joyful rejoicing sound

If you do not know that victory in Jesus
Today is the day my friend,
For here at the end of the path, from your seat to the altar
Is life without end

The Begining of the End

Are you waiting in anxious-anticipation
For the hope that is about to come,
Are you rejoicing in the promise
Of the sudden appearance of God's son

Are you living your life in readiness
Are you fully prepared against that day,
Will you be among God's elect
In that glorious catching away

The wise will not be caught unawares
At that sudden appearance of the thief in the skys,
For they shall be lifted upwards to him
With tears of joy flowing from their eyes

Silence will fill the corridors of heaven
For the space of about half an hour,
When Christ comes with his mighty angels
In all of his glory and power

Angels of light holding back the demons of darkness
Riding in chariots of fire,
Swords drawn and made ready
For the greatest happening to ever transpire

The events that follow the rapture and the great tribulation
Are the binding chain, and Christ's millenial reign,
Then after a small season
The lake of fire, outer darkness, and eternal pain

Yes! Satan's reign is about to end
The resurrection is about to take place,
And the events that follow is the begining of the end
For the tempter of the human race

The Wilderness Man

Out of the quietness of the morning
Penetrating through the stillness that enveloped the land,
Came a peaceful stirring sound
To enlighten the ears of the wilderness man

There on the cushioned carpet of the forest's floor
Beneath shadows of tall pine trees,
He listened to the soothing sounds of rustling needles
As green giants swayed in the gentle breeze

In the distance a lake sparkles like daimonds
As the sun glimmers from each little ripple's crest,
While dark clouds rear their ominous heads
In a rumble of thunder from the west

A hawk screams overhead
As crows glide over pinacles of pine,
The rain enhances the smell of sweet pine air
As the lightning flashes it's jagged line

Water drops fall in rapid succession
From the brim of the hat of the wilderness man,
As he gazes through pillars of pine
And quietness lays like dew upon the land

The wilderness man takes to the game trails
In surroundings peaceful and serene,
As the thunder clouds rumble in the distance
Replaced by a rainbow's colorful scene

On a hillside covered with meadow grass
The wilderness man lays back in the heat of the day,
Taking a rest from his cross country trek
As the sun overhead warms the place where he lay

Then up he jumps moving on down the trail
Deep into the wilderness he goes,
Disappearing into the shadows
As the sun sinks as surely as it arose

Somewhere down an age old trail
The wilderness man moves quietly in the night,
The stars overhead for his guide
As he walks paths bathed in pale moonlight

He walks this place of unspoiled beauty
With no signs or eveidence that he'd ever been there,
Like a ghost, a will of the wisp
He vanishes like smoke in the air

The Call of the Wild

I've drank the pure waters from pristine lakes
I've heard the wolves cry,
I've seen the bear and the moose
I've seen the eagle's fly

I've heard the loon's laughter
I've seen the caribou,
I've fished remote wilderness lakes
Reflecting skys of blue

I've walked the virgin forests
And breathed the fresh clean air,
Awestruck by the enchanting beauty
That can only be found there

I cannot begin to tell you
About this hauntingly awesome place
A rare jewel impossible to describe or imagine
Until you've seen it face to face

Once you've been there
Like a magnet she will draw you back again,
Her breathless beauty will caress you
Like finding a long lost friend

She will steal your heart
She will take you in her arms,
She will hold you spellbound
With her many enticing charms

Once she has you in her grasp
She'll never let you go,
Believe me
I've been there and I know

She whispers to me in the morning
I hear her voice in the wind,
I see her face in every sunrise
And around every bend

The call of the wild
Is there in the mist and the rain,
In the waves that lap the shore
She gently calls my name

The Pause that Refreshes

We all go through life in a scurry
Speeding along at a tremendous pace,
Rushing through it
In an all out race

As we go about our daily routine
Burning up life's highway,
Let us remember to take some pauses
And a few stops along the way

Take time to dream
For it gives life that extra zest,
Reach for the moon and the stars
And belive you can have life's best

Take time to be holy
Take time to pray,
Read and study upon God's word
Believe, trust, and obey

Take time to laugh
For it is the music of the soul,
Listen closely now
I think I'm on a roll

Take someones hand in yours
Give them a warm glowing smile,
Go out of your way to help others
Go that extra mile

Take your foot off the gas pedal
Change your pace before life's final chapter closes,
Slow down my friends
And take time to smell the roses

Blue Fire

The hills and the valleys are a blazing blue fire
Burning clusters of the first signs of spring,
Little blue boquets, beautiful violets
Saphires fit for the crown of the King

Wild flowers spread their beauty across our fields and forests
From early spring to late fall,
But of all the flowers that beautify our world
The little violets of springtime are my favorite of them all

Flowers bring so much beauty to our world
They are a feast for our hungry eyes,
And like multi colored lights they shine out their glory
As they lift their faces to the skys

Soloman in all his glory
Was not arrayed as one of these,
But the rose of Sharon was one of the names
Soloman gave to the glorious prince of peace

And I just know that in the heaven of heavens
And around the throne of the power of powers,
And along either side of the streets of gold and the river of
Life
There's just got to be flowers

A New Heart

I'm trading in this heart of stone
For a new one clean and pure,
For one my lord gives
Washed and made ready for the rapture

Then I'm going to feast my hungry soul
Through the windows of my heart,
And burn thy words upon fleshly tables
And never let them depart

He is my light
And I'm going to let him shine,
A witness burning brightly
Of the light that has filled this heart of mine

You are the light
The burning light within,
Thank you lord for reaching down your nail pierced hand
And reminding me of the price you paid for my sin

O' Holy spirit seal my soul
Give me strength to contiually overcome,
That I may rejoice with the redeemed
In that glorious day of the appearance of God's son

Thank you lord for forgiveness
And for your love so freely given,
Thank you lord for this brand new heart
And the Christian's hope to live in

A Smile

The lord has put joy in your heart
He has given you the gift of grace,
He has placed the peace within
And that smile upon your face

When someone asks about the hope that is in you
And that warm and radiant outward glow,
It's your open door to witness for Jesus
And the seeds of life to sow

When you see someone without a smile
You know what you must do,
Give them one of yours
And most assuredly it will be reflected back at you

It doesn't cost a thing
To give that smile away,
And the rewards are manifold over
More than words can say

Let your light so shine
Like sunshine at midday,
Spread some joy along life's path
Give that smile away

A smile freely given
Is like words fitly spoken,
It's like a flash of light in this dark world
And a needle and thread to the heart that's broken

If God has given you the Christian life
Than go forth and triumphantly live it,
And if he has put a smile upon your face
Go forth and freely give it

The Begining

For everything there is a season
A time to laugh and a time to cry,
A time for every purpose under the sun
A time to live and a time to die

The book of ages
Is both tried and true,
And all that God has promised
He will do

Through the shadow
There is light,
Through death
There is life

To the Christian there is no fear in the valley
For at the other end the gates of heaven are opened wide,
And for those that are saved
Unspeakable joys await on the other side

A home awaits in the great beyond
More beautiful than mind can comprehend,
Awaiting all who trust in Jesus
At the very moment of there earthly life's end

When you walk through the valley of the shadow
You do not walk this path alone,
For Jesus walks with you
With angels on every side to gloriously usher you home

When you close your eyes in Jesus
Go rejoicing in the victory,
For you will open them to Jesus
And all his glory see

Whispers in the Night

In the night watches
He whispered and I awoke,
Then I faithfully wrote down
The words that he spoke

Sometimes his message
Is spoken silently in the night,
Other times it's like pounding thunder
And a flashing bolt of light

Let the ink from my pen flow
To tell the ageless message again,
Of Jesus Christ and the crimson flow
That washes away our sin

There's only one place
That we can experience the overwhelming victory,
And that's at the foot of the cross
And the blood of calvary

Every soul that walks those golden streets of heaven
And along the shores of the crystal sea,
Came through by the doorway
Of the cross of calvary

My soul thirsts for Jesus Christ
My heart hungers for his word,
I was glad when they said unto me let us go into the house of
The Lord
Where God's message may be heard

Honor, glory, and praise
Are the songs that we do sing,
With peace, joy, and love
This message of saving grace we do bring

Praise to the lord of glory
For loving us O' So much,
And filling our hungry souls with goodness
And quinching our thirsty souls from his overflowing cup

And may our souls continually praise him
As long as our flesh holds breath,
And even more so in the city of light
Beyond the shadow of death

Little Girls

With the words - *"I wuv you"*
Heartstrings are tugged,
As they cuddle in our laps
And smother us with hugs

Little pretenders
In a grown up world,
Topped off with angel hair
All natural and curled

These bouncing bundles of joy and fun,
Jump, play, and run

They fill the house with laughter
And squeals of delight,
And thir joyful sounds
Extend even into the night

I walked by her room
And at the foot of her bed,
She was reverently praying
With folded hands and bowed head

On bended knee I heard her pray
God bless mommy and daddy and gramma and grampa too,
And P. S. Lord Jesus
I love you

Sweetness and goodness
With soft golden curls,
Are these God given treasures
Called little girls

Little Boys

Daddy's little shadow
The little fisherman,
Catching the big ones
With a willow stick, a string, and a bent pin

A tree climber
And a critter gitter,
A little leaguer
And a home run hitter

To him
Daddy is always right,
He is his roll model
He's a giant in his sight

To daddy, through his son
He lives his childhood again,
For this little fellow is not only his son
He's his buddy and his friend

And as the son sees his daddy
Down on the floor playing with his toys,
He realizes
That dads too were once little boys

Nova

Bightly shines yon star
Shortly burns it's life,
A silver fire, a dying nova
Proclaiming the birth of Christ

The glory was not in the star
No, it was not in that fire on high,
It was in the event that was taking place below
Beneath that bright lit sky

It was the hope of all mankind
The word made flesh to dwell among us,
The king of king's, the lamb of God
Our lord and savior Jesus

Bringing light and life to a dying world
The kingdom of heaven was at hand,
To restore the link that was broken in Adam
Between God and sinful man

Yes the light in the heavens shone down
Penetrating that silent bethlehem night,
Bringing it's glory to the lord of glory
A fading nova in the presence of his light

Truly Ready

The quest for knowledge is a burning desire
Of both the poor man and the king,
To fill their hearts and minds with facts
On every subject about everything

A very enthusiastic man came up to me
And began to tell of many things,
Of far away countries he had seen
And of their great presidents, leaders, and kings

He would barely catch his breath
Then he would go on and on again,
Of his great oration of many words
There seemed to be no end

You should have seen the things I've seen
And been the places I've been,
Oh I'm so filled with knowledge
I don't know where to begin

I feel I have led a full and wonderful life
And am ready if life should end,
But I never once heard God mentioned
And my opportunity to witness was about to begin

Let me tell you about a wonderful book
And the things that Jesus said,
Of white pages and black letters
And also words in red

The black are the glorious words about Jesus
And the red are the words of Christ,
The book is the holy bible
And the words are the words of life

These words will penetrate your mind and heart
And cause you to seek his face,
These words will convict your soul
And bring you to an altar of grace

Then you can truly say with the redeemed
That heaven is your home,
And rejoice at the trumpet's sound
When Christ comes to receive his own

The Birth and Death of a Season

The silver frost was painted
In the cold predawn hours of the night,
Only to burn off and rise to heaven
In the warmth of the morning light

A miracle was about to give birth
And would soon show it's beautiful face,
In the changing of the seasons
That was very shortly to take place

Upon the golden dawn of day
The black wings of darkness took flight,
Yellow streams bathed the forest's floor
And awoke the silent sentinals of the night

Out of the west a low hum could be heard
Shaking and stirring the rainbow leaves,
Bursting out in joyful song
In the Indian summer breeze

Down they jumped from their lofty perch
And floated their colorful flight,
To roll and tumble through woods and meadow
Spreading their colors bright

Playfully they roamed
Colorfully coating mother earth,
Until they to were covered
By the white cloak of winter's birth

The Silver Crown

Rain fell through the blackness
On a cold December night,
Forming crystal palaces
In the dawn's first glimmers of golden light

Shining, towering, and proud
They guard the glass littered lawn,
Castles all aglow in florescent reds
Reflecting the raging fire of the morning's dawn

Later the sun reaches high in the sky
Transforming the icy world below,
Exchanging it's colorful hues
For a crystal diamond like glow

Then a creaking, cracking, begins to sound
As the wind begins to blow,
And God smiles as he looks down
Upon the silver crown he gave to the world below

Now the only thing left are shattered pieces
Of God's gift of the silver crown,
Glittering, melting fragments, forming shimmering pools
Of tear drops upon the ground

Canvas and Brush

Words carefully chosen and put to ink
Makes beautiful scenes materialize,
In the recesses of the reader's mind
They take on forms he can visualize

A true poet paints pictures
Upon the canvas of the mind,
The hills take shape and the lakes take depth
As he pens each rhyming line

Through scriptive verse
The reader can see what the writer sees,
He can see the wind and the waves in the meadow grass
And the reds and the yellows of the autumn leaves

The dark blue sky, the fluffy puffs of clouds
The mirror image like a mirage in the lake below,
These all become reality in living color
As the rhythmic verses smoothly flow

So imagine if you will
The deep beauty as seen through the poet's eyes,
As pen and paper become canvas and brush
And brings his visions alive

The Changer of Hearts

There is power in the spirit's sword
And if you listen close his whispers may be heard,
Hear ye O' Saints the voice of the lord
And hearken unto his word

This is the power of God unto salvation
This is the gospel of Jesus Christ,
This is the lord's last will and testament
These are the words of life

Quick and powerful
And sharper than any two edged sword,
Are these mighty words
Of our savior and our lord

Piercing even to the dividing asunder
Of the joints and marrow and the soul and the spirit,
And when received in faith
It is saving grace to those who hear it

Be not ashamed of the gospel of Jesus Christ
For this is the changer of hearts,
And make a joyful noise and rejoice always
In the joy it's salvation imparts

The Accepted Time

Now here are a few questions
I want you to ponder on,
Think about them searchingly and deeply
But don't take to long

Where will you spend eternity?
Don't you want that inner peace?,
Forever could start tomorrow
Life has no guarantees

Don't you know that your soul's in jeopardy?
Don't put off what you must do,
Come to Jesus now, just as you are
And let his shed blood cleanse you

With nail pierced hands
Christ reaches out with the gift of grace,
Why do you neglect so great a salvation?
Hell is an awful place

The bible says the accepted time is now
If the spirit is speaking to your heart, come,
Come to the cross of calvary
And be cleansed in the blood of God's son

Don't spurn God's sweet sweet love
Don't hesitate, don't wait,
Reach out and receive life now
Before death seals forever your fate

The Fruit of the Spirit

Inside I have the peace
That only Christians know,
For the Holy Spirit has united forever
My spirit and my soul

I have fullness of joy
In believing and trusting in Christ,
Being washed in the blood of the lamb
God's sin offering sacrifice

I have love in my heart
Placed there by the one who is love and loves us all,
A gift that I received at the altar of grace
When I heeded the spirit's call

I have a burning desire
To tell others about Jesus Christ,
That they would step from darkness and death
Into the light and eternal life

Faith is beleiving
In things we do not see,
And I live in the blessed hope
That one day soon Jesus is coming for me

Little Snow Flakes

Downward they spiral
Sparkling in the night,
Covering everything
In a fluffy blanket of pure white

The moon looks down in wonder
As the wind begins to blow,
And stardust fills the air
In a magical enchanting show

The wind begins to cry
Sparkles are everywhere,
As the crystal snowflakes
Go dancing in the air

Made by the master craftsman
Each is a meticulous miraculous creation of perfect
Intricate design,
A refreshing change of scenery
Created for the enjoyment of all mankind

Those first tiny snowflakes of winter
Are such a beautiful, beautiful sight,
Like millions of tiny diamonds
Sparkling in the slightest light

They are as refreshing as the colored leaves of fall
That the poets feast their eyes upon,
Or the sunshine and the rain
And the rainbow God paints across the horizon

Or as the green forests of summer
That guard the pale blue lakes,
Yes there is nothing more beautiful in all the world
Than God's little snow flakes

If the World only Knew

There is an event
That's about to take place,
That will send shock waves
Throughout the whole human race

An event
If the worldly mind could only comprehend,
The hair on their heads
Would stand on end

Out of the book of truth
Comes the fullfilling prophesy of old,
Which down through generation after generation
Has been told and retold

About the greatest happening
Since the birth, death, burial, and resurrection of Jesus Christ,
An event that will reach down and touch every saved soul since
The begining of time
And lift them and clothe them with spiritual bodys fit for
Eternal life

The graves will be opened
And the dead in Christ shall rise,
Then we which are alive and remain in the lord
Shall be lifted upwards to the lord in the skys

We shall reunite with loved ones
Who have passed on before,
And we shall join hands with Jesus
And fly away through heaven's door

Then we shall dwell with him forever
In a place of unimaginable beauty and peace,
In the land of eternal blessings
Where joy and love never cease

A land where there is no sorrow
Nor heartaches, nor pain,
No tears shall fall on those golden streets
Where we shall sing, forever glory to the king

Most Glorious of All

A rotting log glowing in the dark
In a phenomenon known as foxfire,
And the will of the wisp of swamp gas
Ghostly seepings from the boggy mire

The fireflies that flit through the woods and meadows
Performing eirie rituals in the night,
Little puffs of momentary fire
Of blinking yellow light

The stars that look like shiny holes
Poked in a blanket of black,
And the lanterns of halloween
Staring out from the pumpkins we call jack

The haze of the blue diamond snow
Radiating in the silver moonlight of a long winter's night,
The sun's rays reflecting upward
In the rainbow glory of the northern lights

The reds and blues of a glowing campfire
The lights of a city on a hill,
And of all, the most glorious of all
Is the light of heaven still

The Song of Spring

Running and jumping in playful romps
Over rocks and logs they flow,
The singing crystal clear streams of waters
In the music of the melting snow

Twisting along the forest's floor
Nourishing the earth to life,
With mayapples, violets, and mushrooms
Springtime in all her glory arrives

The morning doves
Calling to God for rain,
And the little frogs, the peepers of the ponds
Lift up their voices and sing

I hear the sounds of the land coming alive
I feel the warm west wind,
I see the robins appear again
And hear the joyful songs of jenny wren

Listen closely to the beautiful melodies
Spreading joy all across the land,
For of all the sounds in all the world
There is none sweeter than these to man

Boss of the Lake

White water lilies and large green pads
Surround and decorate the shallows of the waters edge,
Long stems reaching downward into the murky depths
Securely rooted to a sunken ledge

Cattail moss streamers spiral upwards
Clams and snails pock the silt strewn floor,
Tortoises and catfish lurk in her haunts
And bluegills and crappies and perch and yes more

Dark shadows moving ever so slowly
Vibrating the pads and causing flutters in the cattail moss,
Movements creating instant panic
In all the small creatures of those whose paths that they cross

Giant swirls mar the mirror calm surface
Leaving little whirl pools in their after wake,
And of all the creatures that lurk beneath
He alone is boss of the lake

A hungry frog jumps from the safety of the bank
And amongst the Lilly pads snatches a bug,
And the pads shake and the water explodes
And the frog disappearss like dirt swept under a rug

And the King moves back down through the depths
Triumphantly he returns to his throne,
Undisputed boss of the lake
He, and he alone

Beasty Boss

The damp dew lay beaded upon the matted moss
As a sinister shadow lay beneath the dark waters of the murky
Bog,
Ole boss hog, the beast of the bog
Was haunting the misty morn in the murky waters beneath the
Ghostly fog.

There in the midst of the morning mist
In the murky waters beneath the matted moss,
Moving along just above the mud and mire
Was big ole beasty boss

In northern indiana in kosciusko county
Use to lie the haunts of the big beasty hogs,
There in the backwaters of webster lake
Lurked the lunkers of the mossy bogs

I take my hat off to you beasty boss
For I used to search for you in the misty fog,
Moving slowly over the matted moss
Of the thick green carpet of the backwaters miry bog

Now I no longer frequent her haunts
For she has succumbed to the greedy hand,
Her weed beds have been poisoned, cut up, and destroyed
By the so called progress of foolish man

I long for the haunts of beasty boss
It's a shame that his habitat had to die,
Now he no longer frequents her shady haunts
And so, no longer do I

The Moving Stones

When I walk through the green, green grass
And see the beautiful flowers of the valleys and the magnificent
Wooded hills,
It seems that life should go on forever
But then there stands a stark reminder that that thought stills

It is the stones of marble and granite
Of people whose thoughts were just like mine,
It is the graveyards of the world
That brings reality back in line

Life as we know it comes to an end
And the cemetary lots and their cold stone monuments say it
All,
We all, each one, must come to grips with these cold, cold,
Facts
When we look through and beyond those wrought iron cemetery
Walls

If we can see life as but a passing moment
As a mist that is here and then it's gone,
We would search deeply in our hearts
And see where our life is going

We would want to do what's good and right
Of our time and talents we would want to give,
We would want to leave our mark on the world
In this short span of life we live

Man deep down desires the truth
Life is more than a short span and a cemetary plot,
A cold stone protruding from the earth and an epitaph
All to life is not

For those who find the truth
For those who discover the living Christ,
They shall know victory beyond the grave
In the coming rapture of the bodily resurrection to life

If in this life they are washed in the blood
If they trust in Christ's redemption power,
Death and the grave holds no fear
For this is not life's final hour

For the stones that stand as cold reminders
That our earthly life comes to an end,
Are the stones that shall move when the graves are opened
At the victorious shout of Christ's glorious coming again

More than a Memory

Sadly I miss my grampa as my thoughts go back to him
He's been gone now a long, long while,
But then I think of our long quiet walks in the woods
And I think of his love and I begin to smile

As I walk in the woods where we once walked
I remember how much he loved me,
I run my fingers over my initials
He so lovingly and carefully carved in an old beech tree

I hunt for the mushrooms he loved to hunt
And I go fishing once in a while,
I pick boquets of wild woods flowers
And I reminisce of him and smile

He loved the glory and beauty of God's creation
And he knew the answers to life,
And he wrote beautiful poems about heaven and earth
And Jesus was lord of his life

I loved him so and I still do
He was my grampa and my friend,
And some beautiful day oh glorious day, I'm going to fly away
And I'm going to see my gampa again

P. S. I still have that old ironwood stick
My grampa cut from a sapling tree,
And every once in a while I clutch it and hold it close
For the precious memories of grampa and me

This is a poem I would like to think
One of my grandchildren would write about me someday

Morels

The floor of the forest is a splattered carpet
Of spectacular colors of little woods flowers,
Born of God's nourishment to the earth of warm sunny days
And nightly downpours of refreshing spring showers

There in the shadows of the living forest
In the very lair of the pixies and elves,
At and around the base of the naked trunks of the leafless elms
Grows the majestic yellow morels

It's dead bark hanging down in long stragly strips
The bleached elms bring new life to the woods,
In the spring when the mushrooms appear upon the flowered hills
In the places where the live elms once stood

The dark morels spread throughout the valleys
And the greys add their color to the scheme,
And the long necked mushrooms with their acorn like tops
Add their magical touch to this beautiful scene

Many there be that go in search for this tasty morsel
And seek until they find,
The morels that spread across the flowered hills
In the living forests of God's springtime

Love not the World

The world seeks her own
The Christian the needs of others,
Reaching out to the world with the great commission
Are the faithful sisters and brothers

The world is a magnet
That draws all things unto itself,
But the Christian walks against the flow
In seeking not his own, but anothers wealth

The world seeks to satisfy the flesh
The world follows after it's hearts desire,
The world has hungry eyes
That draws it's captives down deep into it's muddy mire

Jesus Christ's leading is right
The world's leading is wrong,
The music of the world
Is not the Christian's song

The dead leaves of fall
Flow downward from the skys,
But the saved of both the dead and the living
One day to Christ shall rise

When the call is made, when the shout is gone out
When the trumpet makes it's sound
When Christ appears in the clouds to receive his own
The saint's feet shall leave the ground

The world has no attraction
For those who have experienced the new birth,
For the power that holds everything to this terra firma
Cannot bind the saints to earth

The lust of the flesh, the lust of the eyes, and the pride of
Life
Are the three most deadly sins,
And if you forget all else, remember this
Love not the world nor the things therein

God's Gift of Amazing Grace

The earth was created without form and void
And God said: let there be light and there was light,
And darkness removed from the face of the deep
Washed away by the sun's golden light

God spoke from out of eternity
And created all creation and placed it into time,
And the crown jewels of all this creation that he created
Were the living souls of mankind

He created the moon and the stars
The beautiful sparkling gems of the night,
Heavenly scatterings of glittering glory
The glowing fires of the lesser lights

He owns the cattle on a thousand hills
And every beast of the forest is his,
He created the heavens and the heaven of heavens
And all that in them is

God knew that in the flesh we were born to die
God knew Adam's seed of sin was in us,
So he worked out a heavenly plan
The perfect redemption plan of salvation through Jesus

Out of eternity he came
In a stable he became flesh upon this earth,
The creator was born into time
Through the miracle of the virgin birth

He was thirty years old when he began to minister
He lived only to be thirty and three,
For thirty three years our savior walked in time
And then returned into eternity

They took the God of creation
Those religious leaders of that day,
And they crucified him
And placed him in a cold stone tomb to lay

With a great stone they sealed the opening
And placed guards at the entrance way,
But these became as dead men
Upon the dawn of that third day

For an angel appeared from heaven
And rolled the stone back to reveal an empty tomb
Only the burial linens lay therein,
Our lord and savior was risen from the grave
Victor over death and sin

Through the shed blood of Jesus Christ
Through the nail prints in the hands of the creator of the stars,
Through repentance and turning from our lives of sin
This same victory can be ours

We have the atonement
But we must reach out in unwaivering faith,
For only in believing
Can we receive God's gift of amazing grace

This Days Song

Thank you lord for lifting us up
Above this worlds miserys and woes,
Thank you lord for loving us so much
In sending Jesus to save our souls

We thank you lord for our children
And for our grandchildren too,
Thank you lord for directing our thoughts
In channels directed to you

Thank you Jesus for the songs of the heart
Thank you for the joy that you have placed there,
Thank you for the fields of harvest
And the laborers who truly care

Thank you for the minister of the word
And for his family and their dedication to you,
Thank you lord for the family of God
The congregation of the dedicated few

Thank you lord for the new ones coming in
Thank you lord for speaking to and changing hearts,
Thank you lord for the peace that only you can give
And for the body of believers and all it's working parts

Thank you for the talents you have-given
And for the parts that all fit neatly and compactly together,
Thank you for the praise you have placed within
And the gifts you have given to praise you better

Thanksgiving and praise
Is this days song that we sing,
We praise and thank you lord Jesus
Praise thy holy name

Know So

You say that you can't know that you are saved
Well I know that I am,
Because I've been to the altar of grace
And I've been washed in the blood of the lamb

Take hold of reality
Can't you grasp the urgency of it all?,
I'm talking about your soul's destiny
About life's final curtain call

The most precious possesion that you have
Is not your life, but your soul,
And the answer to the question: are you going to heaven?
Is not: well yah I think so

Man you gotta know
The bible says you can know,
I know, that I know, that I know
That Jesus Christ has saved my soul

You ask me how I know?
Because I believe and trust in the blood of Jesus Christ to
Wash away my sin,
This is my righteousness before God
This is the door by which I entered in

He who has the son has life
God can't put it any plainer than that,
And he who has not the son of God has not life.
Your eternal destiny hinges on this one plain and simple fact

Every one of us must stand before God some day
And do you know what God's going to ask each one of us?,
The question and answer which determines your eternal destiny
Shall be
What have you done with my son Jesus

So next time somebody asks you if it is well with your soul
Don't say: yah I think so,
Say yes, and know so

The Storm

We were cruising the peaceful cool blue waters
Scanning the background greenery of endless pines,
Hoping to photograph something wild and beautiful
Eyes searching deep for tell tale signs

When suddenly the light wind that had previously graced the lake
Became deadly silent,
The lake calmed off like a mirror
And I shuddered for I knew what it meant

I looked behind us and chills ran down my spine
From horizon to horizon the clouds were as black as sackcloth,
An angry sky was boiling
And was about to churn the waters into waves of rabid froth

Then the wind began to trouble the waters
We could see the waves foaming at the other end of the lake,
And we were totally unprepared
For that which was about to take place

The wind raced ahead of the menacing black clouds
Raising raging waves into majestic white crests,
Only to crash against the rocky cliffs
And spray over her heights and into her open clefts

We raced for the safety of our cove
But it lay miles away,
And the cliff walls stared out at us
Battered with angry waves and spray

On one side were the wave battered rocky shores
On the other was the vast expanse of the churning lake,
We chose to go for broke and go for home
When in actuality there was no other choice to make

We fought the waves
We rose upon the heights of her crests,
Our hearts in our throats
For fear of sinking into her murky depths

But, praise God, we were about to be delivered from the troubled
waters
A miracle was coming our way,
With pounding hearts we rounded the bend
And entered into the calm waters of our sheltered bay

It was Gods miracles that brought us into the safe haven
It was his miracles that brought us across the foaming crests,
To God be the glory and praise
He saved us from the watery depths

He is my shelter in the time of storm
My refuge is under the shadow of his wings,
I will trust him always
No matter what life brings

Praise the Lord

First Love

Where is that warmth of your first love?
Where has the fire gone?,
Where is the zest you use to know?
Where is the joyful song?

Has the fire gone out?
Are you walking with him today?,
Are you reading his word and intercessing for the saints?
Or has the world enticed you away?

Dear child of the risen king
Lift your eyes to heaven above,
Renew that fire, renew that zest
And return to the joy of your first love

My Treasure

Earthly treasures eluded me
But I sought them just the same,
Yes! I anxiously anticipated that they would come by mail
But those riches never came

My heart was set on the things of this world
I dreamed that great earthly treasures would soon be mine,
I even played the lottery
But I never won a dime

Then one day I was reading God's words of life
And I heard the spirit's call,
And I sought and I found
The greatest treasure of them all

There at the foot of the cross
I sought my savior's face,
And he cleansed my soul and made me whole
Praise the lord for the altar of grace

I now know
That Jesus Christ is the greatest treasure that I could ever find,
For in trusting in his atonement for my transgressions
Saving grace and all the treasures of heaven are mine

The Joys of Christmas

Christmas shoppers filled with the season's joy
Snowflakes slowly falling through the quietness of the night,
Green trees all decorated with garland and tinsel
Cars and houses covered in blankets of pure white

Brilliant blinking colors penetrating the frost covered windows
Flitting snowflakes sparkling like fireflies in flight,
White glitter reflecting red and blue sparks
As the colored lights dance amongst the snowflakes of the night

Souls filled with joy
Hearts filled with love,
In this celebration of the birth
Of our lord God above

Carolers songs float through the crisp night air
Under the setting of twinkling stars and clear clean skys,
Joyful songs touching receptive hearts
As excitement dances like flames in the children's eyes

Joy fills our hearts as we wrap the presents in gay colors
And top them off with bright colored ribbons,
As we anxiously anticipate
The blessings of giving

The gathering together of family and friends
And the thanking of the lord for each and every one,
And the church bells that are ringing
And the souls that are being won

We thank you lord Jesus
For providing the way,
And for the manifold blessings
And for all the joys of Christmas day

The Great Outdoors

Beneath the black oval of the night
Under heaven's star lit dome,
In the shadows of the haunting forest's green cathedral
Is the wilderness I call home

It is a place of peaceful solitude
A place to clear and cleanse the carnal mind,
A place of moon bathed paths
Winding through emerald forests of scented pine

A place of unequaled tranquil peace
A place more beautiful than any I have ever known,
A place where nature and I become one
As I walk her paths alone

The great outdoors is my beautiful home
My windows are the sunrises and the sunsets,
The stars and the moon are my roof
And the grassy fields are my plush green carpets

The darkness that overshadows the night is my drapes
My lacey curtains the morning fog,
The aromatic cedars are my walls and the lakes are my guilded
Mirrors
And my davenport is a fallen log

The wonders never ever cease
Along these beautiful trails that I walk alone,
Out here in God's glorious creation
Where he has so wonderously furnished my home

The Butcher of Baghdad

Far, far away
Their reigns a terrible King,
Known as the butcher of Baghdad
Saddam Hussein

Deep down in the earth
Crawls this cowardly King of Iraq,
The lowest of vermin
Cowaring like a rat

He is a spreading disease
That has to be stopped,
He is a pimple on the backside of humanity
That needs to be popped

This Hitler incarnate
Must most assuredly and miserably die,
For not only what he has done to Kuwait
But for touching Israel, the apple of God's eye

Satan has a room all heated up for Saddam Hussein
Reserved in the hotel hell Hilton,
Where he shall scream forever in pain
For the atocities he inflicted upon men

At this very moment
The bombs are continuing to fall like rain,
As the world prays
For the one that carrys Saddam Hussein's name

All it takes
Is one direct hit,
To rid the world
Of this big zit

Seek and Ye Shall Find

Man proclaims that he seeks peace
But lust and greed controls his heart,
And for every war that ends
Somewhere in the world another will start

Peace will never and can never be attained
By the hands of mortal men,
But the time is coming, it is written
In blood and ink and pen

In the book we call the bible
Are God's words, tried and true,
And in there, peace is promised
And that promise, brothers and sisters, is for me and you

Peace is only a step away
The son of man's step from heaven to earth,
For one day he shall return in glory and power
And usher in the millenium's birth

Then and only then shall man know peace
Far greater peace than he has ever known,
And for a thousand years Christ shall reign as king
And the earth shall be his throne

Yes! God's glorious peace is coming
The peace that only he can give,
Ushered in by the prince of peace, the God of glory
Of whom we praise, rejoice, and live

If you are searching for something
And you want it to be the greatest and grandest thing,
Then end your search with Jesus
And the peace that passeth all understanding

The Wren Continues to Sing

I walked the wooded hills
In search of brown and yellow morels,
Engrossed in springtimes beautyy
Blotting out all else

I heard a buzz and then a whir
Then he began to sing,
The rest was just a blur
And he uncoiled and I felt the sting

I sat down on a log amidst blue and yellow flowers
A wren sang a happy tune,
Springtimes beauty was everywhere
Redbuds and dogwoods were in full bloom

My mind wondered back
My life passed before my eyes,
The sun warmed the spot where I lay
White fluffy clouds floated across the sky

I could hear the water running down the hills
And the flap of woodduck wings,
A flock of geese passed overhead
The wren continued to sing

My eyes begin to close
I thank god for these last few fleeting moments that he has
Given to me,
And for this beautifu greater awareness
In all I hear and see

I say goodby to a beautiful world
That God created and filled with beautiful things,
As the smell of flowers grows slowly fainter
And the wren continues to sing

The Awe and Wonder of It All

Deep in the darkness, dying coals snap, crack, and pop
Glowing embers penetrate the black veil of the night,
Forming ghostly apparitions
That dance in the outer shadows of this erie circle of light

Then the birds begin their morning chorus
As the eastern sky bursts forth into a golden dawn,
And a grizzled, bearded old man rises
Breathes deeply, stretches, and lets out a mournful yawn

Soon last night's embers are rekindled
Bisquits are baked and eggs are fried,
The smell of crackling bacon in an old iron skillet fills the air
And butter and strawberry jam are generously applied

Homefries are heaped up and covered with ketchup
Sassafrass tea is brewing in the pot,
Woodsmoke curls slowly upward
And disappears through a leafy tree top

A fog like cloud hovers over the pond
The dew begins to rise,
As the glory of it all is absorbed and cherished
Through an old man's hungry eyes

He reaches down and lifts a twig from the fire
And places a cigar to it's glowing cherry end,
Creating a puff of smoke and pungent odor
That mingles, drifts, and fades upon silent currents of wind

The old man leans back and smiles
As he ponders a lifetime of the wilderness call,
Loving and living life to the full
In the awe and wonder of it all

The Beautiful Lady

To smell the sweet smells of mother earth
And lay my head upon her breast,
To dance and sing with this gracious host
Who accepts me as her honored guest

To watch the fields of meadow grass come alive
As the waves flow freely in the wind,
To watch the sun paint the eastern sky
Signaling a new day to begin

Where the moon bathed waves
Sparkle silver from every crest,
And dark blue ripples reflect the mother lode
Of the golden sun sinking in the west

That life that beats in this vessel of clay
Crys out for the wild places,
Where ancient cliffs are etched deeply
With wrinkled weathered faces

To lay down in the meadow grass
And gaze at the heavens star filled night,
And awake to watch the dew rise
At morning's first gleaming light

I tried to still her voice
But she cried out all the more,
With the lightning and the thunder she spoke
As her tears began to pour

The wilderness continually pulls at my heart strings
She makes my heart pound like the rolling thunder,
As I stand in awe and admiration of this beautiful lady
And all her magic wonder

The Great Fantasy

Imaginations caught up in the wind
There is no limit to the places they can go,
Far away places of unimaginable beauty
In fantasy lands over the rainbow

To a place where the little people live
In a quaint little village called muchkin city,
Where there is little houses and lots of flowers
And the people are warm and witty

Also there are witches both good and bad
There is glenda the good witch of the north, she's the best,
But there is the evil one all dressed in black
She is the wicked witch of the west

And so the story goes
And begins an adventure unsurpassed,
With a battle of good and evil
Where your held spellbound until the last

Dorothy begins her journey
Skipping down the yellow brick road,
In this greatest imaginative story
That has ever been written or told

She picks up a few friends along the way
And boy can she pick em,
A scarecrow, a cowardly lion,
And an axe carrying tin man

They go to see the wizard of oz
A very great but mysterious man,
Who lives in a place called emerald city
A great walking distance from munchkin land

Well the witch trys to stop them
But to no avail,
For they reach their destination
But by no means is this the end of the tale

The wizard promises to grant their every desire
If they would perform one small task,
And as they conferred amongst themselves
Dorothy said: and what is that if I may ask?

Bring me the witch's broomstick the wizard bellowed
And I'll grant your every request,
And they shuddered and said: in order to do that
We'd have to kill the wicked witch of the west

Well the adventure goes on
And Dorothy is captured and taken to the witch's lair,
But her friends unite in one accord
To free poor Dorothy from there

They broke into the witch's castle
And freed Dorothy from the witch's den,
But they could not escape
Before they were all captured again

Then the witch proceeded to carry out her evil plan
And set the scarecrow ablaze,
But with a bucket of water Dorothy dashed out the fire
And in the process accidently splashed the witch's face

The old witch cursed and cried
And with that she melted away,
And there the story should have ended
What more was there to say

Except that the wizard granted to them their wishes
And the land was once again filled with joy and laughter,
And like all good storys with happy endings
They all lived happily ever after

Where the Eagle Flys

There is a place of unspoiled beauty
A place where the eagle flys,
A remote area of deep blue lakes, clean air,
And bright blue skys

A place where carnivores roam amongst the birch and the pine
Where the scent of cedar permeates the air,
Where the lakes are teaming with walleye and pike
And the beaver and the fisher are there

Ravens and grayjays and whiskey jacks
And moose and bear and caribou,
A place where two kindred spirits unite
Of the great northern wilderness and you

Where the call of the wild seeps into your blood
And flows freely and deeply into your heart,
Where nothing can, or ever will, satisfy your cravings again
Like these places where the rivers start

Where the lonesome wolves howl out mournful tunes
And the loon's echos haunt the rocky shores,
Where the only thing that interupts the peace of the morning
Is the sound of squeaking oars

Primitive beauty beyond your wildest dreams
Peace and solitude that brings tears to your eyes,
It is the land that makes your heart beat faster
The land where the eagle flys

To the Hoop

I warn you
Before the games even start,
This is not a spectator sport
For the weak of heart

It's all about those magnificent young men
And their nikes,
Who fast break and slam dunk
With the greatest of ease

Each trying
To out excell all the rest,
With their three point shots
Of nothing but nets

Bad breaks, bad refs
And bad calls,
Bumps and bruises
And floor burning falls

The smurks, the smiles
And the scowls,
The scuffles, the fights
And the technical fowls

Always aware of the boos and the cheers
Of the rowdy onlookers,
Where close games become heart stoppers, heart breakers,
And gut wrenching tear jerkers

Ah! Basketball
Yea what a wonderful game,
Where a hit or missed bucket can reduce you to tears
Or rise you up to everlasting fame

Now if you want unsurpassed excitement
And this is the straight poop,
Go to the round pigskin
And the hoop

Booger

Society considers the practice
Of putting your finger up your nose,
As socially unacceptable
And totally gross

Are you aware
Of the slime it leaves,
When you wipe your snot
Upon your sleeves

Then there's the constant annoyance
Like a leaky water hose,
Of blurry teary eyes
And a dripping watery nose

Then there's the one you snort in
And hock out,
Or put your finger on your nose
And fire that goober out

And oh yah, there's the big one
Like a long slimey string,
That you let dangle from your finger
Before you give it a fling

Then there's the little ones
That you roll up into booger balls,
And flip'm like marbles
And bounce them off the walls

So cheer up and take heart
All you socially unacceptable slime,
And keep on pick'n and grin'n
It's booger time

Twitch Tail

As dawn's flourescent fire
Sets the eastern horizon ablaze,
The trees explode with vibrant colors
Illumunated by the suns golden rays

The nocturnal prowlers and roamers of the night
Silently retreat to their daytime lairs,
As the early morning risers begin to creep forth
And go about their daily affairs

The oaks bare heavy laden
The beechnuts are bursting forth from their prickly spiked shells,
Butternuts and walnuts are plentiful
The woods is filled with damp pungent smells

Leafy foilage shakes in the tree tops
As watery dew drops fall in torential torents to the forest's floor
Twitch tail is on the move
Seeking to fill his cach from God's bountiful store

Alert to the unusual or unnatural
He listens intently for any tell tale warning,
All the while raining down shredded nut shells
To the tune of a typical twitch tail morning

Endless Wonders

A doorway was opened in the heavens
There was the faint sound of angel's wings,
The clouds began to fill with heavenly beings
Very strange and unusual happenings

The arc angel was about to shout
The trumpet was about to sound,
The graves of the saints were about to be opened
And the alive and saved's feet were about to lift from the ground

What a joyful reunion that will be
When we all reunite up there,
As both the dead and alive in Christ
Lift to meet Jesus in the air

In six days God made this beautiful earth
The heavens, and all that lie therein,
What awaits us beyond this world
I scarce can take it in

For it's been almost two thousand years now
Since the Lord said I go to prepare a place for you,
Heaven must be beyond comprehension
This place of endless wonders we're going to

The creator of the heavens is still creating
Now there's something to really think about,
And all this creation is waiting for us
At the trumpet's sound and the lord's victory shout

The clock is ticking down
We are about to step out of time into eternity,
Into the place of endless wonders
Prepared for you and me

Awesome

He is a lamp unto my feet
He is on my right hand and on my left,
He puts the joy in living
And takes the sting out of death

He is the peace
That only Christians know,
He is the light
At the end of the valley of shadow

He is the bread of life
My cup is always full,
He is the joy and rejoicing of mine heart
The savior of my soul

My meditation of him is sweet
His prescence is ever before me,
His praise is upon my lips
Forever singing of his glory

He is the redeeming lamb
The ever present God of the ages,
Who in his own blood
Has written our names across the book of life's pages

He spoke the worlds into being
He is the creator of all I see,
How awesome
To think he walks and talks with me

The House

Swept and garnished
Every room is spotless and clean,
The light shone in
And not a shadow could be seen

Sixty six pieces of furniture in all
Magnificently deck her halls,
Apples of God in pictures of silver
Ornately decorate her walls

Thirty nine pieces of old
And twenty seven pieces of new,
All are beautiful and perfect
Not too many and not too few

The outside is completely engulfed
In a protective hedge,
An impregnable armour
Of crimson red

When the dark clouds roll in and the winds begin to blow
And terrible storms come across the horizon,
Rest assured within the crimson circle
And turn your eyes upon him

The Principle Thing

King Soloman asked one thing of God
And God did not take Soloman lightly,
For he asked for wisdom, knowledge, and understanding
To rule his people rightly

Because he did not ask for this world's treasures
Or power, or honor, or longgevity,
God gave unto him greater wisdom, greater riches, and
Greater wealth and honor than any man in all history

Get knowledge and with all thy getting get understanding
And get wisdom for this is the principle thing,
Keep your heart always stayed on the lord
And you shall not want for any good thing

If you search for her
Like unto silver and diamonds and gold,
Like the flowers of springtime
Her hidden treasures will unfold

Hold onto her and she will promote you unto honor
Write her across the tables of thine heart,
Lift her up ever before thine eyes
And from thy memory let her not depart

The fear of the Lord is the begining of wisdom
The entrance of his words giveth light,
And whatsoever you do in word or deed
Do with all thine heart and with all thy might

O' What a Joy It Is

There is no better way
For a day to start,
Than to wake up in the morning
With a song in your heart

He is the joy of the sunrise
He is my morning song,
He is the music
Of my all day long

O' What a joy it is to know Jesus
And to rise up in the morning singing,
And to live in the land of the free
And to hear the church bells ringing

I was glad when they said unto me
Let us go into the Lord's house of prayer,
Where we can share our faith, our hopes, and our dreams
With our brothers and sisters there

O' What a joy it is to know Jesus
And to receive his pardon so full and free,
And to live in the blessed hope
Of his return for you and me

My Mother Knows

The angels of heaven rejoiced
That day my mother knelt at the altar of grace,
Confessing Jesus as lord and savior
Destining her someday for a-better place

It was on a cold day, just before my birthday
In February nineteen ninety three,
That my Lord came
And took my mother from me

She rushed towards the light
Her arthritic pain was gone,
She had no more sorrow
Her heart filled with song

Jesus removed her aches and pains
And wiped away her tears,
He gave her back her youth
Turning back the cruel years

She can walk, she can run, she can fly
Echoing Jesus's praises down the streets of gold,
The river of life, the tree of life, the crystal sea
All of heaven's glorys before her eyes unfold

Are there flowers there?
My mother knows,
Do the bird's sweet songs fill the air?
My mother knows

I praise God my mother found an altar of grace
And I thank him for his sweet sweet love,
In taking my mother home to be with him
Into his glorious heaven above

Goose Flesh

There is no greater feeling
Than when God begins to bless,
Have you ever felt his prescence
And the goose bumps rise upon your flesh

Jesus continually touchs our lives
As we bare witness of him,
And I believe the goose flesh
To be the holy spirit's blessing

When two share their faith
When testimonies are give'n,
When someone turns their life around
From the wayward life their liv'n

When someone heeds the invitation
And kneels at an altar of grace,
When someone is walking so close to the Lord
A beautiful glow radiates from their face

When believers pray
When someone asks the way,
When prayers are answered without delay

O' Lord give me ears to hear and eyes to see
And dear God bless my soul,
As I witness of you in spirit and truth
Let those goose bumps flow

The Glorious Gospel

This book is a rock
Holding firm down through the ages,
Vibrantly alive
With the words of life literally jumping from it's pages

Deeply it penetrates the spirit and soul
Pricking the hearts of the readers and listeners thereof,
Expounding and exalting God's beautiful words
Of redemption, forgiveness, and love

Teaching and admonishing
And building us up in the most holy faith,
And giving us peace that passeth all understanding
Through his gift of amazing grace

These words are quick and powerful
And sharper that any two edged sword,
Piercing even to the dividing asunder of joints and marrow
Converting souls unto the Lord

It tells of the birth, death, burial, and resurrection
It's all there in god's wonderful words of life,
His coming, the cross, the empty tomb
The glorious gospel of Jesus Christ

The Miracle of Springtime

The land is a-thirst
The doves coo for rain,
God responds and opens the heavens
And gives us the miracle of spring

Woodducks spook from every pond and puddle
Turtles line half submerged logs,
Dragonflies flit through the air
Snatching mosquitos from the stagnant bogs

The forest's floor becomes a carpet of flaming colors
The redbuds and the dogwoods blossom and bloom,
May apples open their giant umbrellas
The jack in the pulpit appears and up pops the mushroom

Pussy willows and crabapples
Add their vibrant colors to this beautiful scene,
As the miracles of springtime
Turns winter's drab world into glorious shades of green

The earth breaks forth in abundance of life
Beautiful butterflies emerge from cocoons,
The ponds respond with the chirping of frogs
And the wrens add their gay little tunes

The earth is being sumptiously arrayed
As only God could adorn,
For through him her fertile womb is opened
And his miracle of springtime is born

Going On

Now that the burden of the world is rolled away
And you are sealed with the promise of eternal life,
You need to grow in grace
And in the knowledge of our lord and savior Jesus Christ

Study to show thyself approved unto God
Rightly dividing the words of life,
Take your eyes off the world and the failings of man
And keep them steadfastly fixed on Jesus Christ

Walk in the paths of righteousnesss
Order your conversations a-right,
Have nothing more to do with the shadows of darkness
Step out into the light

Look to the bible as your unerring guide
Live by the truths that are found there,
Reach out a helping hand to your fellow man
Always leaning on God in prayer

The path that you have chosen
Is the path that will take you home,
And take courage in this dear fellow christian
You do not walk it alone

Phil

Phil and Tootie, what a beautiful couple
They always encouraged me in all I'd undertake to do,
I shared my poems and my life with them
And they shared theirs with me too

It is to this beautiful couple
I dedicate this poem,
To these two who truly loved others
And you were always welcome in their home

Phil was a hard working farmer all his life
A beautiful person from begining to end,
I'm going to miss him a lot
I couldn't have asked for a better friend

Phil loved God
And I believe he's singing Halleluhahs up there with my Mother,
He was truly one of a kind
There will never be another

I miss him and I know you do too
And I know we always will,
We'll cherish forever the beautiful memories
Of this very special person named Phil

It all seems like a bad dream
None of this seems real,
I know that nothing we can say or do
Can take away this hurt that you feel

In time the wounds will heal
But the scar will always be there,
We entrust it all into the Lord's keeping
And into the hands of his gentle care

Plant and Water

Waiting for loved ones to come home
Are those who have gone on before,
With great expectations
Watching from the other shore

While it is still light
Let us fullfill the great commission,
For there's many more victorys to be won
Before this day on earth is done

There are a lot of people who do not know Jesus
Friends we have the good news to tell,
We need to go unto the world with Christian love
And present the soul saving gospel

Let your light so shine before men
For some you are the only gospel they will ever know,
Be faithful with that which God has given
And let the joy of your salvation show

If we plant the seeds and water them with tears
Being faithful witness's of the prince of peace,
God will open the windows of heaven
And pour out his increase

Joy's Treasures

Heaviness in the heart of man maketh it to stoop
It maketh the countenance sad,
But a word fitly spoken
Lifteth up and maketh glad

He puts the joy in the heart
He flips the frown upside down,
He puts the laughter in the soul
And turns the lives around

Jesus is the joy and rejoicing of my heart
I praise God for the spirit's call,
He is the joy of my life
I stand in awe of the wonder of it all

Nothing thrills my soul like Jesus
Even the very mention of his name,
I rejoice in the joy of my salvation
I am a child of the risen king

All I have or ever will have
Could never compare to that pearl of great price,
For all the treasures of heaven are mine
By grace through faith in Christ

How Great Thou Art

Across the pages of the book of truth
Lies the greatest story ever told,
Where the deep things and the dark sayings
Of the mysteries of God unfold

Although I travel through the depths and heights
And god's mysteries to me are shown,
It will not be until I see Jesus
That I will know as I am known

He is the awesome power
That holds the world in place,
He is the God of wrath
And the loving God of grace

He is the god of my salvation
The giver of life,
The father of creation
And the father of lights

The moon and the stars are the works of his hands
He spoke the worlds into being,
If man would not praise his glory
The very rocks would break forth and sing

He is the giver of gifts
And the giver of grace,
He is the reason
Christians run the race

He created the mountains and the valleys
The sun, the rain, and the bow,
He placed boundaries upon the seas
That they will not overflow

The firmament sheweth his handiwork
The words of life tell his story,
Words of truth to be told and retold
Of Jesus and his glory

And when we come to him in faith
He creates within us a new heart,
Sins are forgiven and forgotten
O' God how great thou art

All That He Is

The angel of the Lord
Encampeth round about those that fear him,
The Lord is the light and my salvation
Of whom should I fear then?

He is the joy of the morning
Whose light is brighter than the rising sun,
He is the light in the valley of darkness
The glorious Lord of my salvation

He lights the pathway of life
And directs our steps in his,
He is our guide even unto death
When, praise God, we shall go to be where he is

He is the light of the world
Who quickens the souls of men,
He is a lamp unto our feet
And the cleansing light within

He is the light of heaven
He is the bright and morning star,
He is the goodness and the righteousness
Of all that we are

His love is more precious
Than silver, diamonds, or gold,
Of all that he is
The half has not been told

In all, he is all
All that he proclaims to be,
The son of man, the son of God,
The Holy Lord God of glory

A Tribute to Orville Breedlove

Orville was a co worker
And Orville was a friend,
He saw what Jesus did for me
And to my church he began to attend

Now one day Orville found out
That he needed bypass surgery,
But he was unsure of his salvation
And he remembered the Jesus he saw in me

The Lord spoke to me
Honest, I heard it loud and clear,
It was plain to me what he said
But it was not audible for another to hear

The Lord said: go see Orville!
I said: what?
And the Lord repeated:
Go see Orville!

I was in the shower at the time
And I dried off and dressed as fast as Ii could,
And drove to Orvilles
Believing for God's good

When I knocked on that door
I was unprepared for what Orville said:,
Where have you been?, I've been praying for you to get here
And whoosh the goose bumps began to spread

Orville told me about the bypass surgery
He was about to face,
And I asked Orville if he was saved
If he had received God's grace

Orville stuttered and said:
I think so,
I said: oh no Orville
You gotta know so

I told him to go the altar
And publicly accept and confess Jesus,
He told me that Friday was the day of the surgery
And with prayer we left it there in the hands of Jesus

Orville called later and said that the doctor had called and
That the surgery had been put off until Monday,
Orville walked up to that altar of grace
And was assured of his salvation that Sunday

Orville came through the surgery fine
And served the lord faithfully for his last five years,
The events that took place that got Orville saved
I recall often with tears

If we walk closely with the Lord
And tune out the world's clutter and noise,
He will speak to us
And we will hear his wee small voice

Orville believed and he reached out
And from the bondage of sin was set free,
I am so glad that I was saved
And Orville seen Jesus in me

Loosen Up

My hand is the pen of the ready writer
I know how to drive the message home,
But a few of my coworkers have threatened to hurt me
If I write another booger poem.

I promise not to write any more gross poems
(Well maybe just a few more),
Hey! Laughter is good for the soul
* Hain't you got no sense of humor

I don't know how many times I've laughed my fanny off
(just kid'n, it's still there),
Over some dry humor
Someone just pulls out of the air

If people look at you like you've lost your mind
Let em stare,
As far as I'm concerned if they * haint got no funny bone
They are the ones who aren't all there

Hey cheer up
There is nothing better for the soul,
Than that which tickles your fancy
And gives you a good ole belly roll

At times I've laughed so hard I cried
That's the good part of the humor we share,
So go ahead and laugh your fanny off
And lose some der-ri-ere

*I found this word in the hillbilly dictionary

Unforgetable

Unforgetable sights and sounds permeate these wilderness haunts
This is the land of crystal clear waters and bright blue skys,
Where the moose, the bear, and the caribou roam
And the ravens and the eagles fly

Where the sound of the loon instills the call of the wild
And every horizon is an uncluttered panoramic view,
And the cedar and the birch shake hands
And gossip at the rising of the dew

Caribou wade the shallow shores
Wolve's howls echo in the pale moonlight,
Black bears roam pine scented forests
And the everchanging beauty of the sunset fades slowly into
The night

O' To contently lean back and listen to the gentle waves
Lapping softly over a rocky shore,
And open ones eyes and look to the heavens
And watch the eagles soar

To walk where moccasins have walked
And to see and to absorb the beauty that they saw,
To walk the trails and paddle the streams
Where the birch and the pine grow tall

Moonlit lakes
And the hum of the mosquito in the night,
The sparkle of gold and then silver
As the sun rises and sheds it's morning warmth and light

Forget this beautiful place?
Never!
For it is unforgetable
A place that will haunt you forever

Well Done

Have patience with me Lord
Reach out and take me by the hand,
Guide me in the pathways
That lead upward towards the promised land

Walk with me and talk with me
And assure me of your love,
Tell me again of the peace and joy
That abounds in your heaven above

Let the joy of thy salvation be felt
Let your prescence be known,
Make me a faithful witness
Of the light to me you've shown

Make me an overcomer
Chastise me lord when I stray,
Correct me with your loving hand
And let me not fall away

Direct my steps in thy steps
Show me the way wherein I should go,
Place my feet on the straight and narrow
And let the radiance of thy prescence show

Let me sing with the redeemed
Let the joyful echos ring,
Hallelujah what a savior
Praise God, my Lord and King

In every failing of my being Lord
I pray grant me the grace to overcome,
That in the book of life, final chapter, final page
Final two words written in red, be Jesus's "Well done"

One More Hug

When a loved one passes on
It leaves so many kind words left unsaid,
Brothers and sisters let us not love in word neither in tongue
But in deed and truth instead

One more hug, one more kiss
One more time to say I love you,
Time is so short
And our passing moments precious and few

Take a loved one by the hand
And make them O' So fully aware,
That they are a very important part of your life
And that you really truly care

As you walk along the pathway of life
Spread some sunshine along the way,
That those who follow after
May rejoice in your day

That they may bask in the afterglow
Of the one who gave you life,
Of the one who gives the flowers and sunshine
The Lord and Savior Jesus Christ

Reach out
And put your arms around that loved one without delay,
For tomorrow brothers and sisters it may be to late
To give that hug away

Let Us Never Forget

They arrayed him in a purple robe
And with a wreath of thorns they crowned him king,
Then they stripped him and beat him
Naked and forsaken he bore our sin and shame

Three rusty nails tore through flesh and wood
They crucified the holy god of creation,
He endured and suffered the curse of the cross
To redeem souls out of every nation

But cold stone walls could not seal him in
For he triumphed victorious over death and the grave,
Miraculously the tomb was found empty
When an angel came down and rolled the stone away

He is God and he is alive
Death and the grave could not hold him,
He openly spoiled principalities and powers
Conquering forever the power of sin

Let us never forget
That God so loved the world he gave his son,
And let us never ever forget
What our Lord and savior has done

To be saved you must come to the foot of the cross
And humbly kneel and pray,
Confessing and repenting and asking god's forgiveness
Yes! Through the blood of Jesus is the only way

If we seek him we will be found of him
The joy of salvation can be yours today,
For at the foot of the cross
Christ is only a prayer away

Into His Hands

When one member of the body hurts
The whole body is in sympathy for that part,
And in instant prayer we go to God
Believing with all our heart

Christian's love for one another
Runs wide and it runs deep,
And we rejoice with those who do rejoice
And weep with those who weep

God knows our joys and our sorrows
Our broken hearts and pain,
And the believer's prayers of faith are answered
When presented to the father in Jesus's name

It is in these darkest times
When we learn to trust him most,
We praise you father, we praise you Lord
And we praise you O' Holy ghost

Thank God and praise God we need not face our trials alone
For lo even unto the end of the world he has promised to always be with
us,
So pray the prayer of faith, and lift those budens up
And place them into the loving hands of Jesus

With A Song In My Heart

Fill me with Jesus joy
Bring a tapp'n to my feet,
Let the songs burst forth
With a live and vibrant beat

Let the arms raise
And the hands clap,
Let the lips praise
And the feet tap

Rejoice O' My soul
Rejoice and cry out,
Make a joyful noise
Give the hallelujah shout

There is a fire in my bones
As my tongue gives you praise,
Let not that fire go out
All of my days

Praise you Lord Jesus
For this joyeous song's beat,
And for the thrilling of my soul
Right down to the souls of my feet

From the tip of every finger
To the tip of every toe,
You are the rejoicing of my heart
And the thrill of my soul

With a song in my heart
I'll praise you with all my being,
And when I leave this world Lord
Joyfully I'll leave it singing

Why?

Why you are not saved
Is more than I can comprehend,
Do you not believe
Or don't you care my friend?

It costs you nothing
Jesus Christ paid the price for your sin,
Salvation is the free gift
Yours for the taking in believing and trusting in him

How can you not believe?
All you need do is to look around you,
Where do you think the heavens and the earth came from?
And who made the oceans so deep and the skys so blue?

Who created life?
Do you think a cataclismic explosion made the big splat?,
Well if so
Who do you think made that?

Do not try to bring God down to your understanding
For with God my friend there is no begining,
He is the "I am that I am"
And to our finite minds he is beyond comprehending

He created and placed us and everything around us
Into the realm of seconds, and minutes, and hours,
But he was, he is, and he will always be
The God of Gods, the Lord of Lords, and the awesome power of
Powers

Two Alternitives, One Choice

Do you want to walk the hallowed halls of heaven
Where there is no shadows or night?,
And walk those golden pavements
Where Jesus is it's light?

Do you want to be clothed with the royal robes
And live forever in joy, and love, and peace?,
Or do you want to be clothed with rotten flesh
And be the maggot's perpetual feast?

Do you want to live with Jesus
Clothed in apparels of glistening white?,
Or do you want to open your eyes
To the demonic terrors of the night?

Do you want to praise Jesus
Where there is no sorrow, nor time, nor tears?,
Or do you want to dwell forever
In nightmares, pain, and fears?

A man can choose
If he so desires,
To escape the eternal damnation
Of hell's unquenchable fires

All that call upon the Lord will be saved
Will God hear your voice?,
There are two eternal destinations
But only one choice

Life without End

You've tried the world, the flesh, and the devil
And did you find lasting happiness my friend?,
Now why don't you try Jesus who gives you fullness of joy
Peace for the soul, and life without end

Don't, I repeat, don't clean up your act
And come to Jesus,
But come to Jesus
Who is your righteousness

He purchased your salvation with a price
You cannot buy it or earn it,
It is a free gift that he purchased for you
You have only to reach out to receive it

The only way
To receive salvation's radiant glow,
Is to be washed
In that precious crimson flow

Our righteousness is but filthy rags
Our goodness won't get us into heaven,
Only by the blood of Jesus
Is salvation found through him

You've heard people say: I'm a good person
I've led a good life,
But heaven's gates open only
For those who have been washed in the blood of Jesus Christ

So turn your back to the world, the flesh, and the devil
And try Jesus my friend,
And enter a whole nother world
Of fullness of joy and life without end

Songs of Fire

We need more songs to cause souls to revive
More songs filled with zest and enthusiasm,
More songs sung with punch and bounce
Like the old fashioned revivals and spirituals have'em

Songs that fill our hearts with Jesus joy
Songs that set the feet a tap'n,
Songs that lift our expectations
In believing god's miracles are about to happen

Songs that kindle the sparks to flame
Song that make us more fully alive,
Songs that make our hearts skip a beat
And cuts through the clutter like a knife

Songs that make Jesus our heart's desire,
Songs that sets our goals much higher,
Songs that sets our souls on fire

Songs that make us more fully aware of the needs of others
Songs that put our feet and hands to our prayers,
Songs that send us out into the world
Seeking not ours but theirs

Songs that take the lukewarm hearts
And brings them to a boil,
Songs that make us want to give our all
In blood, sweat, and toil

Songs of fire
Songs that rekindle and revive,
Songs that wake up the soul
And makes us fully alive

The Way Back

You've wandered, you've strayed
You've fallen away,
Of God's words of truth
You no longer obey

I tell you of a truth
I've been there,
And it's a scary thing to be outside the fold
And no lnger under God's loving care

But listen for I tell you there is hope
You need not be lost forever in that merciless black hole
For beneath the altar where you were first saved
God's mercy continues to flow

But unless you put on the whole armour of God every day
The devil's fiery darts will come penetrating through,
And your soul will gradually corrupt
And your thoughts toward God will be seldom and few

I tell you again, if your mind is not stayed on Christ
You will utterly fall away,
You will wake up one morning wondering how it all happened
And ask yourself in tears, how O' How could I have lost my way?

But if we wrap ourselves with garments of light and truth
Putting on the breastplate of righteousness,
And shodding our feet with the gospel of peace
God will put his helmet of salvation upon us

And with the shield of faith
We will thourouly quench every fiery dart of the wicked one,
And with the sword of the spirit
Every battle, great and small, will be victoriously won

All that We Are

We are more than flesh and bone
We are more that hearts beating in vessels of clay,
God made each one of us different and unique
In our own special way

He gave us personalities and talents
And clothed us without and within,
He gave us a soul and a spirit
And placed within us a need to know and worship him

He floods the soul with joy
And infills us with his holy spirit,
He has made available to us the knowledge of amazing grace
And to all who have ears to hear it

This totally awesome God
Now grasp this if you can,
Has extended his gift of amazing grace
To the likes of sinful man

And by the light of all that we are we reflect the glory of all that he is
Through the gifts and talents that he has given,
God miraculously takes our total indivduality
Amd makes us vessels of honor and glory to him

A Glimpse of Heaven

I was reading in revelation the other night
And through John's eyes I saw heaven for the first time,
Imagine a city of transparent gold paved with streets of
Transparent gold
With Jesus's light making all of heaven to shine

The river of life flowing through it
The sea of glass glistening like an emerald,
The tree of life and it's twelve manner of fruits
No sun, nor rain, nor heat, nor cold

Only peace and joy and rejoicing
Seeing loved ones again,
Talking with Paul and Silas
And John, and Peter, and James

And seeing and walking and talking with the lamb of God
I would shed tears of joy but there are no tears there,
I cannot comprehend that this beauty, and joy, and peace is
Forever
But this to you I will declare

I Tom, saw the city of New Jerusalem
And I saw paradise,
As I caught a glimpse of heaven
Through John's Eyes

A Warning

If you like darkness that can be felt
If you love sulfur's acrid smell,
And the worms crawling in and out of your burning flesh
And you are fully determined to go to hell

Then don't open the holy book
Don't pick up this rock that's held firm down through the ages,
No don't look inside it's covers
And most certainly don't read the words that are scribed across it's
pages

For people have been known to be convicted and converted
By merely the reading of the gospel of Jesus Christ,
You could find yourself saved and sealed by the holy ghost
Where the only thing to look forward to is heaven and eternal life

This is the book of truth
This is the greatest story ever told,
Inside are the words of life
Treasures far exceeding silver and gold

Be ready when you read this book
For a life changing experience,
I read it for the first time a long time ago
And nothing, I mean nothing has been the same since

Yea this word is quick and powerful
And it will convict you of sin,
It will seep into your bones, prick your heart, and lift your soul
So beware before you read, " you could be born again"

Don't

Don't climb a tree without testing each and every limb
And even worse don't do it with a running chain saw,
For you may find yourself holding a hollow limb
And your body in a terrifying free fall

Now here's another one
And this is really dumb,
When you catch a dogfish
Don't try to pick him up with your forefinger and thumb

When walking through a swamp
Test out each and every step on the solidity of the land,
You may find yourself shorter than usual
Sinking in quicksand

And when you relieve yourself in the woods
There are things you ought to leave be,
Don't wipe on poison oak, poison shumak, or nettles,
Or any leaflet three

Don't straddle a rattlesnake
Don't stand up in a canoe,
Don't walk into an apple orchard with bee hives
Or you might wind up with a lump or two

There are a lot of common sense laws
You shouldn't break or bend,
Like don't try to swallow before you chew
And don't spit into the wind

Don't wait to go to shore
Until your eyeballs float,
And whether standing up or bending down
Don't try to pee over the side of the boat

I've got sixteen needle size teethmarks in my thumb
And I'm guilty of all these things that I wrote,
Yes I'm the guy who climbed the tree, straddled the snake
And drained the thing over the side of the boat

The Land of Dreams

This is the land of the free
The land where dreams come true,
The land of America, the land of old glory,
The land of the red white and blue

To the soldiers who gave their all
In honor and glory we sing,
For the freedom we have in this god blessed nation
Let the liberty bell and the church bells ring

Our country was founded upon God
And the freedom to pursue our heart's desires,
This land is our land
Where sparks of hope become blazing fires

Here there is nothing you cannot be
There are no mountains to high,
You can reach for the moon and the stars
And pluck them out of the sky

Let your voice be heard
Let your arms raise,
For all that America is and stands for
To God be the glory and to God be the praise

This is the home of the stars and stripes
A land filled with stardust and moonbeams,
A nation truly blessed of God
Where your free to pursue and achieve your dreams

Nuts

They say I'm going the wrong way
Down a one way road,
And that I'm one brick shy of a load

I was out in the back yard
Rocking in my rocking chair like old folks do,
Playing solitare
With a deck that lacked a few

I had a bag of marbles
Clutched tightly in my hand,
And I lost my grip and they spilled out
And went down a gopher hole in the sand

I got up to find them
And yes I had lost my marbles and was off my rocker,
But hey, my wife ain't wrapped to tight
But no ones knocking her

I'm a bubble off center
I ain't all there,
Somethings missing
But I don't know where

They came to take me away
I really didn't want to go,
But they got me to laughing
Ha ha, hee hee, ho ho

I had this backward jacket on
You know, where they tie the sleeves in the back,
And guys in white were frantically chasing me
Yelling something like: "Catch that escapee from the boobie hatch

Hey! The world's okay
But I think I'll go back to the loonie bin soon,
Cause there ain't nothing funner
Than bouncing off the walls of the rubber room

Fully Alive

Have you ever walked into a woods
Just before sunrise,
And sat down on a log
And watched the morning come alive?

Listening to the click click
Of the chipmunk's telegraph alert,
And the fox squirrel's bark and the red squirrle's sbuzz
As the dew rises from the damp clean earth

To listen to the distant hooting of a great horned owl
And the scream of a hawk and the cawing of crows,
To smell the faint sweet smell
Of the multi flower rose

To feel the sun's warmth drive out the chill of the morning
To watch the honeybees visiting the wild woods flowers,
To hear the hypnotic hum of the mosquito
As you sit totally engrossed in the enchantment of the wee morning hours

To watch the clouds turning different shades of pink, red, and yellow
As the hand of god paints his glory across the skys,
Sights and sounds and smells
Gloriously bringing the beauty of the morning fully alive

Angelic Voices

Everything is covered in a blanket of pure white snow
The ribbons and wreaths are hung,
There is holly and bittersweet and mistle toe
And christmasy songs to be sung

Ornaments reflecting flaming colored lights
The scent of pine is in the air,
There are smiling faces and joy filled hearts
And the laughter of children everywhere

Yule logs burn brightly
Popcorn garlands wrap trees of green,
Peace falls over the star studded night
The countryside is transformed into a christmasy scene

Candy canes and packages with bright colored wrappings
Cold, clean, clear, crisp skys,
Turkey, and ham and all kinds of pies
Family and friends and children's excitement filled eyes

Then we hear the melody of the carolers
Spreading Christ's messages upon the wind,
Reminding our hearts of the true reason for the season
And to turn our eyes upon him

Wise Men

The wise men, the magi, the kings of the east
Journeyed from kingdoms a-far,
With treasures of gold, frankincense, and myrrh
Following a wandering star

Over the little town of Bethlehem
The star stood still and cast down it's silvery glow,
Down upon the blessed event
That took place in a manger below

The kings opened their treasures
And presented their bountiful offerings,
Kneeling before this baby boy
Lord of Lords and King of Kings

No life would ever change the course of the world
Like that one wrapped in swaddling clothes,
God the Son, the Son of God
Sharon's beautiful rose

In this present world
Two thousand years after Christ's atonement for sin,
Lives are still being changed
As wise men continue to seek him

Step Out

Do you want that heavenly peace?
Do you want that sweet release?,
Come to Calvary
Come to the altar of grace, the foot of the cross
And set your soul free

There is victory in Jesus
He will set your heart on things above,
He will fill your soul with joy
And lavish you with love

Jesus gave his all for you
Turn from your life of sin,
Come to the altar and witness to the world
That the light of heaven's come in

Stand up
And step out from where you are,
Come to Calvary,
To that bright and morning star

Live the life of miracles
Experience the victory,
Know what it's like to be born again
And your burdens lifted free

Step out, kneel down, and reach up
Look full into his wonderful face,
And receive the greatest gift of all
God's gift of amazing grace

The Last Great Adventure

I've ventured through thick forests
And canoed down wild and beautiful rivers,
I've fished and hunted this glorious land
And experienced many and varied adventures

I've been to the Canadian wilderness
And my heart still yearns for her,
But one day O' Glorious day
I will experience the last and great adventure

Through the bible I've caught only a faint glimpse
Of all of God's beauty that awaits,
But one day I shall know as I am known
As I step through those pearly gates

Rivers and seas like emeralds of glass, citys of translucent gold
Endless, fantastic, marvelous, beautiful sights,
Glory more magnificent than this world has ever known
Where the light of heaven outshines the northern lights

When the death angel comes to call
Don't be terrified by his sight,
Believe and trust in the promises of Jesus
And go towards the light

Let the anticipation of the great adventure
Take away every fear of death,
And let us praise our redeemer, savior, lord, and king
From our first to our last dying breath

Make your calling and election sure
And in the last great adventure your joy shall be full,
Beyond the portals of time
In life eternal

Goodby Uncle " Pud " I love you

The Fat Man and the Hare

A bag full of goodies
And a great big heart,
His belly jiggles when he laughs
Jolly old fart

For a rabbit
To lay an egg would be a phenominal feat,
But believe me when I tell you
What comes out of the backside of a rabbit you wouldn't want
To eat

A fat chimney duster in a red and white suit
Real funny,
But wait till you hear the one about the colored eggs
And the legendary Easter bunny

Now I know what comes out of the backside of a rabbit,
And believe me when I tell you
Chocalate and hard boiled eggs ain't it

Now I wrote this poem
To be read just the way it's writ,
And those droppings along the bunny trail
Are nothing but bunny—doo

Enough said
And with that this poem now ends,
Of the fat man and the hare
Two myths that became legends

Put Your Hand in His

Why have we fallen in love with stuff
That rots, corodes, and rusts?,
The world's treasures
And it's many enticing lusts?

Our Lord offers us eternal rewards
Of everlasting love,
Treasures that fade not away
In his kingdom up above

If we spend each day
Filling our own selfish desires,
How then shall we escape
Hell's unquenchable damnation fires?

Jesus is reaching out
His desire is that none be lost,
Reach for heaven's gold
And forsake this world's dross

Joy and peace and love
Are the greatest of all treasures,
These all await the repentant soul
Who chooses Jesus over worldly pleasures

His hand is reaching out today
Won't you put your hand in his?,
Follow where he leads
And be a rflection of all that he is?

There is no greater treasure
Than that which God has to give,
Put your hand in his
And live

O' Glorious Day

How can we ever begin to comprehend
The fullness of God's love in all that he has done,
When in his infinate mercy and grace
He offered up his son

The story's been told and retold
And then told again,
Of the telling of it
There is no end

Of how Jesus came to this earth,
Through the miracle of the virgin birth

How he lived his life
And was crucified,
The cold stone tomb, the seal upon it
And the watch that was placed outside

But three days hence
Before the dawning of the breaking of day,
An angel came down and broke the seal
And rolled the stone away

And that which the witnesses saw,
Was the greatest miracle of all

The tomb was empty
Jesus was not there,
Accept for the burial linens
The grave where they laid Jesus was bare

He was alive and appeared unto many
And afterwards asscended to his heavenly throne,
Gone to prepare a place for us
And one day, O' Glorious day, he's coming back to take us home

Hubie

Hubie would reach down deep into his pocket
And offer up a piece of wrapped sweetness,
And from out of his heart
He would offer up Jesus

His witness was consistent
He preached to everyone,
Even in the hospital
The doctors and nurses had nowhere to run

Whoever he would come in contact with
He would ask about their spiritual welfare,
He was sincere and he was concerned
Hubie really did care

He loved God and he loved people
And he truly loved to preach,
No one within the sound of his voice
Was out of God's reach

He knew the word of God
And God blessed his word through him,
He would tell you about the joys of Jesus
And the consequences of sin

No sugar coating
Hubie always told it like it was,
God's faithful witness
Who was an inspiration to all of us

We shall truly miss him
His jolly laughter and his warm friendly smile,
He was not only our acquaintance and brother in the Lord
But he was the friend who would go the extra mile

A Sense of Humor

I believe that a sense of humor is vital to life
And that there is at least a smidgen in each of us,
And that a warm friendly smile will melt the coldest heart
And that laughter is contageous

If it tckles your fancy
Let out a giggle,
Loosen up the old funny bone
And chuckle a little

Come on
If it strikes you funny let it roar,
Don't hold back, let it go
Laugh till you can laugh no more

Get a new lease on life
Give a few ho-ho's,
Let that belly jiggle
And forget your woes

A sense of humor is a lot of fun
Come on and give it a try,
Laugh until your belly hurts
Laugh until you cry

Music of the Soul

Childhood memories recollected
But barely so,
Of the many wonders
Of days of long ago

Of a bucket and spoon
And a sand box,
Of swimming and fishing
And collecting rocks

Of going bare footed in the sand
Of dancing in the rain,
Of playing in the autumn leaves
And of looking forward to winter again

Of snowblall fights and snow forts
And the making of snow men,
Of ice skating
And downhill sledding again

Through youthfull eyes
The world looked O' So grand,
As we anxiously awaited and anticipated the changing of the
seasons
Through God's miraculous transforming touch upon the land

Laying back and looking up
With an imagitive creative eye,
Watching white fluffy clouds change their shapes
As they journey lazily across the sky

O' To ponder
Upon those youthful days of long ago,
When joy and laughter
Was the sweet, sweet music of the soul

"Bumps of Fire"

The deep things and the dark sayings
All of God's hidden treasures of old,
To the converted heart, like a spring flower
Miraculously unfold

Have you ever felt the spirit's fire
Of goose bumps running along your flesh?,
Of the tears of joy
Of overwhelming happiness?

Peace, love, and amazing grace
Are God's precious gifts to man,
To be enjoyed throughout his lifelong journey
On his pilgrimage towards the promised land

Joys unspeakable and full of glory
Blessings poured out upon us,
As we rejoice in our awesome god
And the manifestation of his son Jesus

Goose flesh!
Of all God's blessings I shall never tire,
And O' How I love
Those little bumps of fire

Jenny

Leafless trees and lifeless sounds
What a dreary scene,
But then the brush begins to stroke
With splattering shades of green

The days are getting longer
The snow is melting from off the land,
And this brown muddy mess that now appears
Is but a canvas in the master's hand

If the winter blahs are weighing you down
Then listen intently for those first signs of spring,
For the time the ponds scream out
And Jenny begins to sing

God is painting his springtime colors
In wild woods flowers all across the ground,
And the ponds are bursting forth with life
As little bug eyed amphibians begin to sound

Look for God's miracles
In all the phenominal glorys of the arrival of spring,
And listen intently for those sweet melodys of joy
That only Jenny can sing

Not Just a Line

Roses are red
Violets are blue,
I've made up these words
Just for you

Yah! Right!
You say you've heard it before,
Well hang in there
There's more

I love you
And that's not just a line,
The sweetheart of my youth
Is still my valentine

Through thick and thin
We've always kept our vows as husband and wife,
And you are and will always be
The love of my life

Yes! Roses are red and violets are blue
Are statements that are absolutely true,
But so also dear Alice are those three little words
I love you

Happy Valentines Day
from your everlove'n hubby

Beware

I love to tickle the old funny bones,
With off beat dry humored funny poems

No! This is not going to be one of those,
That embellishes upon the gross things
That inhabits your nose

With the soul of a poet
And the heart of a clown,
Have I ever let you down

If it's funny I'll write it
So don't get all bent,
If I write about toe jam, arm pits,
Or belly button lint

I try not to be gross
But you know me,
If it's thunk, it's wrote
For all to see

So keep an open mind
And your barf bag handy,
Cause the next poem
Could be just one gross of a dandy

The Wanderer

Jesus came
To seek and save that which was lost,
Come to the altar of grace
And kneel at the foot of the cross

He left eternity
And entered into time,
But not for to seek
The ninety and nine

He came for the wandering daughter
And the wandering son,
Are you the lost sheep?
Are you that one?

Jesus is still preparing a place for us
A place of unending joy and peace,
Where the cares of this world
And all pains and tears cease

If you ever make a vow to God
Make sure it's one you keep,
And when Jesus comes again to claim his own
Don't be that wandering sheep

He is There

Why should I attend church
When the great outdoors is my cathedral?,
Where God's beauty is spread out before me
And the sermons are never dull

We as the body of Christ
Need each other,
We are the family of God
Each sister and each brother

I was O' So glad when they said unto me
Let us go into the Lord's house of prayer,
Where we can share our joys and our blessings
And our burdens are lifted there

It is a place where the truth is heard
The glorious gospel's good news,
And tears of conviction appears in lost souls eyes
As white knuckles grasp old wooden pews

Let us not forsake the assembling of ouselves
In the Lord's house of prayer,
For where two or more are gathered in his name
He is there

Beautiful Choice

He is the truth and the life
He is the only way my friend,
There is hope in no other
Salvation comes only through him

How can you live in this world
Without Christ?,
Don't you know that he loved you so
That he died that you might have life?

What in this world
Could entice you away from eternal glory?
Open your bible to Mathew, Mark, Luke, and John
And with an open heart read the whole gospel story

And if God puts conviction into your heart
To believe,
Kneel where you are
And ask and receive

And salvation's joy
To your soul he will impart,
And he will send the comforter
To dwell in your heart

Now listen to me, if you were a-thirst and were offered an
Ice cold drink
Wouldn't you drink thereof,
God offers eternal life through the shed blood of his son
I can't understand anyone rejecting such love

God is calling
Won't you listen to his voice?,
Life
What a beautiful choice

You Ain't Seen Noth'n Yet

The deciples looked upon the temple
As a marvelous work to behold,
As we also marvel
At all of God's creation of old

The seven wonders of the world
The oceans, rivers, lakes, and seas,
Plush green valleys and snow capped mountains
God's endless wonders seemingly never cease

You were born
You came, you lived, you saw,
And at the end of life
Just when you think you've seen it all

Now I'm not a gambling man
But this to you I'll bet,
Of all your eyes absorbed before
You ain't seen noth'n yet

For those who continually used his name in vain
And never repented of their sin,
And for those who were converted
And lived their lives for him

Each has the hereafter to face
For the one hell's horrors awaits,
The other has all the joys and wonders
That lies inside those pearly gates

One gave all that he had
The other took all that he could get,
To both I say
You ain't seen noth'n yet

The Never Fading Light

Flaming yellow fire
Sinking slowly into the horizon,
Streaking clouds with veins of gold
As we bare witness to the breathless beauty of the setting sun

Pinks and reds
Replaces the flaming yellow gold,
As the sun sinks deeper and deeper
Causing the darker crimson colors to unfold

Then that beautiful painting flickers, fades,
And then it's gone,
But it is not lost forever
For in the memory it lingers on

Our thoughts go then to deeper things
More beautiful than the setting sun,
Of the gift of life, of Jesus Christ
And our heavenly home when our day on earth is done

Of the place where there is no sun
But the light of it is lighter than day,
And that light is Jesus
The light that never fades away

O' So Beautiful

At the eastern edge of the woods
Delicately clinging to a web a spider has spun,
Dew drops of gold
Reflect the glory of the rising sun

Puffs of white fluff
Float across a sea of blue skys,
As God continues to delight and enlighten the soul
Through the windows of the eyes

Out of the darkness overhead
We see twinkling eyes of light
Diamonds sparkling
Imbedded in the black velvet of the night

Then there is the white fire
Of gleaming ripples upon the streams,
And the shimmering glittering sparks
Of snowflakes dancing in and out of silvery moonbeams

The sweet fragrance and deep beauty of a flower
And the most beautiful music ever heard.
Praising, rejoicing, uplifting songs
That could only be sung by a little bird

Rainbows bursting forth in all their majestic colors
Glorious to their beholders eyes,
Casting mighty flourescent arcs
Against a background of blackened skys

And O' So beautiful
Is the sunshine after the rain,
And the peace
Beyond the pain

It's Hallelujah Time

If you have been sealed by the holy spirit
If you have been grafted into the vine,
Rejoice with exceeding great joy
For it's hallelujah time

It is a time for shouting
A time to confess Jesus before men,
Go tell the world of the miracle of Calvary
And the appropriation he has made for your sin

The miracle worker lives
He dwells in the hearts of all who believe,
All you need do is open the door
And ask and you shall receive

Christ's desire is that none be lost
He wants to save you,
His arms are opened wide
What are you going to do?

He awaits without
Awaiting your invitation,
Open the door of your heart
And let the Lord of life come in

Let the tears of joy flow
Become a part of the vine,
And praise glory to the God of creation
It's hallelujah time

My Everything

He is my all
He is my everything,
He is my every heartbeat
And the songs of joy I sing

He is the joy of my salvation
The rejoicing of my every breath,
He is the giver of life
Who has triumphed over sin and death

Praise you Lord Jesus
Praise thy holy name,
Praise you for entering into my life
And forgiving my sin and shame

You have changed my world forever
You have turned it upside down,
You have loved me into life
And turned my life around

Of all the wonderous joys of thy salvation
My soul shall forever sing,
Thank you Lord for coming into my life
And becoming my everything

What's Holding You Back?

Is your name written down
In the lamb's book of life?,
Have your sins been blotted out
Have you been washed and cleansed in the blood of Jesus Christ

Who in their right mind
Is more than I can tell,
Would choose eternal damnation
In the firey pits of hell?

Are you holding back
Hanging on to some dirty habit or dark desire?,
Then ask yourself this question
Is the nicotine, drugs, or booze worth the eternal damnation
Of hell fire?

What prevents you from coming to the Lord
Is it that cigarette in your hand?,
Nothing, I mean nothing
Should be allowed to come between you and the promised land

In hell the fire cannot be quenched
And the worm never dies,
The darkness is the darkness that can be felt
And the voices are the damned's wailing crys

Don't miss out on heaven's joys
Because of some unclean habit you can't seem to break free of,
Come to the altar of grace
And be washed and cleansed in the fountain of love

Heaven is the one and only wise choice
Lord lift the scales from their eyes that they might see,
All the glorys of heaven and the horrors of hell
And the stark reality of eternity

Masterpieces

A little lake nestled deep in the woods
Like a mirror so calm and still,
Whose silence is broken only by the deep bellow of a bullfrog
Or the haunting cry of the whipperwill

The fresh clean smell of the damp morning air
The dawn's first faint glimmer of golden light,
Masterpieces one and all, painted forever in the memories
Of smells and sounds and sights

Dark blue violets, dogwoods, and multi colored woods flowers
Water gurgling over rocks as little streams flow through deep
Cut erosions
Large raindrops raise bubbles upon the lakes calm surface
As flashes of light precede cracks of thuderous explosions

Refreshing sweet odors follow after the rain
And drift slowly through majestic trees that have outlived
Our father's fathers,
Royal kings of the green shaded forests
Whose time weathered faces stare back from the pale blue waters

Spell binding, captivating, scenes to be recalled over and over
Beautiful memories that fade not with time,
Masterpieces each and every one
Painted forever upon the canvases of the mind

Utterly Awesome

Winter is crisp and clean and summer is lazy and wonderful
And O' So beautiful are the colored leaves of fall,
But when God ushers in his springtime
We are in for the most glorious season of them all

Spring has arrived
Filling the land with all it's magic wonder,
Morrels are bursting forth from the damp clean earth
Raised to life by the sun and rain and thunder

A flowering quilt is spreading over the land
The dogwoods are sporting their white petaled best,
The earth is coming alive
Awakening out of it's long long winter's rest

The spirea bushes are covered with yellow blossomss
The redbuds are in full bloom,
Everything is adorned in springtime's garments of glory
And jenny wren is singing her joyful tune

In this time of utterly awesome wonder
When life so beautifully and abundantly abounds,
Our hearts beat faster and faster
To God's springtime miracles of sights and sounds

Elm

Their gray naked bodies stand straight and tall
In long thin strips their outer skin sags to the ground,
They are the dead guardians and keepers
Of the magnificent golden crown

Of a rare disease
They died long ago,
But in the springtime their dead roots reach down
To create and bring forth life from the dark realms below

The dead feeding the living.
What a spectacular sight,
When all around their rotting roots
Yellow and gray morels burst forth into the warm sunlight

Haunting ghostly apparitions of the morning fog
Dewdrops gleam a-top yellow gold,
Mayapples, flowers, and apple blossoms bloom
As springtimes mysteries of life unfold

Tall ghostly specters standing firm in the mist
Surrounded by yellow sponges,
Graveyards of naked gray and peeling bark
Standing guard over the incredible edible fungus

Dorothy

Dorothy as we knew her
Has been absent from us a long, long while,
In the nursing home her mind was gone
Yet she continually greeted us with a smile

The other night the angels came
And ushered her to her heavenly home,
Her mind has been restored
And now she smiles before God's throne

The funeral was a beautiful tribute
To a soul entering into life,
Not a mourning for the dead
But a rejoicing for one alive forevermore in Christ

Two sisters sang that beautiful song
Titled "In the garden",
Emotions overflowed from singers and listeners
As tears of joy were shed for the victory that Dorothy had won

A poem written by a loving granddaughter
Was read aloud by the preacher for all to hear,
And in every heart was felt her love
And in every eye there glistened a tear

Thank you Lord for that christian lady
Who you predestined to be my mother in law,
Who faithfully prayed for us when we were lost
Till we heeded the spirit's call

Yes Lord we thank you for Dorothy
And yes we are saddened that she has been taken from our midst,
But we praise thy holy name
That in your book of life, her name was on that list

The Pen and the Pearl

The word of God is quick and powerful
And sharper than any two edged sword,
More powerful than lead and steel
Is this life giving gospel of my Lord

All I have or will ever own
Cannot buy everlasting life,
For this prize can only be attained
Through faith and trust in the cross of Jesus Christ

God's written word
Speaks of amazing grace and eternal life,
And of his most precious only begotten son
The pearl of great price

It speaks of mysteries
That have been hidden since the begining of time,
In a parable
It tells of new bottles for new wine

With pen and ink
The Bible was written by holy men filled with the holy spirit,
And spirit led men down through the ages
Have preached this gospel so that all the world may hear it

So then of all
The pen and the pearl are the greatest powers of them all,
For only through the penetration of God's word
Can one receive the spirit's call

Yes pen and ink is the sword of the Lord
Dividing asunder the thoughts and intents of the heart,
Powerfully piercing through marrow and bone
O' God, how great thou art

The Wild Places

The tackle box is full
The old canvas duffle bag is packed,
Fishing poles have been slid into a tube
And I've grabbed up my old fishing hat

Lake and road maps have been gone over and over
The face stubble's starting to show,
Check lists have been checked and rechecked
And I'm more than ready to go

As the excitement of Christmas is
To a little child,
So to me
Are the remote places of the wild

Walleyes, northern, and smallmouth bass
Lurk in the depths of her clear blue waters,
Moose and bear roam the deep dark forests
And her lakes swarm with beaver and otter

There is nothing in the world like the wild places
Unspoiled by human hands,
Far from the hustle and bustle
Of this world's unyielding demands

Anticipation permeates electricity in the air
As a bush plane awaits our arrival,
Ready to transport us deep into the canadian wilds
Far away from, it all

Raw beauty, simple and awesome beauty
Beauty not created by human hands,
God's beauty carved in stone
An awesome creation of unspoiled wilderness land

A Love Letter

For the sheer joy of living
The little birds sing,
As we also lift up our voices
To all the miraculous wonders that each day brings

Halleluah what a savior
Together with the birds we rejoice,
They in beautiful song
And we in joyful noise

Lord we lift our praises unto thee
Each in our own way
I pray accept our songs of joy and love
That we sing to you this day

Words without music
And music without words,
One is the lyrical praises of man unto his maker
The other the beautiful melodys of the birds

Bless us O' Lord
As we continually praise you on high,
Hearts overflowing with love
From your feathered friends and I

The Golden Years

Hearing aids, tri focals,
And getting up three or four times in the night,
Weak kidneys and full bladders
And all the other symptoms of the old age plight

Crows feet
And middle age spread,
Bags under the eyes
And hair a thin'n a-top the head

The bones creak
As Arthur sets in,
Sometimes I arrive
And wonder where I've been

What little hair that's left
Is riddled with grey,
My thoughts are all foggy
And have gone astray

The stars and my teeth
Both come out at night,
In order for me to hear
You have to holler with all your might

I can no longer bend over
Or tie my own shoe string,
And on a quiet night
You can hear my arteries hardening

Many things I have forgotten
I can't remember much so I'm told,
So I have come to the conclusion that no one can master
This art of growing old

Channels of Love

Why are our eyes fixed on the temperal
Tangible things we can see and touch,
When we need to seek the eternal
And turn our eyes upon Jesus

I asked O' God how can I show you my love
For so wonderously setting my soul free?,
And you answered
What you do unto others you do unto me

So to show our love for the Lord
We need to open our hearts to our fellow man,
And love our neighbor as ourself
And reach out a helping hand

By this the world will know that God dwells within us
When we openly love the sisters and brothers,
For from out of the inward joy of the converted heart
We must open up and give of ourselves to others

By far the greatest gift of all is love
But secret love is sin,
So let's give that love away dear sisters and brothers
Let us be channels of love for him

Grasp This

Most of the world
Does not grasp the urgency of eternal values,
They live for the here and now
Doing the don'ts instead of the do's

The obituary columns are full
Filled with the old and the young,
Death is not discriminatory
And it comes to each and every one

If you grasp nothing else grasp this
There is more to life than that which we see,
This day could be your very last
And then where would you be?

Hell is real and heaven is real
Eternal torment or everlasting life,
Choose this day whom you will serve
The devil or Jesus Christ

The choice should be easy
But let this thought help you choose,
Hell is a place where the fire cannot be quenched
Choose Jesus and do the do's

Heaven

There is one thing you must believe
One thing I want you to know,
And that's the beauty that lies beyond
In the place where christians go

When our eyes close upon this earth
They will immediately open to a most glorious sight.
To a land of endless wonders
Where Jesus is it's light

Where there are no clouds
Nor sorrow, nor pain,
There is no sunshine there
And there is no rain

There is no heat
Nor cold,
It is a place
Where all the mysteries of life unfold

A place our Lord and savior
In love prepared for us,
Where life is beautiful
Thank you Jesus

Paul, the Sparrow, and the Thorn

There is a story
So I've heard,
A beautiful story
About a little bird

Whose little body
So pitiful and forlorn,
Was pinioned in a bush
By a prickly thorn

She could not free herself
From this painful prison,
But with her very all
She gave back to the world the gift she was given

She sang and she sang
With all she had left,
She filled the air with her beautiful melodys
Even unto her last dying breath

Paul was buffeted with a thorn in his side
Yet he served faithfully to the very end,
And if you listen closely you can still hear the melodys of
That sparrow
Drift slowly upon the wind

What Must I Do?

You ask
God what must I do?,
And God says come
And I will pour out my spirit unto you

To be saved you must believe
But believing is not enough,
You must become a vessel of the infilling
And outflowing of God's love

By grace are you saved through faith
It is by nothing that you have done,
For the cross of Christ would be null and void
If you could be saved by naught but by the blood of God's son

You are not saved by good works
But those works will follow after you,
For when you are filled and sealed with the holy spirit
You will want to please God in all you say and do

Now is the day of salvation sayeth the Lord
Come to the altar and seek his face,
And receive the greatest gift of all
God's amazing gift of grace

From The Cradle to the Grave

He stepped down from his heavenly throne
To fullfill the heavenly plan,
He came to earth to defeat the serpent
That caused the fall of man

The man of sorrows walked this earth
The shadow of the cross ever looming before him,
He was the lamb, the sacrificial lamb
Mankind's only hope for the atonement of sin

His thirty three years upon this earth
From the cradle to the grave,
Would change the lives forever
Of all who would believe and trust in the gift that he gave

He was born
To instill hope in all,
In all who would believe
And heed the spirit's call

Thank you father for the cradle
And Christ's victory over the grave,
And of sins forgiven and forgotten
Because of the price that your son gave

The Angel's Song

Could you ever imagine
That so much joy as shared by the whole human race,
Could be attributed to one small package
Of utterly amazing grace

Emmanuel, God with us
The baby Jesus,
What an amazing gift
Our father in heaven gave to us

Peace on earth
Good will toward men,
O' What sweet music to the shepherd's ears
That must have been

So many miracles marked that blessed event
The virgin birth, the appearance of angels, the kings from afar,
The glad tidings
And Bethlehems's star

Joy, peace, and good will
Was the song the angel's sang way back when,
My friends that Christmas message still stands
And as long as the earth remains it will never end

Bags of Bones

These bags of bones
That we now live and breath and walk around in,
Will soon be transformed
Into the glorious likeness of him

As also the streets of this earth
That we now trod,
Will be traded in
For those golden streets of God

And all this decaying beauty
That we now see,
Will be exchanged
For the endless wonders of eterity

Where our faith in all that we have believed
Will suddenly materialize,
Where all that our Lord has ever promised
Shall appear before our eyes

And nothing, I mean nothing
Can compare to that beautiful sight,
Our first glimpse of heaven
Where bags of bones become vessels of light

He Liked to Drink Alone

A little man he was
Being only five feet tall,
Walked into a bar
And started a brawl

He walked up to the biggest man there
And kicked him in the shin,
And when he bent over
He busted a beer bottle under his chin

The little guy weighed
About a hundred and ten,
And when he lookd around
There were two - two hundred and fifty pound men

They were coming at him
And their fists began to double,
And there was no smile on their faces
And it looked like he was in trouble

One big man swung a hammy fist,
But the little guy was to fast
And the big guy missed

The other man grabbed, and said:
A-ha a-ha, I've got you at last,
Then there was the sound
Of breaking glass

Another beer bottle appeared
In the little man's hand,
As he scratched one very big man

Now the other fellow
Reached out for the little man,
And there was the crunch of sinking teeth
In a big fat hand

Now the big man began to yell
And the little man reached for a bottle of beer,
Glass flew and the big man fell
And the rest of the bar did cheer

And the little man said that he liked to drink alone
And everybody stood clear,
As he saddled up to the bar
And drank a cool glass of beer

As he walked out
They looked at him in awe,
For such a little man
He was walking mighty tall

Boot Hill
"The Ballad of Navajo Joe"

He was lean, he was mean
They called him Navajo Joe,
He wore tight blue jeans
And a six gun way down low

He swaggered when he walked
His steel gray eyes revealed no fear,
His body was hard as stone
He had broad shoulders and a tiny rear

All those he called out
Now reside a-top boot hill,
His reflexes were fast as lightning
And he always went for the kill

Then one day
He called out a handsome young stranger,
What he didn't know was
That this man was a Texas Ranger

Joe's gun slid from it's holster
Faster than usual that day,
But in less time than it takes to blink an eye
The stranger's gun had sent five bullets Joe's way

Joe's fingers opened
And his shoot'n iron slid from his grip,
Every bullet found their mark
And the Ranger's peacemaker returned to his hip

On top of boot hill a tombstone reads:
The fastest gun in the world,
Rides on the hip of a Texas Ranger,
Joe took him on and now Joe's gone
Done in by a handsome young stranger

One Sweet Kiss

How do you put into words
The joys of two hearts that became one,
About a beautiful girl of eighteen
And a boy two years shy of twenty one

Something very special is happening
And this is what I want you to know,
I am still I love with that beautiful girl
That I met forty years ago

It all started
With one sweet kiss,
And now it has accumulated
Into forty years of wedded bliss

In the begining years
God gave us five little bundles to love,
And they in turn gave us many more
Of these God given gifts from above

Yes we have had many, in our forty years
Of joys and sorrows,
But we rejoice together
In that we have placed God in all of our todays and tomorrows

Through joy and laughter sorrows and tears
We have walked this earth as one together,
We have experienced all of our wedding vows
Of sickness and health and the bad, good, and better

At forty years of age God loved me into his kingdom
And I know that God's love never ceases,
And after forty years of living with you dear Alice
I want you to know that I still love you to pieces

See You Later

Earth to earth
Dust to dust,
Temperal earthen vessels
He has made of us

One glorious day
We must lay them down,
And commit these bodys of clay
To the ground

When I leave this earth
I'll not say goodby,
I'll say see you later
And please don't cry

I'm traveling the upward road
Trusting my soul to Jesus Christ,
Knowing that one day soon this vessel of clay
Will be traded in for one of glory and eternal life

Praise God I love you all
And I said it before and I'll say it again, I'll not say goodby,
Only see you later
And please don't cry

Turn

The lesbians and gays
Want a special day in which to honor them,
They had better be careful for they might get their wish
And their just dues for their abominal sins

Sodom and gomorrah
Were citys of like passions,
And God said enough is enough
And rained down fire and brimstone upon them

Men with men, women with women
Unseemly acts of disgust,
God gave them up to dishonor their bodys
In putrid displays of lust

If God can't stomach the acts of lesbians and gays
Why in the world should we,
But we as Christians need to pray for them
That they may somehow someway break free

They must want heaven and eternal life
They must want to break free from this deviate life style
That they now live,
They must want all the good things of heaven and earth
That only God can give

And then and only then
Can they receive God's forgiveness for sin,
And be washed in the blood of the lamb
That was shed on the cross for them

Turn, I say turn
From this abominable to God and man way of life,
And turn your eyes to the heaven of heavens
And fix them steadfastly upon Christ

Think About It

The sun was but a shadow
The moon failed to reveal her light,
The stars in the heavens fell like ripened fruit
Spiraling through the black hole of the night

There were great earthquakes
From which all of mankind fled and hid their faces,
The islands and the mountains shook
And removed from out of their places

Prophesy was being fullfilled
That great and noteable day of wrath had come,
The lamb, the judge of the quick and the dead
Had declared that the day of grace was done

Out of the heavens great hail stones fell
Each stone about a talent by weight,
And men continued to blaspheme God and not repent
Not grasping the end and their eternal fate

They had not believed
And they had missed that upward flow,
Now, unprepared
They shall receive the dragon's warm welcome below

Are you following after Jesus
Or are you following the crowds?,
Are you prepared
For that sudden appearance of the God of glory in the clouds?

Will you be lifted upwards with the saints
Rejoicing in that glorious flow?,
Or will you choose the latter
And all the horrors that await below?

Open the Door

I want to tell you
About a love so wide, so deep, and so high,
About a love that was spent willingly
About the one who gave his all for you and I

About a king
Who gave up everything,
He laid his all on the altar of sacrifice
And of him and to him we shall never cease to sing

No amount of nails could hold him to the cross
It was his love for us that held him there,
He is the lamb of God
Who took all our sins and griefs to bare

He is the Lord of glory
Heaven's shadowless light,
Who loves us all
With all of his heart, mind, soul, and might

If you are tired of being dead within
And of your lifelong bondage to sin,
Then open up your heart's door
And let the Lord of life come in

Father and Son

The alarm was set
It would go off just a little before sunrise.
But there would be little or no sleep
For this little guy's eyes

Daddy had promised to take him fishing
And they had gathered some worms the night before,
He lay there wide eyed
Imagining that distant shore

He was saying his night prayers
And telling God all of his desires and wishes,
And at the end he asked one more thing
And that is that he and daddy would catch lots of fishes

All through the night
He lay there wide awake,
Occasionally glancing out the window
In anxious anticipation of the dawn to break

Then the birds began to sing
And a faint glint of red spread across the horrizon,
He was about to partake in an awesome outdoor adventure
Of bonding between father and son

They scarfed down some eggs and toast
And a couple of rolls,
And grabbed up all of their fishing gear
And a couple of poles

Excitement was building up
In the little boys eyes,
As father and son arrived at the lake
Just a little before sunrise

Fog hung over the lake like a cloud
Paddles dipped and tugged and dipped,
Then the anchors were set, hooks were baited
And just as quickly stripped

They baited up again
And watched their bobbers go under,
They set their hooks and pulled them in
Engrossed in all this awesome wonder

They fished for hours and hours
And there was not many a fish that got away,
As the boy thanked God
For the wish that he had received that day

And when the sun sank down
And the day of fishing was over and done,
There was written forever in the memory of a little boy
A wonderful day of bonding between father and son

Light My Fire

Let my footsteps
Leave light wherever that they go,
And when my heart searches for the words to speak
Let it be seeds of life I sow

May all my ways please you O' Lord
Let it be no other way,
Place your conviction upon my heart
If ever I begin to stray

Write your words
Upon the tables of my heart,
Place them in my memory
And let them never depart

Make my heart tender
To the needs of those around me,
And give me the confidence and wisdom
To open their eyes that they might see

Let me be able to convey to them
In a way that they might believe,
That they may be pricked in the heart
And seek an altar that they might receive

I know that those souls who are convicted and converted
And experience the transformation of the new birth,
Are the only treasures
That will follow us from this earth

Let you r light shine out O' Lord
Let my life honor you always,
Let it be all you would have it to be
To your honor, glory, and praise

Smile, Reach Out, and Share

A word fitly spoken
Is like apples of gold in pictures of silver,
And the souls that are being won for Jesus
Are treasures that will last forever

When you look upon a person
Whose continence is down and sad,
Remember that heaviness in the heart maketh it to stoop
But a good word maketh it glad

Smile at passerbys
Who knows what trials they are facing today,
Speak encouraging words
Lift some burdens away

Reach out a helping hand
Go that extra mile
It doesn'nt take much effort
To offer up a smile

Share the Lord
Reach out and touch some hearts and souls,
Give them a glimpse of what could be theirs
In the one who is greater than all their cares and woes

My God

My God is not a God
Of wood or metal or stone,
But my God is the God of everything
He and he alone

My God, the son of our father God
Was born of a virgin womb,
My God, the creator of all things
Is the risen Christ of the empty tomb

My God
Instills hope of glory within me,
In every living thing
It is my God I see

My God
Is the God of hope, the God of joy, and the God of peace,
He is the God of the impossible
His miracles and blessings never cease

My God is forever my God
For my sins he offered up his son,
I rejoice and praise my God
For all for me he's done

The Warming Of Days

Love blooms
Hearts flutter and take wing,
Spring
What a wonderful thing

April showers
And little blue flowers,
Blue skys
And little blue butterflys

Ponds bursting forth
In concerts of praise,
As the little peepers thank God
For these warming of days

The bees are a buzz
The birds busy building nests,
As the earth yawns
And awakens from it's long winters rest

It is in wonderous joy
We sing,
All praise be unto God
For his glorious spring

The Road Less Traveled

Going against the flow of the world
Is not the easiest path to go in,
But the road less traveled
Is the one that I have chosen

I rejoice in the straight and narrow
For it leads towards the promised land,
With my Lord my God
The king of kings I have taken my stand

I'll take no detours along life's way
There is no looking back,
He is a lamp unto my feet
And the light upon my path

Joy unspeakable and full of glory
The way to eternal life,
Peace that passeth all understanding
Are all yours in Jesus Christ

Yes! The straight and narrow
Is a very dusty road,
For it is the road less traveled
That leads to the streets of gold

Fluffy

*She's not snooty
High minded or stuffy,
She's a down home girl
We lovingly call fluffy*

*She's a good friend
Come hell or high water,
But if you cross her
You're gonna face the flyswatter*

*As far as fears
Loretta travels different roads,
It ain't spiders and snakes that scares her
It's frogs and toads*

*She's a good person
With deep felt feelings,
And we've given her a lot of rough times
In our day to day dealings*

*She's took it all in stride
With a great sense of humor,
Now we wish her the very best
In what retirement has in store for her*

*You've brought a lot of joy to others
And I reckon that's what we're here for,
Enjoy your years of rest Loretta
You've earned them and more*

Music of the Heartstrings

Love, faith, grace, life
These are more than words to us,
For we have placed our hope and trust
In the everlasting arms of Jesus

We are here to celebrate life
We thank God for every breath,
For he is the resurrection and the life
Who rose victorious over sin and death

The beauty of God's creation becomes even more awesome
When seen through born again Christian's eyes,
For we who love him live in the blessed hope
Of the promise of paradise

Church bells are ringing, congregations are singing
Praising glory to the author and finisher of our faith,
Trusting and believing in the promises of Jesus
To which we cling and firmly embrace

Joy to us is not in the satisfying of the eyes and flesh
Nor the accumulation of earthly things,
But it is the loving of the Lord and the loving of others
That plucks the music of our heartstrings

Grandchild

The smile of a grandchild
Excels the grandeur of a sunrise,
Their beauty
Is more glorious than rainbows and blue skys

Beauty beyond that of the soft petaled rose
Unrestrained laughter that bellows and rolls,
Pure sweet music that comes from their toes
Bubbling up from the very depths of their souls

Loving and giving
Hugging and forgiving,
They bring endless joys
Into these lives we are living

Their energy is unending
They love to create,
And best of all
They think grandparents are great

Gold, diamonds, money, and fame
None can compare to that one precious name,
And when they look at you and smile
You know that name is grandchild

The Fading Sounds of Summer

Crickets are the stradevariuses of the night
With tree frogs adding a few strums to the fray,
Bullfrogs sound off like big bass drums
And the birds sweet songs announce the breaking of each new
Day

We hear a little ditty from katydid
And the shrieking shrill whine of the locust,
Honeybees are all a-buzz
As skeeters suck blood till they bust

The sky is speckled with honking v's of high flying geese
A blue heron lets out an awkward squawk,
A shadow moves swiftly across the earth
As eardrums are pierced by the shrill of a hawk

Mallards chuckle gleefully amidst flossy cattails
Through the thicket comes the whistle of woodduck wings,
Beautiful reds and yellows are replacing the green summer leaves
As nature's concerto continues to sing

The colorful flowers and this scenery of green
Is being ornately replace by a covering of pure white,
As the wind hums mournfully through needles of pine
Of summers gentle passing into the long winter's night

Uncle George

He left loved ones behind
They refuse to say goodby,
For they know they shall see him again
In the great by and by

We miss him terribly
Our hearts are saddened that he is no longer with us,
But we rejoice that his pain and suffering has ended
And that he is in the glorious prescence of Jesus

I believe my mother and my uncles
Are singing amazing grace,
Rejoicing in the Lord
Looking full into his wonderful face

In the land of uncloudy day
All their pain and tears have ceased,
They walk those golden streets
In joy, and love, and peace

We cry for my uncle's abscence from us
But we rejoice for where he's at,
We love you unc
But then you always knew that

Yes!

This is the season we celebrate the virgin birth
God incarnate, the word made flesh,
The God of creation, the Christ child
Our only savior Jesus

He came to save souls
To open the gates of heaven to all who would believe,
He stands before heart's doors
Ready to enter in to any who would rejoicingly receive

Say yes to Jesus
Let his sweet peace flood over your soul,
As all that stands between you and heaven
Is washed away in the crimson flow

Ask: Jesus come into my heart
Jesus come into my life,
Jesus I want you to be Lord of all
I believe that thou art the very Christ

Jesus become the light of my life
I accept the spirit's call,
Cleanse my soul of every dark spot
Jesus I believe and I surrender all

From the virgin birth to calvary's cross
I believe that you are the holy one,
For the blood covering and cleansing of my every sin
I here and now trust in all that you have done

I hunger for the unspeakable joys
Of sins cast away as far as the east is from the west,
My answer, sweet Jesus, to the spirit's call
In tears of joy is "yes"

So Some Say

You think you've come a long way
And I guess you have, reaching the big four "O",
But believe me
You've still got a long way to go

Some say life begins at forty
That's what some tell,
You just tell them some
To go ——— fly a kite

Forty is a new begining
A new lease on life,
You are more settled in
A more devoted loving wife

Denny's happy
That you are not fat and portly,
What the heck
So what if your forty

Adjust to the situation
Someday little rug rats will be hollering "Grandma sue"
And "Grandpa Denny",
So look at it this way
You are only one year older than Jack Benny

I love you sue
    Your dad
        Happy fortieth

Believe, Repent, Receive

The answers to life
Are not in sensual pleasures and earthly things,
But in the savior Lord God messiah
Jesus Christ, Lord of Lords, king of kings

The words of life through Holy Spirit conviction
Causes that a man be born again,
Reading, believing, heeding and receiving
Of the blood cleansing washing away of sin

Jesus is the answer my friend
There is no other way,
Turn to him, trust in him
Give your heart to him today

God loves you
He sent his son to die for you,
Believe, repent, and receive
Is all that he asks you to do

Why is salvation so complicated?
Jesus purchased it for you on a blood soaked tree,
Let your lips be filled with praise and rejoicing
To the lamb of God who sets souls free

Seeing's Believing

A slight breeze on a warm summer's night
Beneath seemingly endless skys,
Comets sizzle and streak
Through a dark sea of sparkling eyes

Cool sand oozing between toes of bare feet
Dancing in the rain,
Walking knee deep through waves of meadow grass
And gathering mushrooms in the spring

Listening to the rumble of bullfrogs
As their drums beat throughout the night,
Glimpsing the mystic union of sun and ice
Creating an amphitheatre of northern light

Thermometers plunge
Causing thuderous echos from freezing lakes,
Pine trees
Adorning myriads of white symetric shapes

Trails wind through hills and hollows
And along side cool blue pools,
All who see and still not believe
Are members of the congregation of fools

The Forever Child

The forever child
Was both God and man,
The word made flesh
Was how it all began

The king of kings left his forever home
That souls could be born anew,
And one day soon he is coming again
To receive those faithful few

He stepped down from his heavenly throne
And put off his royal robes of white,
To be born in a stable wrapped in rags
One holy star lit night

The forever child
Gave his all for us,
When on the cross he paid the penalty
For all our sins and lusts

He that hath the son hath life
In the holy book it is written,
And he that hath not the son of God hath not life
For the spirit of God is not in him

Christmas is and should be
The joyeous celebration of Jesus's birth,
The greatest hope
To ever grace this planet earth

Aunt Jo

Aunt Jo was fun to be around.
She had a sense of humor that just wouldn't quit,
Also she had an ornery streak
Which she blended into her humorous words of whit

She would get that devilish twinkle in her eye
And scrunch her face all up,
Just before she unleashed her dry humor upon you
Which was God's gift to her in a full cup

We miss you auntie
As you join the many loved ones who have passed on,
Emerging from the valley of the shadow
Into the everlasting dawn

You've left you wheel chair behind
To walk upon a distant shore,
Your troubled earthly life has ended
Your suffering is no more

We truly miss you
And all of our love goes with you,
As you enter into that land of uncloudy day
Where the skys are always blue

Something from Nothing

*If the world and the heavens were created by a cataclysmic
Explosion
That means they had to be created by something,
But the truth is
God created it all out of absolutely nothing*

*One little round blue spec stands out
From the whole vast array of the universe,
God's awesomely beautiful creation
Of the green planet we call earth*

*Who else can make something out of nothing
Except the living God,
He even fashioned the first man "Adam"
Out of a muddy ole dirt clod*

*Then he caused him to sleep
And took from him a rib,
Then he made eve from Adam
And that's no fib*

*He is the awesome God of miracles
Beyond all human comprehension,
A rainbow, a snowflake, a new born baby
Is just a few I could mention*

*We are not to try to bring him down to our understanding
As scientists continue to try,
But we as Christians accept by faith
What they believe's a lie*

*But whether they believe or not
God is who he is,
And I believe and that's all that matters
And he is mine and I am his*

Tear Drop

From heaven to earth it fell
From out of a clear blue sky,
One drop, one tear
Fell from on high

He weeps over the world
A world lost in sin,
If only, if only
They would turn their eyes upon him

The lamb of God
God's only begotten son,
Shed his blood
For the evil deeds that we had done

What, what is the question
Is your soul worth?,
Of all that you posess
It is your greatest treasure on earth

His nail pierced hands are reaching out
The father, the spirit, and the son say "come",
Come to the altar of grace, the cross of calvary
Before another day on earth is done

Settle forever the eternal question
Come give your life to him,
He who shed his life blood
To wash away your sin

A tear fell from heaven
My Lord weeping for the lost,
For all who have not knelt at the altar of grace
And been washed in the blood of the cross

Worth It All

It hurts so much
When loved ones pass on,
It seems so final
We look around and they are gone

We draw comfort from family and friends
Holding tight to precious memories,
Knowing that our loved ones are in the prescence of the Lord
Abiding in his perfect peace

No more tears, no more pain
Oh what wonders they must be experiencing,
Their beauty and health restored
Oh what praises they must be singing

Golden streets and golden palaces
Glowing in Jesus's light,
Heaven and all it's glory
Has got to be an incredible magnificent sight,

Just being there
Where faith is transformed into sight,
Bathing in the everlasting love
Of our savior Jesus Christ

The Tree

Colorful wrappings, fancy ribbons
Gifts beneath the Christmas tree,
Shoppers fill the streets and shops
Singing Christmasy songs with joy and glee

It is the time we celebrate the birth of our Lord
The air is filled with the fragrance of pine,
But the gifts that lie beneath these trees
Are symbolic of another tree and time

For the greatest gift of all
Was purchased on the tree of calvary,
With nail pierced hands
He holds it out to thee

If you believe that he is who he says he is
Ask and receive the gift of eternal life,
Open your heart, believe and trust,
And receive the risen Christ

Green trees and gifts
Cross beams and nails,
All reminders
Of the one who never fails

We thank you Jesus
For taking our sins to that cruel tree,
We thank you father for so loving us
That you sent your son to set us free

Yes, he is who he says he is
Of this rest assured,
For he is the savior, Lord God all mighty
Jesus, the living word

Beyond the Comfort Zone

Reach out to those in need
Get out of those easy chairs,
Get off your duffs
And put actions to your prayers

Leave your comfort zone
Adorn the Christian smile,
And out of sheer Jesus joy do all that it takes
Then go that extra mile

Jesus loves you
And he loves others through you,
He will add his blessings
Unto everything in his name that you undertake to do

So go beyond the comfort zone
Bless others in his holy name,
And I guarantee that their lives and yours
Will never again be the same

Oh what blessings God has in store
And not just for you and me alone,
But for all who would take the courage
To go beyond their comfort zone

To the Max

The old adrenilin is really pump'n
The signs of spring are everywhere,
Warm showers are drenching the land
A fresh clean smell is in the air

Warm west winds are prevalent
The earth is about to explode,
Morrels are taking form
Readying their mother lode

God's rainbow sprinklings
Are spreading high and low,
Blanketing the hills and valleys
With a mixture of colorful flow

Bass are cruising the warming shores
Bluegills are circling and fanning out oval pockets,
Fly lines are whipping the air
Shooting out dry flies like soaring rockets

Morrels are popping
The bass are biting,
Life is so beautiful
Living is exciting

The rivers are begining to swell
All of life abounds anew,
It's time to paddle and explore the waterways
In my kevlar mad river canoe

Retired and layed back
Ladened with plenty of time,
I intend to enjoy to the max
All of the joys and adventures of God's glorious springtime

The Greatest Miracle of Them All

While squirrle hunting one hot august day
I found myself with a massasuga rattler coiled between my feet,
I'm sure that God was there
Ain't his miracles neat?

While on top of a twenty foot ladder
Cutting limbs with a chain saw,
Having left just one
That was the one that broke my fall

Another day on a large wilderness lake
There came a storm and heavy wind,
Our fate was in his hands
And he reached out and saved me again

Then there was the time the battery hoist broke
And over a ton of lead and acid hurled my way,
With no time to think or react
God intervened again that day

And then there was the time the angel spoke
And told me to go to a friend in need,
Did he assure that friend that day?
Oh yes he did indeed

But the greatest miracle of all
Was not in the miracles of the saving of my life,
But it was the miracle of the saving of my soul
Through the shed blood of Jesus Christ

I thank God for all the miracles
And for all that he has done,
But I thank him most of all
For life everlasting through his son

Praises Never Cease

I know where I am, I know where I'm going
And I know where I'm coming from,
And I praise my God for the past,
Present, and the blessings yet to come

He is my lamp, my light,
My God, and my friend,
He is the living word
He is life without end

Throughout the trials and dark times
Through all the troubles we bare,
As also through the joys and good times
We know that our Lord is there

My heart ponders
Upon all the many awesome wonders we shall see,
Beyond this land of the sun and stars
In the true land and home of the brave and the free

Oh what praises we shall voice there
What beautiful songs we will sing,
As we come face to face
With our Lord, God, Savior, and King

Into the place of endless beauty
Into the place of perfect peace,
Where angels and saints sing out their joy
And praises never cease

B. W. C. A.

Glowing embers ward off the chill of the night
Your day of the paddle is done,
Then your visions turn to the morrow
And waking to the warmth of the morning sun

You listen to the soothing sounds
Of gentle waves carresing a rocky shore,
And the wilderness wail of the loon and the howl of the wolf
Leaves you craving even more

Lodgepole pines whisper in the breeze
Of Indians and explorers of long ago,
Of birchbark canoes winding silently
Hearts pounding to the beat of the river's flow

Against a background of glorious blue Eagles soar
High above this land of God's magnificent creation,
The bear and the moose walk the ancient trails
Of a long ago Indian nation

Smallmouth, Walley, and northern team in her clear blue waters
Panoramic views scan her horizons with uncluttered Glory,
She is the most beautiful unspoiled, unpolluted place on earth
And with every splash of the paddle you become a part of her
Never ending story

God's Masterpiece

Distant storms
Sunshine and beautiful rainbows,
Rock strewn rivers
Of raging waterflows

Bighorns
Antelope and buffalo,
Panoramic majestic mountains
Clothed in blankets of snow

Magpies and marmots
Winding canyons and sheer cliff walls,
Elk and deer
And spectacular waterfalls

Water spewing geysers
The Eagle and the Osprey are there,
Bubbling foul smelling sulphur pits
Black and grizzly bear

Beauty beyond description
Ornately and uniquely carved in stone,
God's masterpiece - unexcelled
"Yellow stone"

Hobby Horse

It was used
But she didn't seem to care,
She couldn't of been happier
If it had been a real live mare

When she saw that old horse
She filled the house with joy,
She loved it so
I believe it was her favorite toy

She's older now
But I bet she still remembers those days,
And all the fun she had
With pretense of whinnys and neighs

She rode the open range
On that old wooden nag,
Of those days and times
There is no price tag

Oh what joy filled the air
As she giggled and laughed with glee,
Bouncing up and down on that old horse
My granddaughter "Wendy"

Free

No more smoke filled break rooms
No more time cards to punch,
No more 8 to 4
No more brown bagg'n lunch

Sun rises and sun sets
Fishing mirror calm lakes,
Canoeing gentle rivers
And walking amongst the snow flakes

Taking grandkids camping
Every now and then,
Taking them fishing,
For a walk, or for a swim

Bible study and visitations
Quiet places and prayer time,
Putting thoughts down on paper
And getting the verses to rhyme

Touching souls with Jesus
Church and Sunday school,
Living life to the full
Always by the golden rule

Loving neighbor, family, and friends
Reaching out a helping hand,
Speaking words of encouragement
Doing daily all that I can

Free to pursue hobbys and intrests
Free from the daily routine,
Free to wake up filled with the joy of the morning
Just free to do anything

My Golden Spring

The birds are singing of all the wonderous joys of the morning
Pussy willows and crocuses are blooming again,
The red breasted robins are arriving in droves
As we absorb all of God's breathtaking beauty of spring

Red buds and green weeping willows
Dogwoods and flowering fruit trees,
Hills and valleys adorned in quilts woven of wild woods flowers
their sweet smelling nectar attracting busy little bees

The sky is so blue
The clouds so fluffy and white,
The lakes so calm and clear
And the stars so sparkly and bright

Grandchildren's laughter
Makes my heart skip a beat,
Just knowing I'll have time to spend with them
Is just oh so neat

Yes! This is my golden spring
I've just turned sixty two,
Retired and ready for all that life has to give
So little time and so much to do

Thank you father for this time to reflect
Upon all that you are and all that you do,
And for all the blessings, and gifts, and miracles
Of making each day so special and new

Time to enjoy life to the full
Time is such a precious thing,
I thank you again father
For this gift of my golden spring

Treasures

He is the light
Of heaven's golden glow,
He is the sparkle
In every flake of snow

He waved his hand across the heaven's
And created a beautiful bow,
I can see his hand in everything
Every where I go

He is the God of creation
There is no denying that,
Science cannot prove
Their theory of one big splat

God is real
And what I know is true,
He changed my life
And he can change yours too

This world's treasures
Are but dung and dross,
Compared to the treasures
That are yours at the foot of the cross

All We Need

All I have is your word
Your word- a rock steadfast and sure,
All I have is your word
Tried, true, and pure

O' God I have your word
In my heart I know that that is enough
For your promises are mine
No need for signs or other stuff

I need not see you
To know that you are there
Your word is all I need
To let me know you care

Your word dear God
Transforms darkness into light
Every verse a stepping stone
On the pathway of life

We have your word dear God
A garden of life giving seed,
We have your word dear God
And that is all we need

Do the Do's

It is a daily battle
To fight the demons within,
The darkness that holds back the light
The hidden cancers of sin

Powerful
Are the flesh's dark desires,
The spirit indeed is willing
O' God how shall we escape hell's unquenchable fires

To overcome these demons of darkness
That lurk and plague the mind,
We need an open bible
For God says: seek and ye shall find

Commit your works unto the Lord
And your thoughts shall be established,
Deny thyself, take up your cross
And fullfill your life with God's do list

For as mike warnke once said
And I'm sure he won't mind if I use his quotes,
If you do the do's
You don't have time to do the don'ts

Not Mine

I pray dear God
For beautiful poems to write,
I pray that they be sparkling
With your precious words of light

I pray that they be as refreshing
As the spring rains,
And let the melodys be as beautiful
As the songs the nightengale sings

Let me write with a sweet smelling savour
Like as unto new mown hay,
And let it be as glorious as the rising sun
That brightens our each new day

Let the verses flow
Let Jesus be in every line,
Let the world know
That these words are yours not mine

O' God I pray
For beautiful poems to write,
And may every verse sparkle
With heaven's precious light

Words of Fire

So little time
So much to write,
A poet's heart
Overflowing with God's words of light

How can I reach the lost I asked?
In God's vocabulary there is no such word as can't,
He said: take of my precious seeds of life and go
And liberally water and plant

I pray his thoughts
Be in every verse I write,
I pray these be not just words
Of black written on white

I pray no honor
Be bestowed upon me,
But God be honored
In all these words you see

And may these words of verse be written
Always with his message to impart,
And the fire thereof burn within
To melt the coldest hardest heart

God's Best

To walk out on ice crystal clear
And hear it's thunderous roar,
As freezing ear splitting cracks
Unravel and travel from shore to shore

Falling symetric shapes
God's white diamonds of shimmering light,
Moonbeams and stardust
Set ablaze these sparkles of sheer delight

Giant puffs of fluffy white clouds
Floating lazily across robin egg blue skys,
Shimmering blue pools
Reflecting mirror images back to awestruck eyes

Hot summer days
Warm refreshing showers,
Strawberries and rassberries
And rainbow colred flowers

The beauty of autumn leaves
Transluscent rainbows,
Hiking, camping, and fishing
And canoeing winding river flows

Fireflies moon us
With blinking butt lights,
Treefrogs and bull frogs
Peep and rumble throughout the hot summer nights

Going for a swim, getting a tan
Being outside for any excuse or reason
Just enjoying life to the fullest
God's best of every season

Jenna

Josh is popp'n his buttons
Trish is all aglow,
Now I'm going to tell you why
As if you didn't already know

Jenna was born
Beautiful and gorgeous,
A miracle from above
God's blessing to all of us

Grandma sue is so happy
She's jumping for joy,
She didn't care wether that grandbaby
Was a girl or a boy

Jenna's got grandmas and grandpas
And great gramdparents too,
She's going to be spoiled
But that's what we were born to do

She is a little angel
God's special gift to both of you from above,
To be nourished and raised
With all of your love

J.E.M.

I carved her initials
In an old beech tree,
J.E.M.
For all to see

I would have carved in the date
But I didn't have time to linger,
For you see when I got done with her initials
My knife folded on my finger

Actually what I done
Was real dumb,
And it wasn't my finger
It was my thumb

It hurt like @!%*
And blood was everywhere,
I didn't even put the dots between her initials
So Jem is what you will see there

Now I'm going to tell you where it's at
That I surely am!,
It's just a stone throw
From J.J. Jam

Solo

The canoe glided silently and swiftly in the rivers gentle flow
The sweet smell of pine permeated the air,
Streaks of gold filtered down through the tree tops
Diamond drops of dew hung glistening everywhere

With double paddle in hand
He masterfully manuevered his little canoe,
Gliding along flower strewn river banks
Under and oval canopy of turquoise blue

He stopped on an island
Fried some mushrooms and brewed some tea,
Listening to the sounds of nature
As he sat down and leaned his back to a tree

The setting sun
Put on a spectacular display,
As he erected his tent
Washed his dishs and stowed them away

With tent facing to the east
He awoke to the morning sun's warm radiant glow,
And after a hearty breakfast of bacon and eggs
He was off to new adventures in the river's beckoning flow

Guardian Angel

O' Guardian angel
You knew what it took.
And you were there
When I opened the book

You were there
When the words rose from the pages,
When I was introduced
To the glorious rock of ages

You were there in my youth
When I commited my life to sin
You were there
When I gave my life to him

You were there
When I knelt at the altar of grace,
You were there
When the change took place

Thank you Lord for my guardian angel
You appointed to watch over me,
And for all the miracles you bestow in my life
To bring me closer to thee

Our Legacy

The final chapter of our lives
When our earthly days are done,
When the last line of the last page is written
And we, like vapor, rise toward the son

In minds and hearts
The memories of our lives live on,
For our children and children's children
We are and always will be a part of their heart song

Let's give them beautiful memories
Let's make them precious and dear,
Let's give to them our love and our time
So even when we're gone we will always be near

May we be good-listeners
And hear their every hope and prayer,
And may they always know
That in body or spirit we will always be there

Love is the most precious gift we could give
Whether rich or poor,
If we give our hearts
We could give no more

Travis

Travis is my grandson
A very loving little guy,
I asked: why oh why Lord
Did he have to lose his eye?

At first I was angry
Then you brought me to my knees.
My heart hurt, I cried
Only in you could I find peace

The prayer chain was activated
Churchs everywhere lifted Travis to Christ,
I accept now that they took his eye
In order to save his life

We ask for a cure for this cancer
Through this you brought me back where I should be,
I pray have mercy on the little guy
And make him cancer free

In the holy name of Jesus Christ
Father we raise our prayers to you,
May Travis continue to see the sunrises
And all his life your skys of blue

The Day of Grace

God we love you
And we offer up our praises,
You are a rock
Standing firm down through the ages

You are forever the same
Praise your holy name,
We needed a savior
And we are so glad that you came

We know O' Lord of heaven and earth
That your work on the cross was not in vain,
For you reconciled us to the father
As you took upon yourself our sin and shame

We know that you died on the cross
But we also know that you rose again,
Assuring every believer
That they too will do the same

Let's get the gospel message out
That others may enter in,
For the day of grace my friend
One day, all to soon, will end

The Dogwood Tree

I found it on the fenceline
A little sapplihg of a tree,
God's miracle of the third day of creation
This one made just for me

I transferred it to my yard
Where it bathed in sunshine and rain,
Ever reaching upward
God's beauty to proclaim

As the years rolled by
It grew and grew,
Spreading it's magnificent beauty
Beneath God's matchless skys of blue

Clothed in snow white petals
She was adorned as a beautiful bride,
This is a tree many say
Like upon which my Lord was crucified

Springtime just wouldn't be the same
Without the dogwood's bloom,
For it is God's reminder of the cross
And the victory of the empty tomb

Here Am I

He is the light on my path
He is my heart and soul,
Where he leads I will follow
Whereever he beckons I will go

He is the light of my life
All of his promises are yea and amen,
His love lifted me and changed me forever
He is my God, my savior, and my friend

All that I ever hope to be
Even all that I dare,
All that I am and all that I have
I entrust to his loving care

Of the manifold options in this world
Jesus is my choice,
O' God of heaven how I love you
O' How I yearn to hear your voice

Open the doors dear God
My heart is open to your call,
I lay before you, my Lord my God
My heart, my life, my all

O' Fleeting Poem

I want to write a poem
But I know not where to start,
I pray that it come from the very depths
Of what God places within my heart

I know that I am not worthy
But I pray for this one poem,
That will touch the world of the lost
Before I'm ushered home

I pray for tears
To swell up in grown men's eyes,
I pray it bring conviction and conversion
And change peoples lives

Jesus, O' Precious name of Jesus
It's got to be about Jesus,
He is everything
It's got to be about him who died and rose again to free us

O' Fleeting poem
Into the very depths of my heart I'll search you out,
And Jesus, O' Precious Jesus
Of your honor, Glory, and praise every verse shall shout

Full Cup

Sometimes I pray and my faith falters
It seems my cup is only half full,
God says cease not and don't give up,
and I will send you a miracle

My God is the God of miracles
So the bible does tell,
My God is the God of the impossible
And he is alive and well

Although things may seem impossible
And sometimes with man this is true,
But with God all things are possible
There isn't anything he cannot do

So continue to pray
Don't give up,
It is God
Who will fill the cup

Half full
Is not his way,
Never give up
And cease not to pray

Alcaholic

Sometimes I know your down
Sometimes you're on the brink,
You reach for the bottle
You believe you've got to have that drink

I'll guarantee you
That there is a better way,
Now listen closely
To what I have to say

Jesus
You say you've heard it before,
Well you've never heard it like I'm going to tell it
So hang in there and I'll tell you more

He left his home in Glory
And died on the cross for you,
God loved you so much that he gave his son
To take the punishment for the sins you do

Drink in Jesus
And you will never thirst again,
He will break satan's bands asunder
And his shed blood will wash away your sin

He is the living waters
He is the only way my friend,
You need Jesus and Jesus only
With him you'll never need that bottle again

I've shown you the way
And my friend it is Jesus,
Are you ready to reach out
To the one who frees us

Maybe this poem is to long
But I want the message to come shining through,
That Jesus is stronger
Than the bands that bind you

Metamorphosis

When a soul finds Jesus
The angels sing,
The whole of heaven rocks
With a joyeous ring

Glory to the king
Another soul has entered in,
Glory to the king
Forever praise to him

A pull on the heartstrings
A tear falls at the sound of his name,
A soul steps out from the pew
Like metamorphosis a life takes on a miraculous change

Born again
What a wonderful phrase,
Born again
Praising Jesus all his days

Where the end is truly the begining
Where God's wonders stretch out forever before you,
Where the angels and the redeemed sing out his praises
And the skys are always blue

Endless Joy

O' To wake up one morning
And be on that other shore,
Free from the aches and pains and sorrows of this world
And be with Christ forevermore

Weeping may endure for a night
But joy cometh in the morning.
O' What joys await
All those that have been born again

While I patiently await my change
He is become my morning song,
He is the melody
Of my all day long

The golden years are only golden
If you know Jesus Christ my friend
So find an altar and be washed in the blood
And experience the endless joys of being born again

Yes there is endless joy
But it can only be found in him,
It is the endless circle
With he who has no begining nor end

No Greater Joy

The world says
When I see it I'll believe it
The Christian says
When I believe it I'll see it

The great "I am"
Is the ancient of days,
Worthy of all honor
And worthy of all praise

He truly is an awesome God
He is the creator of all that we see.
He is a holy God
Creator of all that we do not see

He is the one, true, and only God
The world would have us to believe otherwise,
But they are blinded by the serpent
That castaway father of lies

Praise, honor, and Glory
Rise up, sing, shout, rejoice,
Let us praise him with all of our being
With a resounding joyful noise

Praise to you always father
We praise you in our daily lives and prayer,
Casting before you in humble adoration
Our every joy and care

There is no greater joy found anywhere
No, none we will ever know,
Than the joy received
Beneath that crimson flow

Send Me

Angels walk this earth
This I not only believe, I know,
For one spoke to me one evening
To the saving of a praying soul

I'll never forget that experience
No, not as long as I live,
Next to the salvation of my soul
This is the greatest gift God could give

He used me to plant and water
I praise God that I went,
I will always be greateful
That it was me that he sent

This man was praying
That God would send me,
And I thank and praise God
That you set this soul free

I know dear God that he is rejoicing
Up there in heaven with you,
And dear God, know this
That I shall never forget that mission you sent me to do

Love

My Lord
He's coming again you know,
Are your wicks trimmed and your vessels full?
Are you continuing in Christ to grow?

Ten commandments God gave to us
To keep our hearts from sin,
Ten commandments we must not break
But obey to honor him

Don't let your feet get attached to this earth
Let your heart be fixed on things above,
And let the world see Christ's infilling
And the overflowing of his love

Without love we are nothing
No matter what we do,
The bible says that God is love
Is the God of love in you?

Love O' God
Is the greatest gift you gave us,
For you so loved the world
You gave us Jesus

Space

Piling higher and higher
Enough is enough of this snowy fluff,
I'm buried up to my crotch
In this blasted white stuff

Cabin fever has set in
I'm like a boiling kettle that's about to spout,
I'm getting stir crazy
I've got to get out

I set here like a turnip
Every day,
T.V. is my entertainment
My brains starting to decay

I'm miserably trapped
Snowed in at home,
All day long
I set here and groan

Enough is enough
Sure, I know one day this will all melt,
But I've devised a plan
To deal with this hand I've been dealt

I've orderd some snowshoes
And I'm waiting for them to arrive,
So I can get out once again
And feel fully alive

Every day, anxiously
For the mail I do watch,
For those snow shoes
That will put space between the snow and my crotch

Debts Forgiven

I pray dear God that the life I live
Be lived to honor you,
That every thought, word, and deed
Give honor to whom honor is due

Jesus love
O' It don't get no better than this,
Jesus love
Is pure heavenly bliss

Christ's salvation cannot be contained
Is just too big for any vessel to hold,
It must overflow with abounding joy
As the new replaces the old

To be born again
Is not just a phrase,
It is a lifestyle change
To be triumphantly lived the rest of your earthly days

It is getting your name written down
In the lamb's book of life,
It is the receiving of debts forgiven
By the one who paid the price

Rat Pack

This poem is written more or less
And matter of fact,
To tell you about the fabulous four
That make up grandpa's rat pack

I've watched them grow up
They are all teen agers now,
And each one in their own special way
Is a living breathing doll

They are like spring flowers
Blossoming into full bloom,
Like beautiful butterflys
Emerging from a coccoon

Perky and full of ginger
That's jama to a T,
A beautiful heart
And perty as can be

Wendy's a fireball
That's mellowed out a lot,
But don't get me wrong
This gal's still hot

Elizabith's the quiet one
Bursting with personality,
A beautiful spirit, a beautiful girl
Inward and outward for all to see

Ashley is drop dead gorgeous
And everything about her shows it,
The biggest problem is
She knows it

So let's go camping guys
Are you ready for some summer fun?,
You are grandpa's rat pack
And I love you, each and every one

Ugly Dude

I don't know whether I was dreaming
Or not,
But I awoke out of a sound sleep
And got up off my cot

I had thought I heard a noise in the night
I grabbed my gun and stumbled down the hall,
And in the very faint light
Guess what I saw?,

There was this ugly dude staring back at me
I raised my gun and he raised his,
And then I shot and heard a crash
I was so close I couldn't miss

My whole body was shaking
I broke out in a cold sweat,
I looked down
And my pants were wet

I flipped on the light
And there was no body there at all,
For the ugly dude I shot
Was the mirror on the wall

Little buddy

Travis is heavy on my heart
He has had to endure so much,
Dear God we pray for a miracle
To end this cancer's clutch

We lift him up to you
Every single day,
We want to see these trials over
And he be normal in every way

Dear God you've broken our hearts
We pray you mend them once again,
And touch my little buddy
And remove this affliction that's upon him

We look to you for answers
We look to heaven above,
If you give us naught but crumbs
We'll accept them with your love

We thank you Lord
No matter what the answer,
For my little buddy
And his cancer

My Lady Fair

To show
How much I care,
I wish to write a poem
For my lady fair

I used to buy you candy
Or flowers for valentines day,
But I decided a poem
Would be a better way

We're growing older
We're not as young as we use to be,
And that's perty obvious
For all the world to see

But inside
Your youthful beauty lives on,
If I was musically inclined
I would sing you a song

I love you so much
I can't express it in words,
But I have a song in my heart
As sweet a melody as the music of the birds

You are as beautiful to me
As when we first fell in love,
I'll cherish and love you always
As God's gift from above

Love is so wonderful
Love is when two become one,
On behalf of you I thank the Lord
For taking the rib of Adam and creating woman

Beyond Measure

If you
A Christian be
Come
Rejoice with me

For the treasures
That are ours,
Beyond the earth
And stars

This is not all that there is
This is but a shadow of things to come,
The good things of this world are but dung
Compared to the inheritance we have in God's son

Beyond the realm of understanding
Beyond what you've ever seen or known,
Heaven is brightly shining
In the glory emitting from Christ's throne

O' How our hearts yearn
To look upon the face of our savior,
And to receive of the endless wonders
Laid up there for us beyond measure

Trials

No matter what trials
Upon this earth we are to endure,
Our inheritance in the Lord
Is true, steadfast, and sure

Because he is at my right hand
Though these trials be not fully understood,
I must accept them, that out of them
Will come God's ultimate good

To thank him for all things
This we must,
For he is loving and good
And fair and just

We are never alone
No matter what the trials might be,
He is beside us, before us
And he has made his abode in you and me

We must have faith
And trust him more and more,
The trials are to strengthen us
And make us stronger than before

Without the trials
We would become weak and lukewarm,
But with Jesus we shall shine forth as the rainbow
After each and every storm

I pray for a closer walk with thee
For I know that the trials must come,
And I pray to endure to the very end
And to hear those precious words "well done"

Listen

Wild strawberry blossoms
Are blooming everywhere,
The music of the returning birds
Is floating in the air

If you listen closely
You can hear the new borns sing,
As the ponds come alive with these little peepers
And their joyful concerto of spring

Heaven fills the earth
With springtimes sweet, sweet song,
And we, caught up in it all
Rejoice and sing along

God hath said: as long as the earth remains
The seasons will come and go,
What god has promised in his word
We believe and know as so

Spring's covering of beauty spreads
As winter's power wanes,
The earth bursts forth in newness of life
Nourished in April's saturating rains

Coccoons are opening
Colorful butterflys take wing
Trees are budding, flowers are blooming
As all of life praises God for spring

Never shall we cease to be amazed
At all the many wonders god has given to us,
Springtime's glorious newness of life
And our forever life in Jesus

Pure and True

In the hope of life eternal
My soul does firmly cling,
Christ has put a song in my heart
Of which, with a joyful noise I sing

O' The joy we have
No man can take away,
As we share the gospel story
To those we meet along life's way

Life is a journey
Which ends in the promised land,
Are all your thoughts and walks
Guided by his hand?

Walk in the son shine
Step out of the shade,
Walk in the footsteps
That Jesus made

Daily read, daily pray, and daily give his love away
Make him the center of all you say and do,
Keep your eyes upon him
And your heart always pure and true

Blessed Hope

The next major event on the prophetic time scale
Is the long awaited, anxiously anticipated, catching away,
It is the fullfilling in us of Christ's victory over sin and death
It is the blessed hope of resurrection day

It is the day of the Saints of God
Dead or alive with no exception,
The day when corruption puts on incorruption
The wedding day of the bride's reception

We shall be changed
Every born again believer shall rise,
We shall lift at the trump of God
And go to meet our Lord in the skys

To those left behind
There shall be weeping and nashing of teeth,
The seven year tribulation of wars, famines, pestilence, and
plagues
Shall initiate the dreaded coming of the mark of the beast

Be ready always to give an answer
For the hope that burns within you,
Of the blessed hope
Of Christ's return for his faithful few

For the miraculous catching away
For that great and glorious day,
For rapture's hope fullfilled
In all who trust and obey

Our eyes are turned to the heavens O' God
As our hearts burn within us,
For the time mortality puts on imortality
And we are clothed upon like Jesus

Praise God

From fifteen months old to twenty months old
Travis went through hell on earth,
As he suffered through transfusions and chemo
To fight a cancer he had from birth

His right eye was filled with cancer
It was just about to explode,
If it did it would enter his brain
And kill him so I'm told

They removed his right eye
This was the only way to save him,
But then they found a spot on the optic nerve of the other eye
Things were looking pretty grim

It took months of chemo to shrink it down
And when it finally did we thought his trials were done,
But then we were told they found another spot
And we were devastated to hear the location of this one

Deep down our hearts ached
This one was upon his brain,
I don't see how the little guy
Could endure much more pain

It turned out to be a cyst
Which they say he'll probably carry all his days,
Today travis is declared cancer free
To God be the glory and to god be the praise

Thank you father for the brothers and sisters
Who took our burdens and cares,
And lifted them up to your heaven of heavens
Where you heard and answered our prayers

Encourager

Many people are discouraged
So many disheartening things are happening today,
We need to reach out a helping hand
And send some encouraging words their way

We need to see the need
And to be instant in prayer,
We need to let them know
That we will always be there

A word fitly spoken
Is like apples of gold in pictures of silver,
We have promised to love our neighbors as ourselves
Brothers and sisters it's time to stand and deliver

Heavyness in the heart of man maketh it to stoop
But a good word maketh it glad,
You have the power to ease the burdens
And lift up that soul that's down and sad

Don't you have a smile to give?
To encourage that one that's down,
Won't you give them one of yours?
To replace their saddened frown

Reach down into the depths of your heart
And pray to God that they be the right words that you choose,
And with love give them to that hurting soul
And pray that they ease their heartsick blues

O' Saints of God
Let those uplifting words be heard,
Reach out and touch that one
That has need of the encouraging word

He Rose to Victory

Friday he nailed our sins to the cross
Saturday he set the captives free,
Sunday he rose to victory

He came from glory
Through the miracle of the virgin birth,
He gave up heaven for a short season
To dwell for a time on earth

For the first thirty years
He grew in stature and wisdom,
For the following three
He preached repentance and the inward coming of the Kingdom

Jesus gave his all
Upon calvary's mountain,
That we might attain the victory
Through the blood of the cleansing fountain

Good Friday was a black Friday
In which Christ suffered the agony and shame of the cross,
But for this very reason is why he came
To seek and save that which was lost

All who come unto him
Even as many as the Lord our God shall call,
Will in no wise be cast out
For the son of God died for all

Friday he nailed our sins to the cross
Saturday he set the captives free,
Sunday he rose to victory

Cleansed

Christ took our sins upon himself
And nailed them to a tree,
Every sin repented of
Is ushered back to the cross of Calvary

As far as the east is from the west
This is what he said,
They are cast away
Forgotten, buried, and dead

New life he has given to us
The old is dead and gone,
The tunes we use to sing
Have been replaced with a new song

Clean in every way
The father now looks at us through the blood,
Clean in every way
Washed in the cleansing flood

Christ suffered the curse and the shame
So that none need be lost,
Come to the altar of grace
And kneel at the foot of the cross

There is power in the blood of Jesus
I've heard the thunder roll,
There is power in the blood of Jesus
To the saving of the soul

Don't let your hopes be dashed
Don't let your soul be cast away,
Come to the altar of grace
And know God's peace today

What If?

What if Jesus was not the Christ?
What if the crucifixion was the end?,
What if there were no resurrection?
What if there were no redemption from sin?

If there were no savior
There would be no reason for life,
No reason to be moral
No reason to have just one wife

No reason why gays can't marry
No reason for laws and commandments,
No reason for living
Life would make no sense

I thank God for the salvation plan
I thank God for Jesus Christ,
I thank God for heavenly mansions
And for the hope that lies beyond this life

There is no what if
The bible is God's word,
And lives are being changed daily
When the words of life are heard

Jesus is real, heaven is real
The blood of Christ washs away sin,
The way of the cross
Is just as powerful today as it was way back then

There is no what if
It is all true my friend,
Heaven is real, Christ is real
And in him and through him is life without end

Yuck You Say

Rattlesnake steak
And alligator tail, escargo
And blubber from a whale

Carp and coot
And pickled pig's feet,
Just to name a few
Of seldom eaten meat

Quail and pheasant
And frog legs too,
Squirrel and rabbit
And snappin turtle stew

Berries of all kinds
Blue, black, razz, and straw,
Bluegills and bass
And mushrooms spring and fall

The wilds provide our tables
With tasty morsels fare,
Peachs, plums, and apples
And also the pear

Cherrys, puffballs, and pawpaws
Readily available to rich and poor,
We thank you God for your tablefare
You provide from your bountiful store

Some of these are real good
Some will make you gag,
So let your taste buds tingle
But don't forget your barf bag

One Word

As I witnessd of my father in heaven
Of how he healed Travis oh so neat,
He blessed me with goose bumps
From the top of my head to the soles of my feet

Our God truly is awesome
I know he doesn't always give us what we ask for,
But he gives us his very best
We could not ask for anything more

No matter what
Even though the answers are not fully understood,
God's answer
Brings about the ultimate good

Trust and obey
Pray every day,
Beleive and receive
God's best is on the way

Our God truly is awesome
For as I continued praising him,
The goose bumps returned and ran their course
Oh what mighty victorys through him we win

If we would only beleive
And trust and obey,
Our truly awesome God
Will send miracles our way

One word cannot describe
My Lord, my God, my King,
But awesome is the one I choose
Above every other thing

Surrender All

He healed the sick, made the deaf to hear
And made the blind to see,
He raised the dead, cleansed the leper
And died for you and me

He turned water into wine
He walked on a boisterous sea,
He calmed the winds
He paid sin's price on Calvary's tree

He showed us the way
He made the lame to walk,
He preached the good news
And made the dumb to talk

He died and was buried
And rose to life the third day,
He is the Son of God, God the Son
The truth, the life, the way

From heaven to earth he came
To pay the price for sin,
From earth to heaven he rose
With the promise he'll come again

He cast out devils
And gave gifts unto men,
He set the captives free
Forgiving and forgetting our sin

He is the glory and the power
The one, true, and only way,
There is salvation in no other
Surrender all to him today

The Best is Yet to Come

Guys drink water
And girls drink tab,
Trying to prevent
The middle age flab

But nature takes its course
And guys get a big gut,
And women your little behind
Becomes a huge butt

Your perky pair
Becomes a saggin twosome,
And your vericlose veins
Become very gruesome

Some get grey and some go bald
As old age takes its toll,
Arthritis, reumitism, and gout
And the wrinkles begin to prominently show

Tri focals, false teeth, and hearing aids
And so many things we can't remember,
Our April of life has passed
And we are racing headlong into December

But one day we shall mount up
O' Yes the best is yet to come,
And we shall take up wings of eagles
And fly away with God's Son

We shall renew our strength
Though now for a season everything seems blurry,
We shall run and not faint
And we shall walk and not be weary

Written in Granite

Terrorism came to the shores of America
Cowardlly acts rocked our free nation,
Innocents of thousands died this day
And our tears shall never dry from this day's sin

Souls crying out
Families torn apart,
Raw inward pain
Of hurting hearts

The sleeping giant has been awakened
You made a huge mistake bin laden,
You may think that heaven awaits you
But Satan's got a warm place for you and Saddom

New Yorkers have become even closer
As also our nation and many others,
For it was not only Americans that died
But many nations and peoples of different colors

This has made the many as one
To wipe terrorism from off this planet,
For those nations that support these evil deeds
Your names are written in tombstones of granite

You think your God will welcome you home
And yes he surely will,
For your God is Satan in disguise
And your expectations he will never fill

Yes you have awakened a sleeping giant
And you will now feel the wrath of these many nations,
And you will soon come to realize
The horrible fate that you and your followers are now facing

Victory in Jesus

Wether it be read
Or wether it be heard,
Eternal life
Is found through God's word

God loves us so
That he gave us the life of his son,
That we might through him
Victoriously overcome

Confess and turn
From your sin filled life.
And be filled with the holy spirit
Spreading the love of Christ

Knowing that one day soon
You will be with him,
In a place of endless joy
No longer condemned

As mortals of flesh and blood
How can we express our gratitude and love,
To an all powerful, all knowing, ever present
God of heaven above

We must read, beleive, retain,
And obey the scriptures as God's holy word,
Never straying, always praying
Assembling with others where God's message is heard

O' Jesus we thank you
For all that you gave,
And for the blessed hope
Of victory over the grave

God Bless America

We are the United States of America
No act of terrorism can tear us apart,
We are one nation blessed by God
With God's word written on our heart

If we ever fail to acknowledge that fact
God will let our enemys triumph over us,
We are blessed because we are a godly nation
Honorable, peace loving, and just

We are the protector of peace loving nations
We are the symbol of that which is right,
And if tyranny and terrorism comes to their shores
They have the U.S.A. and God to fight

I praise God that he blessed and continues to bless our free nation,
And that the statue of liberty is there
To show those coming to our shores the way in

A new beginning
Free from persecution and strife,
Her torch held high
To show the way to a better life

New York we love you
Where our forefathers came before,
And where others can find the freedom
That can be found upon our shore

Terrorism must be stomped out
It has no place in this world of ours,
And the United States will continue to fight it
With all of her stripes and stars

Slime Pit

You say you are a good person and that you are gay
I want you to listen and I want you to listen well,
Your goodness won't take you to heaven
But your sin will take you to hell

When God says turn
He means a one hundred and eighty degree turn,
Walk away from your sin filled ways
Or seal your fate and eternally burn

Good works come after salvation
Salvation is through the blood of Jesus Christ,
Come to the altar of grace
For by grace through faith comes life

You cannot earn salvation
Climb out of the slime pit in which you now wallow,
Let Christ cleanse you of all unrighteousness
And afterwards the good works will follow

You can break free
God is ready to forgive the repentant soul,
He is ready to mend the broken heart
And restore it and make it whole

Read your bible through and through
Don't be eternally damned by this abominable life style,
God loves the sinner but hates the sin
Repent and God will erase your condemnation file

This gay life of vile affections
Is an uncleanness you can overcome,
But you cannot do this on your own
Only through the blood of God's son

A lot of good people have opened their eyes
In a place they don't want to be,
While there is life there is hope
Repent and God will set you free

Now is the day of salvation
Now is the accepted time,
Come to the altar of grace
And let the blood of the lamb wash away the slime

Oh So Wrong

They use God's name to condone their evil deeds
They are the lowest of earthly scum,
Brainwashed into thinking their reward is in heaven
When their earthly journey's done

We are to pray for our enemys
But O' God it's so hard to do,
When we have witnessed the sorrow they've caused
And proclaiming it all for you

We are Christians
Washed in the blood of our Lord,
At peace with peace loving nations
But those that live by the sword must die by the sword

We must not allow terrorism to exist
We must stamp it out everywhere,
To the uttermost ends of the earth
We must show peace loving nations we care

He that hath the son hath life
God can't put it any plainer than that,
He that hath not the son of god hath not life
Our hope rests upon that one simple fact

The majority of Muzlims I beleive
Are peace loving but O' God oh so wrong,
If only they could come to the knowledge of the truth
And join us in singing the victory song

Jesus is the way, the truth, and the life
If this were not so life would be pointless,
God said without the application of the blood of his son
No man shall enter into his rest

What's It All About?

We pray for our missionarys everywhere
And the gospel message that they give,
That those in the false religions of this world
Would come to know Christ and live

They do not know that they are dead while they live
They do not know that the torments of hell awaits,
For they do not know the keeper
Of the keys of the pearly gates

I thank you God for the laborers
That you have equipped and sent,
For the faithful few with willing hearts
That took up their cross and went

In faith they have gone out
Going whereever you send,
Assured that your guardian angels
Are standing round about them

The world is dying
And one day soon time shall be no more,
Today is the day of salvation
Today is the open door

Don't wait, don't hesitate, don't procrastinate
For you don't know when your life shall end,
Jesus is the answer
He wants to be your brother, savior, and friend

He awaits you with outstretched arms
His nail pierced hands are reaching out,
Reach back and walk the walk and live the talk
For this my friend is what life is all about

For the Love of We

Jesus I love you
I am so glad that you came,
For you install hope within us
As we place our trust in your name

You are who you say you are
I know beyond a shadow of a doubt,
For I have seen your miracles
Of souls changed from the inside out

I beleive in the virgin birth
For I have seen the miracles of souls being born again,
I know you have the power to forgive
Because you have lifted my burden of sin

I feel your presence
As we gather in your name,
I feel assured of your salvation
O' Lord I am so glad that you came

You are the only hope of a world without hope
We must share that hope with those around us,
For you have given to us a gift more precious than life
Hope, joy, love, and peace, all in your name O' Jesus

O' God what we do not see
Is more real than that which we do,
Heaven and hell, and angels and demons
And eternity in glory with you

O' Lord I am so glad that you came
For you came for your love for me,
O' Lord you came also for your love for others
You came for the love of we

Hang Jaw Beauty

From emerald greens
To rubys and golds,
Like a beautiful spring flower
Falls beauty unfolds

God we stand mesmerized
Looking on in awe,
At these changes
Of the vibrant colors of fall

Autumns metamorphic transformation
Is a reflection of the glory of its maker,
The earth and the heavens
Awesome creator

God through these changes
Reaffirms our beleif,
As we see his miraculous touch
In every leaf

Hang jaw beauty
Ever changing before our eyes,
As we gaze at these many colored tree danglers
God has painted against the backdrop of blue velvet skys

Rainbows to Diamonds

The sky is filled with the rainbows
Of many colored leaves,
As they don their beautiful coats
Painted by frost and freeze

They leave their lofty perch
To fly freely through the air,
Floating gently to the ground
And peacefully settleing there

Laughter can be heard
As children come to romp and play,
In these gigantic piles
Of soft beds of colorful array

Then the leaves scatter to the winds
Knowing not where they go,
Frollicking merrily
Skipping to and fro

Summer and fall comes to a close
Displaying their unique phases as they go,
And these quilts of many colors
Are in turn covered in blankets of sparkling pure white snow

Ever Changing

Flowers and bird songs
Rainbows and diamonds,
These are the four seasons
God has given to us my friends

Flowers are springtimes
Glorious carpet,
Bird songs are summers music
Sung from sunrise to sunset

Rainbows are falls colorful display
Of god's painting of the leaves,
His glory
Magnificently displayed in the trees

And winter with its bitter cold
Has a beauty all its own,
As snow flakes sparkle like diamonds
Reminding us of God's great white throne

Coating every thing in sight
Making all things clean and bright.
As the cloak of Jesus
Which no fuller could make whiter white

These are the four seasons
God has given to us,
Always beautiful, ever changing
Like what Jesus does in us

A Fading Giant

All nations that forget God
Will be turned into hell,
Only God can heal our nation
Only God can make it well

We need to ask god for his blessings
We need to get down on our knees,
We need to honor our country and flag
And put God back in this land of the free

Abortion, pornography
What has happened to justice,
The gay lifestyle is condoned as normal
It's no wonder God is judging us

You hand out condoms
And take prayer out of the schools,
You let the false religions and the atheists
Set the rules

We are supposed to be one nation under God
We have become a sodom and gomorrha in God's eyes,
We need the way, the truth, and the life
Watching over our sovereign skys

You can recognize the one true God
Or you can have it your way,
But if you continue to leave god out of our nation
America will continue to be the enemy's prey

In tears we pray for those in authority
That God would take the scales from their eyes,
That they might see and correct their errors
Before our great nation fades and dies

Love is Everything

Cling to the Lord
With your whole heart pledge him your love,
For he is the light of heaven
Come down from glory above

His love
Can lift us above worldly despair,
His love is unconditional
His love is always there

The cross
The symbol of sin and shame,
Became the symbol of salvation
Symbolic of Jesus's glory and fame

O' Jesus
We love you so,
For you have brought hope into a world without hope
And in you a greater peace we will never know

You gave so much and we give so little
May the paths we walk honor you,
May our thoughts and words and deeds
Glorify and magnify you to whom our all is due

Love O' God is everything
Open our hearts to receive and to give,
That our lives may be full in you
In this earthly life we live

Dear Bin   (A Letter to Osama)

Osama Bin Laden
You are a boil on America's butt,
A real pain in the posterior
Whose time is just about up

You say you are going to destroy America
Well your eye will never see it,
For you are a festering sore
One big putrid zit

You're going to be pinched and popped
Before your plans are carried out,
You're going down screaming into hell
Of this there is no doubt

You are one sick puppy
How can anybody so smart be so dumb,
In murdering innocent people
You are the lowest of earthly scum

You say you've done it to please your God
Well your God is not the same as mine,
And if it is true that there is but one God
I don't buy your sanctimonious line

Drugs and power are your God
Jesus Christ is mine,
You chose hell and I chose heaven
You will have all of eternity to pay for your crime

God bless America is the song that I sing
In the land of the brave and the free,
God Bless America
My country tis of thee

Sincerely Up Yours

Childlike Faith

A child needs to have childhood dreams
Innocence lasts but for a short time,
They need other children to play and dream with
To rob them of that is a horrible crime

Let them beleive in Santa Claus
The jolly fat man O' so merry,
The Easter bunny and leprechaun gold at rainbow's end
And that tooth filching money leaving fairy

Let them enjoy their childhood as a child
Living out their magical flings,
For all too soon they grow up
And put away these childish things

Then they can beleive in greater things
True and real and glorious,
Like God and heaven and Jesus Christ
And the guardian angels assigned to watch over us

Remember God said unless we become as a child
We shall in no wise enter. Into his glory,
For we must beleive with childlike faith
The birth, death, burial and resurrection's story

God is o' so real, heaven is real
And his holy angels are encamped all around us,
More real than that which we see
Are the father, the spirit, heavenly angels and Jesus

The things of God are forever things
Heaven awaits all who beleive,
Knock and it shall be opened, seek and ye shall find
And ask and you shall receive

The Gift of Christmas

Christmas is a time of miracles
We think of that first Christmas of two thousand years ago,
When the Christ child was born to the Virgin Mary
And heavenly angels sang the good news to the shepherds below

We celebrate anew
Every Christmas day,
The coming of our Lord
With tinsels and garlands array

It is a time for giving
A time to celebrate Christ's birth,
A time to rejoice and sing Halleluahs
Of our savior come to earth

Special gifts for special people
To remind us of the special gift God gave to us,
The holy one wrapped in swaddling clothes
God with us, the Christ child Jesus

Christmas is more than getting and giving
It is receiving of the greatest gift of all,
Our Lord come down from glory
To rescue us from the fall

Thank you father
For the gift that you gave,
When you offered up your son
Our lost souls to save

No greater gift could we ever receive
God O' God we love you so,
We thank you again for the gift that you gave
On that first Christmas of two thousand years ago

Spring Eternal

We ponder the joys of life
As the colorful flowers begin to bloom,
We listen to the sweet sweet melodys
Of the little wren's joyful tunes

To see the naked trees once again
Majestically clothed in glorious shades of green,
And the fruit and flowering dogwoods
Add their spectacular touch to springtime's awesome scene

There is no portrait more beautiful
Than God's masterpiece of spring,
When tadpoles emerge as peepers
And in syncronized symphony begin to sing

Red breasts are blazing
Joyful signs of life are everywhere,
The smell of easter lillys and crocuses
Permeate the air

Spring puts zest and bounce back into your steps
It makes you feel so complete and whole,
It makes you feel so fully alive
In body, spirit, and soul

Joy bubbles up from your very toes
As the beauty of spring surrounds you,
It makes you want to dance and sing
And put more energy into all you say and do

Jesus our Lord God and savior, our all things creator,
To you we contiually praise and thank for everything,
For we know that one day soon we shall rise up singing
Into the breaking day of your eternal spring

Mary's Baby Boy

My Lord, my savior
My God, my all,
Was born into this world in a lowly manger
Upon a bed of golden straw

Born the king of angels
Born of a virgin,
Born according to prophesies foretold
Born to live a life without sin

Angels heralded his coming
Spreading the good news through lowly shepherds,
Peace on earth and good will toward men
Blessings of encouraging words

Kings brought their treasures
And laid them before him,
Shepherds came
To laud and adore him

Jesus was the greatest person who ever lived
Born through the miracle of the virgin birth,
The God of heaven left his home in glory
To dwell among men upon this sin filled earth

He was born through the lineage of David
That great grandson of the moabite Ruth,
He was born in a lowly stable
God, King, Savior, the way, the life, and the truth

Praise and halleluahs should continually be upon our lips
For he was born to live a life of miracles and to die for our
sin,
His life is the greatest story ever told
And only in him and through him is life without end

Quite a Dame

Of all the women in all the world
One stands out from them all,
Next to my wife she's my favorite
With two centerfolds on my wall

She is not quite what you would call a lady
But she is quite a dame,
She makes us laugh
And this is her call to fame

She has that God awful horse laugh
And her hair is always a mess,
She won't win any beauty contests
Of this we must confess

She brings a lot of joy to others
She is the joker in the crowd,
She is bratty and witty
And boisterous and loud

We laugh so hard it hurts
Her zany antics could kill us,
You like to cut up and your full of ginger
Amongst other things dear phyllis

Yes! She's my idle and her centerfolds grace my wall,
She's a comedian extrordinair
And a treasure to us all

This poem was written to honor her
She who deserves her place of greatness in the hall of fame,
This most outstanding lady (Yes I said lady)
That dizzy diller dame

The Good, the Bad, and the Scuzzy

One got frightened by a chicken
One got sick and puked in her bed,
One slipped and fell in the mud
Another got bumps all over his head

One lost the lens out of his glasses
One lost her shorts in the river,
One got a splinter in her finger
Just a little sliver

One shattered the bathroom window
When a baseball went astray,
Another got sunburned on the river
On a tube float on a hot summer day

One locked the keys in his truck
What a dunce,
For he not only did this
But he did it more than once

We all got soaked in our leaky tents
By torential downpours of rain,
And we met a little black boy
Who said hollywood was his name

We've been raided by raccoons
And visited by scuzzy boys,
We've had some rowdy neighbors
Keeping us awake with their all night party noise

Grandpa and his notorious rat pack
In spite of it all have had a lot of fun,
With swimming, hiking, and campfire chats
Just soaking up the summer sun

The Words of a Poet

The words of a poet
Stirs the inner being, painting
A clear picture
Of what the poet is seeing

Creating a thing of beauty
Is the poet's delight,
To knit verses together in his mind
And take pen in hand and write

Words can make you happy
And words can make you sad,
Yes words can be used
For the good or the bad

Words can paint a beautiful picture
As they enter heart and soul,
Words when fitly spoken
Can achieve a miraculous goal

When the clouds linger on and on and on
Turn your imaginations to skys of bonnie blue,
Of the sun creating sparkling diamonds
In honey drops of dew

The poet is an artist
Who paints with words instead of a brush,
As he writes in vivid colors so breath taking
It causes the birds to hush

He transforms his visions
Into beautiful works of art,
In hopes his readers are touched and moved
Into pressing them upon their heart

Come to the Cross

Precious are thy words o' God
Written for all mankind to see,
Words o' precious words of life
Written to set souls free

Words of life transforming power
That seep down into the very depths of your soul,
Words that draw you to the cross of calvary
That cruel tree of long ago

Come to God
Make that life changing step,
From the pew to the altar
Where God forgives your debt

The altar is the symbol of the cross
A standing invitation in churchs everywhere,
Where souls can come and kneel beneath that crimson flow
Where Jesus took our sins to bear

For without the blood applied
Without the knowledge of why Christ died,
We shall be found guilty before God's eyes
When the books are opened and we are tried

Precious are thy words o' God
Precious is the blood of the lamb,
We repent and of thy salvation we are confident
For it is upon the solid rock we stand

O' God you cause that a man be born again
You apply the blood of the lamb that washs away sin,
For when a repentant soul turns and forsakes his wicked ways
You rain down your mercy upon him
    Jama's 14th birthday

Beautiful Soul

Oh so beautiful is the soul
Whose heart's door is opened to let the light of heaven in,
And the miraculous change that takes place
To that person within

But ever more beautiful
(Of this I have no doubt),
Is the light of heaven within
Shining out

When to others
Their Lord and saviour they show,
Seeing redeemed faces
Transformed into angelic radiant glow

God's reward to us
Is to see those faces light up,
As the living waters
Overflows from the rim of their cup

Peace that passeth all understanding
Hearts surrendered to Jesus Christ,
The light of heaven
Becoming the light and fire of their life

No treasure on earth
Is more precious than the eternal soul,
And witnessing
Should be our highest priority goal

The transformation that takes place
Within that person who steps out and goes forward,
Is the faithful witness's
Tears of joy reward

The Rumble and the Roar

Brushed alluminum, bright shiny steel,
And eye blinding chrome,
Two wheels of awesome energy and power
And a world of endless wonders to roam

The wind in your hair
Bugs in your teeth,
Your buns vibrating in the saddle
Of this iron horse beneath

Roadways without end
An open throttle in hand,
Free spirits
Experiencing the highways and byways of this glorious land

Yamahas and kawasakis,
Riding the backroads
With hondas and harleys

Fresh air fills the lungs
360 degrees of uncluttered view,
Engines rumble and roar
And fade into the blue

Greeting fellow bikers
As you travel along,
With one common bond
Of the open road song

Things

It's good to own things
But don't let things own you,
For we are bought with a price
And we need to give our time and honor to whom it is due

The lust of the eyes
Is sin,
To want and to crave
Those things made by the hands of men

We should be seeking
Those things which are not seen,
Grace, mercy, love, and the God of heaven
These things are those which we should glean

He gives us good things
Things to enjoy each new day,
Things to praise and honor him
In all we do and say

He said that no good thing would he withhold
From them who walk upright,
Who are chaste in thought, word, and deed
And are walking in the light

So be content with such things as you have
For he hath said that he would never leave nor forsake you,
Praise him with all that you posess
For in so doing you give him the honor that is his due

Yes we all posess things
But truly they are not ours,
For we cannot take them with us
Beyond the earth and stars

Angel's Song

*You've danced with the devil
And walked the world's way,
You are the prodigal
That Jesus came to save*

*God's most beloved only begotten son
Went to the cross for you,
He gave his life blood
To give you life a-new*

*Love not the world
Neither those things there in,
Turn and be forgiven
Be washed of all your sin*

*God's pen is ready to write your name
Into the eternal book of life,
When you open your heart's door
And receive Jesus Christ*

*He says all who call upon him shall be saved
And in no wise be cast out,
Make your choice this day
And end all your fears and doubt*

*Sing the song of the redeemed
In joy lift up your voice,
And according to God's holy word
The angel's of heaven rejoice*

*Don't put off this day that which you know you must do
For you know not what tomorrow will bring,
But know this that when you open your heart's door to Jesus
The holy angels sing*

Silence of the Rocks

Bearing precious gifts
The kings of the east came from a far,
Guided through the night
By God's miraculous creation of a wondering star

And as it came to rest above the inn
Where Mary, Joseph, and baby Jesus were,
The kings came and bowed down and worshiped him
And presented him with gifts of gold, frankincence, and myrrh

Lowly shepherds
Were tending their flocks as usual that night,
When lo and behold round about them
Appeared a heavenly light

And a heavenly host of angels began to sing
Peace on earth good will toward men,
A savior is born unto you this day
In the city of Bethlehem

Lord of Lords
Creator and sustainer of everything,
If we do not praise you
The very rocks will break forth and sing

You are the king of kings
The wisest of the wise,
And I thank you father, son, and holy ghost
For the plan that you devised

Praise God for the silence of the rocks
As church bells begin to ring,
And congregations all across this land
Sing praises to their Lord, their God, their king

The Change

There is a day coming
When the dead in Christ shall rise,
And also all in Christ
Who yet remain alive

He is coming in all his glory
And the graves of the saints shall open,
And they shall receive of their reward
Of the stedfast hope they have in him

Spirit and soul shall reunite
With a body that cannot die,
So it is written, so I beleive
In our God who cannot lie

To die is for soul and spirit to be with Christ
But the body is consecrated to the earth,
Until that day of the rapture of the saints
When Christ returns for his church

Soul, spirit, and body
Will then receive of that glorious transformation,
As earthen vessels of dust and ashes
Are changed according to the promises of Christ's salvation

Heaven is every soul's hope
Yes! He is coming, he is opening heaven's door,
And he is bringing with him
All those who have passed on before

We shall not all die
Now do not think this strange,
For we shall not all die
But all in Christ shall receive the change

Those bodys of corruption in the grave
Those bodys who yet remain alive,
When Christ comes for all that are his
Shall be caught up and changed as they rise

We live in the blessed hope
Of Christ's return for us,
And the incoruptible transformation
Of corruptible flesh and dust

Praise him
Whom through all blessings flow,
Praise him all saints in heaven
And all saints below

Victory Song

Are you ready?
Are you sure?,
Is your heart
Clean and pure?

Have you been to the cross?
Have you knelt beneath that tree?,
Have you been washed in the blood?
Has your soul been set free?

Do you believe?
Have you turned to the ancient of days?,
Have you turned and repented
Of all your wicked ways?

If so lift up your voice
And give the victory shout,
For God has promised, and he cannot lie
He will in no wise cast you out

You're heaven bound
O' how I love that sound,
Standing on the rock of Christ
There ain't no higher ground

Let the floods come
Let the waters flow,
I am Christ's and he is mine
He has redeemed my soul

The Ultimate Gift

I've been to the magic kingdom
Magiccal things you can see, experience, and feel,
But for the most part
These things are superficial, artificial, unreal

Beautiful, yes, beautiful
A man made awe inspiring sensation,
But it cannot be compared to the unseen
Of God's ultimate masterpiece of creation

The heaven of heavens
The paradise promised by Jesus,
The home that lies beyond this world
Created by God for us

I go to prepare a place for you
This is what he said,
If I go I will come again
For all who are spirit filled and led

He who has the son has life
These things have I written unto you,
That you might believe and know without a doubt
That all that is written of me is true

The bible is the book of truth
Every word inspired from above.
Believe and receive his ultimate gift
Purchased on the cross by the God of love

It's Up to You

Do you chew, do you drink?
Do you smoke?,
Do you swear?
Do you do dope?

You are the light of your children's world
These are God's precious gifts to you,
Are you raising them in the admonishment of the Lord
Knowing they have placed their love and trust in you?

They need to know about heaven and hell
They need to know you love them,
They need to know about Jesus
And the terrible consequences of sin

Don't let God down
For he knows your every thought and deed,
Teach them right from wrong
These are little followers that you must lead

We each have only one life to live
Let's live it right,
Let's teach them the way in which they must go
Let's lead them to the light

Super Glue

Josh and Trish, two becoming one
Joining together in love,
In the sight of man
And the God of heaven above

A lifetime commitment
For better or for worse,
Josh is making his vows
And Trish is making hers

The glue that holds a marriage together
In sickness and in health.
Is your love for one another
In poverty and in wealth

You have vowed to protect and cherish
Till death do you part,
Two becoming an inseperable one
In soul, spirit, and heart

Yes! Love is the glue
Through sunshine and stormy weather,
Love is the glue
That holds a marriage together

And with an added little blessings
God has given you an angel to look after,
An energetic bundle
Of golden haired joy and laughter

May your home always be blessed
And God always be praised,
And may your lives always be filled
With joyful happy days

Live It

We put him last
Who should be first,
He who loves us so much
That it hurts

We eat steak
And throw him a bone,
He who has gone to prepare a place for us
Our heavenly home

When Christ comes into your life
And you experience the change.
Do not fail him
For this is not a game

This is life and death
Believe and do not doubt,
For what you have found
Is what life is all about

Love him more than life
For he gave his life for you,
And honor him all your days
In all you say and do

He will establish your thoughts
As you commit your works unto him,
With a new heart
Pure and cleansed from sin

May this little light of yours
Be forever lit,
God gave you the Christian life
Now go and live it

A Psalm of Praise

I praise the father
Who gave his son for me
Who went to the cross willingly,
I praise the holy spirit
For he is Christ's promise who dwells in me

I praise you for your word
I praise you for the preachers that I've heard,
I praise you for the missionaries that you've sent
Who with compassion for souls willingly went

I'll praise you in the morning
And at noonday too,
I'll praise you in the evening watches
And in the nighttime I lift my praise to you

I praise you for answered prayer
And that when I kneel that you are there,
I praise you for the daily miracles
And for all your loving care

I praise you and I thank you
For coming into my life,
For bringing me out of darkness
Into your wonderous light

I thank you and I praise you
For all you mean to me,
My praise for you dear God in heaven
Is for all eternity

Cleansed for Service

Take the garbage out of my mind
And out of my heart,
And take of your light and your love
And fill every part

Emptied out
And filled to overflowing,
Reading, kneeling, praying
And constantly growing

Becoming a faithful witness
Upon the highways and byways,
The lost being found
To the Lord's honor and praise

Witnessing miracles
All the days of my life,
Spirit filled and spirit led
Cleansed by the blood of Christ

Rejoicing on my pilgrim way
Lips filled with praise,
Trusting him with all
All my days

Change of Life

Those things I used to love
No longer thrilled my soul,
I was a dinasaur who outlived his time
Lost without a goal

I knew I must change or die
I no longer hunted and trapped,
I still camped a little and fished sometimes
I just had to learn to adapt

I knew new interests and new purposes
Must now fill my life,
Then " halleluah " I discovered something far better
Than anything I had before
In the Lord and savior Jesus Christ

He came to me
Through the reading of his word,
And what I read I beleived with all my heart
And when he spoke, without a sound I heard

I trusted him with my all
And experienced the miracle of rebirth,
I will rejoice in his saving grace all my days
And will continue to do so to the day my feet leave this earth

Trials

We thank you for yur blessings
And all the wonderful things that you do,
We thank you for the trials
That strengthens our faith in you

We thank you Lord for all things
For you would never do anything to hurt us,
And we know that all things work together for good
For those who are called according to your purpose

All that we are and all that we will ever be
When we surrender all to you will never be the same,
Praise " o' God " praise
We sing praises to your holy name

You say if God were by your side
There would be nothing that you would be afraid of,
Now let me tell you
Inside of you dwells the all powerfull everpresent God of love

No trials will he give to us
That are greater than we can bare,
Even up to and through the valley of the shadow
Our loving God is there

We praise you o' we praise you
For every trial you bring us through,
Thank you God for who you are
And who we are because of you

All

Jesus gave his all for me
All to him I owe,
Where he leads I will follow
Where he beckons I will go

The debt he forgave
I could never repay,
All I can do is take this life he gave to me
And live it day by day

He gave his all
To forgive my sin,
Now I must live my all
To honor and glorify him

O' what a wonderful life it is
This life he gave to me,
May it continually shine forth his glory
For all the world to see

O' yes he gave his all
That we may have it all,
O' what a wonderful wonderful life that awaits
In answer to the spirit's call

It is for him
This life I live,
All
No less to him I give

What do you require of me o' Lord
Except my all to you,
May my all honor you
In all I say or do

Not Forgotten

I thank God for all the people that have ever been
For all who are now and all that will ever be,
That he not only died for them
But that he also died for me

When I came to know him
He took the book and wrote down my name,
And he nailed to the cross
All my sin and shame

How can we not
Praise him,
Who took upon himself
Our punishment for sin

Thankful
Yes and I shall ever be,
For of all the people in all the world
He hasn't forgotten me

I thank you Lord
For who you are and for all you mean to me,
For caring enough to go to the cross
To set my soul free

Church Bells

I am so thankful
That I was born in this land of the free,
Where we are not persecuted nor condemned
For what we beleive

God is so good, he is so good
The church bells throughout this land are ringing,
Of thee o' Lord God of heaven
The redeemed are joyfully singing

I thank God
For washing away my sins,
I thank him always
For family, health, and friends

There is so much to be thankful for
I am thankful for the faithful everywhere,
For travis and God's miracle cure
In answer to our prayers

Thank you father
For the many treasures in heaven yet untold,
Thank you father for your many miracles
Which you daily to us unfold

I thank you God for the big bang
When you created everything,
Thank you father for this land of the free
Where the church bells continue to ring

Time

*What will it be like
When time shall be no more?,
What will it be like
On the other side of heaven's door?*

*What will it be like
To no more walk this sod?,
What will it be like to stand beneath the tree of life
Beside the river of God?*

*We are pilgrims upon this earth
On a journey toward the promised land,
What will it be like to walk on the sea of glass and the streets
Of gold
Where there are no oceans nor beaches of sand?*

*To be in that awesome place
Where time is replaced by forever more,
And to take in all the endless wonders
That spread out forever on that distant shore*

*To look on the face of our savior
As he takes us by the hand,
And walk through the Garden of Eden
In this awesome place called the promised land*

*O' what will it be like
To stand on that distant shore?,
And take in all the beauty and wonder
Where time is no more?*

*Where pain, suffering, and death
Have been done away,
And Christ is the light
Of this endless wonder of uncloudy day*

More Blessed

It is more blessed
To give than to receive,
This is one of the first things I read
When I first came to beleive

Angels came
And gave the good news,
"A savior is born unto you"
Jesus: King of the Jews

Our father in heaven
Gave us his son,
And his son gave us salvation by grace
Through the cross when our victory he won

The wise men gave gifts
To this miracle born in Bethlehem,
Born the savior of the world
Born the approriation for our sin

Giving is God's way
This Christmas remember all he gave to you,
And with the love of God in your heart
Make it your way too

Christmas is God's gift to us
What we do with it is our gift to him,
Jesus took our sins to the cross
And opened the doorway to heaven

This Christmas
Let's remember all that he gave,
From the miracle of the virgin birth
To the miracle of the empty grave

The Giver

Dear God
And father in heaven,
Empower this vessel
To be a channel for your love

May all my thoughts
And all I say and do,
Wherever I go
Bring honor and glory to you

Evangelism
Is a life lived for the one above,
A lifestyle turned from worldly ways
To one of brotherly love

We may be the only gospel
Some people will ever know,
May your word take deep root
And continue to blossom and grow

Let not pride enter in
I pray to humbly serve throughout this life I'm live'n,
With all the abilities you blessed me with
With all the God given gifts you've given

May every moment, every dollar, every thought and deed
Be precious in thy sight,
As I walk the walk, talk the talk
Shining forth your light

May the giver and sustainer of life
Be always in every decision I make,
As I give praise, honor, and glory
To the giver of every breath I take

The Dove

The spirit came down from heaven
In the form of a dove,
The very symbol
Of peace and love

Peace and love
The Lord God of heaven above,
Showers us with blessings
Of peace and love

The world thinks that christians are teched in the head
When in reality they are touched in the heart,
For what the God of heaven
Inside of us did impart

Jesus is God, the prince of peace
Jesus is God the son,
God is love
And it is by this love that we overcome

The spirit came down from heaven
And rested upon the son of man,
Filled to overflowing
He ministered with miracles all across this land

Good tidings of joy and peace
Were the angel's message upon his birth,
As the God of heaven became the son of man
To walk in the flesh upon this earth

We worship the God of peace and love
As we celebrate Christmas from year to year,
But in our hearts we celebrate daily
Of the time our God drew near

Go To Now

We thank the father
For the gift he has given to us,
For he so loved the world
He sent his son to save us

Those who don't accept him
Must be desirious of a warmer climate,
You're walking on shakey ground
If you haven't made that decision for Christ yet

Who knows for sure
What your tomorrows will bring,
A heart attack or stroke
Or you may get run over by something

Life has no guarantees
It could end tomorrow,
And where then will you awake?
Don't let it be in everlasting sorrow

He has given you a choice
Heaven or hell awaits,
Ponder your decision wisely
Will it be where the worm never dies?
Or safe inside those pearly gates

Will it be where there is wailing and gnashing of teeth?
Or where the streets are paved with gold?,
Will it be where the fire cannot be quenched?
Or the place where it is neither hot nor cold?

Go to now, do not hesitate
Do not procrastinate,
Now is the accepted time
Tomorrow may be to late

Praise my saviour

Blessed Assurance

Do you know without a doubt
That you are saved and destined for heaven?,
You can know, you can be assured
For in the holy book it is written

If you will confess with thy mouth the Lord Jesus
And believe in thy heart that God has raised him from the dead,
If you believe the testimony written of him
All the words written in black and all those in red

If you have confessed your sin
If you have opened your heart and let him in,
If you have turned
And living your life for him

These things have I written to you
That believe on God the son,
That you shall know that you have eternal life
So it is written, so it is done

These things have I written unto you
That you may know that you have eternal life,
These things I assure unto you
That believe on the name of Jesus Christ

You can know
You can be assured,
Read first John five, verses twelve and thirteen
And take comfort in the assurance of God's word

Blessed assurance
Jesus is mine,
O' what a foretaste
Of glory divine

Praise Him

Angels, angels, angels
Angels all around,
We are not alone
For angels walk this ground

O' that men would praise the Lord
Who sends his angels to watch over us,
O' that men would praise the Lord
Who gave us the victory through Jesus

Peoples lives change forever
When they kneel to God and pray,
Born again, praise to him
To walk with him every day

For his wonderful works unto us
We praise him,
We praise him for all of his wonderful works
He bestows upon the children of men

He satisfyeth the longing soul
He who is fair and just,
His mercy endures forever
To we who are but ashes and dust

Praise him, praise him
He is so good, praise his holy name,
We praise him for his goodness
As we witness to the world of his awesome fame

Praise him, praise him
Angels in heaven praise him,
Praise him, praise him
All ye children of men

Blink

We have a watch
Let's keep it vigilant every day,
The bible says he's coming back soon
No matter what people say

As you wait for the trump of God
As you wait for the archangel's shout,
Let your lights shine bright
Let your fires not go out

Paul believed it could happen in his day
We believe it could happen in ours,
Our hope burns brighter each new day
And each night as we look beyond the stars

We have a watch
For that which we hope, we will receive,
In our hearts we know he's coming
And we shall never cease to believe

We are waiting patiently
Fires burning bright,
Waiting for the heavens to open
To receive us into his light

The gravestones are shaking
Feet are lifting from the ground,
All in anticipation of the archangel's shout
And the trump of God to sound

Watch and be ready
He is coming in a time you know not when,
And lift your eyes to the heavens
And let not your lights grow dim

Words

Open my heart, spirit and soul
Fill my pen with heaven's light,
Let the power in the gift you've given
Break forth in the words that I write

Touch souls dear Lord
Let the secret things be known,
Let your words take deep root
As the seeds of life are sown

May the hearts be open and tender
And the tears of joy flow,
May they receive of thy salvation and grace
And may they thy peace that passeth all understanding know

Thy word o' God of heaven
Spoke the worlds into place,
Thy word o' God of heaven
Speaks of thy salvation and thy grace

Beautiful words, wonderful words
Words of truth that was spoken of old,
Powerful words, words of life
From the greatest story ever told

May the words that I write
Show forth to all the living,
That you are a merciful God
Tender, loving, and forgiving

And that if they would humble themselves
To kneel at an altar and pray,
The greatest treasure they could ever attain
Would be theirs today

A New Song

Old songs become new songs
When you open your heart and let Jesus in,
Old hymns become new hymns
When the blood of Jesus washes away your sin

He is my God, my friend, my life, my love
And he has become my song,
Music bubbles are bursting in my heart and soul
And my feet are tapping as I'm humming along

O' what a melody
He has placed within me,
The rhythm is so beautiful
So full of joy and glee

Jesus is my song
There is no more beautiful music that's ever been wrote,
There is no lyrics that makes your heart skip a beat
Than when Jesus is in every note

Yes! He has put a melody within me
Yes! He is my song,
O' yes, o' yes he is the music
That's got my fingers snapp'n and my feet a-tapp'n along

Praise, joy, love, glory
So many songs to choose from,
So many hymns all about him
With joy filled hearts to be sung

Open your mouth and make that joyful noise
Singing praise to the ancient of days,
Sing glory to the Lord of glory
Sing a-new the songs of joy, glory, and praise

Big Splat

What if there is no God?
What kind of question is that?,
There is no way science can prove to me
Everything was made in one big splat

The big bang theory just doesn't cut it
Scientists can't prove everything came from nothing,
God is the only logical explanation
The only way nothing can become something

If there is no God
There would be no universe,
There would be no sun, no moon, no stars
And there would be no God's green earth

If there is no God
Which they insist,
The human race
Would not exist

Our God is!
If he was not, everything would cease to be,
Look around
For he is in everything you see

If there is no God
There would be nothing at all,
No angels, no Jesus, no heaven
And no big blue marble

Divine creation, think about this
Big bang theory, think about that,
God
Or one big splat

Creator

Only God could create
That myriad of symmetric shape,
That tiny little white magical miracle
Known as a snow flake

And that beautiful arc against a backdrop of black
With it's radiant red, yellow, and blue glow,
That promise from God of long ago
Known as a rainbow

Hills and valleys covered in different shades of green
To hear a new born baby cry,
To watch the puffs of white fluff
Lazily drifting through a beautiful sea of blue sky

Brilliant flowers of vibrant colors
Busy little honey bees,
Multi colored leaves
Adorning all the different kinds of trees

As little windows, the stars shine out in the blackess of the night
The moon he created for a radiant glow,
The sun he created for light and for warmth
For all of us creatures here below

Awesome is our God
In everything that we see,
Awesome is our God in the unseen
Which by faith someday we will receive

One o' one glorious day
Every knee shall bow before the throne of the king,
The awesome God of heaven and earth
The creator of everything

The Greatest

There is a power greater than all others,
That one,
That one which our father in heaven used
When he sent to earth his only begotten son

It knows no evil
There are no obstacles in it's path,
It is greater than God's anger
And greater than his wrath

What is that one power
That is greater than all others combined?,
That one
That has withstood the test of time

What could be more powerful
Than the bombs that were dropped on Japan?.
What could be more powerful than the creation of the universe
And the creation of earth and man?

Power beyond belief
Power that makes an enemy become a brother,
One power
Greater than all other

It is the power that takes a tarnished soul
And removes the dross,
The same awesome power
That held Jesus to the cross

The greatest power that will ever be,
Is, or ever was,
If you haven't guessed by now
That power is love

Do the Do

If you want to get something out of life
You've got to put something into it,
If there is something worth doing
You need to be doing the do of it

Quit doing the don'ts
Good things don't come on a silver platter
Get off that duff
And start doing the things that matter

God gives the breath of life
God giveth and God taketh away,
Stand in the light and do that which is right
Rejoicing in your every God given day

Life can be o' so beautiful
If you live it right,
Step out of the darkness
And step into the light

God accepts you for where you are
And condemns you not for where you've been,
Take of your God given talents and gifts
And use them to glorify him

Do the doing of it
Do that which is right and good,
Remember the woman and the alabaster box
Who done what she could

Do the doing of it
And remember it's not about you,
It's all about Jesus
To whom our all is due

Letter to the Rat Pack

I'm on the other end of life
Closing in on three score and ten,
For that beautiful "rat pack" that always brings joy to my life
Their life is just about to begin

I pray only good things for them
Dear God lead them in the right direction,
Keep their hearts pure and right
Gently chastising them with thy correction

I pray that drugs, alcohol, and nicotine
Will never be a factor in their life,
I pray whereever life takes them
Their eyes never stray from Christ

I pray that the lives that they live
Make the world a better place,
And that Jesus, the guide of their youth
Watch over, protect, and keep them safe

Joyfully live each day as it comes
Live it to the full,
And you will find if you live it in the Lord
Life will never be boring nor dull

Life is what you make it
Sometimes up and sometimes down,
No matter what, keep the faith
And keep your feet planted on solid ground

Life for each of you is just begining
With all of it's joy and trial,
Step out in faith and take the journey
And take Jesus with you in every mile

Wendy's birthday

Written with love
Grandpa

Fear Not

Above and beyond the celestial heavens
In a dimension that we cannot see,
Lies the heaven of heavens
Where souls and spirits are set free

There we shall see Jesus
And Peter and Paul and John and James,
And friends and neighbors and kindred spirits
Of thousands and thousands of other names

A place where we shall forever
Sing of our joy and praises to the king of kings,
Walking upon the crystal clear sea of glass
Experiencing all of heaven's unimaginable awesome things

A place of endless wonders
Streets of translucent gold,
God will wipe away all our tears
In this place where the half has not been told

Growing old is not a bad thing
It just means we are getting closer to our forever home,
It is not the aches and pains of ageing
But it is for the heaven of heavens for which we groan

If Jesus be for us
What then shall we fear,
When we come to the valley of the shadow
Just remember that our Lord is ever near

Take him at his word
He said he would never leave nor forsake you,
Live life to the full in every stage of it
Till the day you rise like the morning dew

In Jesus's Name

Those that do not pray in Jesus's name
Where do their prayers go?,
They are tossed to and fro
And go to a place I do not know

Jesus said in the holy scriptures
No man cometh unto the father but by me,
How then can our prayers reach unto heaven
If we do not come dear father in Jesus's name unto thee

God said: you shall have no other Gods before me
You are the branch and I am the vine,
Jesus is the one, true, and only God
And I am his and he is mine

Father, son, and holy ghost
Is the God head of the mysterious three,
One God in three persons
Jesus, my only hope is in thee

If I were to pray in God's name only
My prayers will not be heard,
For there are Gods a plenty
According to the scriptures of God's holy word

Whoever we pray to other than Jesus
Is God with a little g,
And unless it's in the name of the son of God
Your prayers will just return unto thee

Now don't tell me to pray
Unless it's in Jesus name,
For without him all religion is vain
And I will not play that game

Praise his holy name

No Other Name

Jesus will be honored in all I say and do
Else it will not be said nor done,
For I will not dishonor
My father's only begotten son

I would not give my prayers to someone
Who does not pray in Jesus's holy name,
I will pray in no other
And I pray others do the same

He that hath the son hath life
He is the life, the truth, and the way,
He that hath not the son of God hath not life
There is no other name in which to pray

If Jesus is the son of God
Why would you pray to another?,
There is no what if
And there is no other

I know in whom I beleive
I have answered the spirit's call,
He is who he says he is
And I pledge him my life, my all

A-men

Abomination

United States of America take warning
All nations that forget God shall be turned into hell,
Remember Soddom and Gommora
And the reason that the fire and brimstone fell

Thou shalt not lie with mankind as with womankind
It is abomination,
In the levitical law punishable by death
Do not allow this pollution of our "in God we trust" nation

Men with men, women with women
Dishonouring their bodys in unclean lusts,
Vile affections of unnatural acts
Deserving of whatever punishment God deems just

Do not condone same sex marriages
Why do you think they call them queer,
These acts are condemned by the higher power
Be careful what you allow with fear

Let's keep our nation clean
With God her soverein king,
Let the scriptures be our laws
And once and for all let's condemn this ulnclean thing

Pray for our leaders

The Atonement

Where there is life there is hope
If you have fallen back in sin,
Repent and overcome
And give your life back to him

Seventy times seven he asks us to forgive
Jesus will do no less,
Confess your sins and turn from them
And he will cast them as far as the east is from the west

We have a hope steadfast and sure
The hope of glory is ours,
We have a mansion not made with hands
In that paradise beyond the stars

We thank you for taking our place
On the cross of calvary,
We thank you for the atonement
That you willingly took to set us free

We thank you for the hope you've given to us
Of someday being with you,
In a place of unimaginable beauty and peace
Where all that you promised is true

The day of atonement was overshadowed
By the fullfillment of the promise of life,
When good Friday, earth's darkest day
Gave way to Easter, her brightest light

The Third Day

The hammer blows that drove those nails
Pierced through Mary's heart,
The earth quaked and the sun was darkened
As the veil of the temple from top to bottom was torn apart

And they wrapped him in fine linen and laid him in a sepulcher
And rolled a great stone before it's opening,
They placed a seal upon it and posted soldiers to guard it
As if any grave could hold our Lord and king

For behold there was a great earthquake
And the angel of the Lord descended from heaven,
He rolled the stone away and sat upon it
And for fear of him the keepers shook and became as dead men

And he said to the women who stood by
Fear not: for I know that ye seek Jesus who was crucified,
He is risen from the dead
The sepulchre is empty, Jesus is not inside

And quickly they fled the sepulchre
To tell the good news to the disciples, as joy replaced their grief,
And the disciples beleived not until he appeared unto them
And Jesus upbraided them because of their unbeleif

Good Friday is the dark day that Jesus died
Easter Sunday is the glorious day he rose again,
Upon the cross at Golgotha, the place of the skull
Jesus paid the full price for our sin

That third day the gates of heaven opened wide
To receive all who would come unto him,
Come and kneel at the altar of grace
And be shed of your burden of sin

The Sacrificial Lamb

Confess it, your forgiven, forget it
If God doesn't remember it why should you?,
It all goes back to the cross
Evaporated like the morning dew

Repent, turn, and do it no more
Gone is what Jesus said,
Washed away by the blood of the lamb
Erase it out of your head

There is forgiveness at the foot of the cross
Do you have the courage to go there,
The altar is the symbol of that tree
Where you can take all your burden and care

To receive it youv'e got to beleive it
Youv'e got to reach out for it,
If Jesus is pulling at your heart strings
It is time to answer the call of the spirit

Go to now
For now is the accepted time,
And shout with all joy that Jesus, eternal life,
And all of heaven's treasures are thine

Live life like it was meant to be lived
Live in the blessed hope of that which is to come,
Looking to the author and finisher of your faith
Yearning to hear Jesus's "Well done"

I thank the trinity of heaven
For their perfect salvation plan,
All glory, praise, and honor be to my Lord and saviour
For becoming the sacrificial lamb

Two Years Early

I married the most beautiful girl in the world
Fifty years ago on this day,
And we are still together
No matter, come what may

She captured my heart
Which I willingly gave to her,
Three months later we said our vows
The next fifty years are just a blurr

Five gorgeous daughters
Seventeen grandchildren, and two great grandchildren
Life don't get no better than this,
God gave me my heart's desire
My every prayer, my every wish

If I had life to live over
I would not,
Life has been too beautiful
And I'm very happy with what I've got

Fifty years, fifty years
My how those fifty years flew by,
We survived the good and the bad
But it has been mostly good for you and I

I love you Alice
More and more each day,
And even more
Since Jesus came our way

Jesus gave us greater purpose
To live this wonderful life,
You were and are the most beautiful girl in the world
And I thank God you became my wife

Our 48th wedding anniversary

Beautiful Name

Who was it that taught you your bedtime prayers
Of now I lay me down to sleep,
I pray the Lord my soul to keep?,

Who was it who calmed your boo hoo's,
And kissed your boo boo's?

Who prayed at your bedside when you were sick?,
Who taught you that there was no problem you couldn't lick?

Who did you' run too
Besides daddy that is,
When you were ready
For your bedtime hug and kiss?

And when it was bedtime
Who tucked you in?,
It was probably mom
Nine times out of ten

Who was willing
Her all to sacrifice?,
Who loves you
More than life?

It is mothers who ease us through our every pain, "mother"
What a wonderful beautiful name

So Good

Awesome, o'how awesome
I've said it many times before,
O' for a thousand tongues
To praise him even more

God is good. he is so good
We praise him and we entrust him with all our burdens and cares,
With the faith that moves mountains
We go to the one who listens to and answers our prayers

O' how we love him, o' how we praise him
O' for the words to come forth from my tongue,
How do we tell of his wonderful goodness
There are poems to be written and songs to be sung

He is the one who made the mountains
He can move our mountains from before us,
There is no other name in heaven or earth
More precious than the name of Jesus

An everpresent help in time of need
When we call upon him he is there,
When we have a praise or concern
We go to him instant in prayer

O' to express the fullness of God's goodness
The heighths and depths, o' if only I could,
To reach down into my heart and soul
And o' to tell how God is so good

Praise the Lord
Psalm 107

Bestest Friend

Who corrected you
With just a look?,
Who took you fishing
And baited your hook?

Who took you camping
To all those neat places?,
Where you had loads of fun
And met lots of new faces

Who taught you to play poker
And the teacher looked at you with a grin?,
Because you thought
Jack, queen, king, came after ten

Dads make you laugh
And dads make you cry,
But they only spanked you when you needed it
And you thought that was only when pigs fly

Dads have a very special place in our hearts
Sometimes gruff, but they have their tender side,
And if they would ask their children how much they loved them
They would say this much, with arms opened wide

This is a very special day
A day set aside just for him,
Daddy
Your bestest friend

My Prayer

I pray give me the souls to seek
Give me the words to speak,
Give me the paths to walk
And chide me to walk the talk

May I always be instant in prayer,
And where there is a need and I am able
May I always be there

Write your words
Upon the table of my heart,
And may I speak those encouraging words
Your hope to others impart

Keep me on the straight and narrow
Try me and chastise me,
Remind me often of your love
That I may reflect that love for others to see

Let me not fail you
If I begin to falter remind me of your saving grace and salvation's
price,
And draw me back
Into the loving arms of Jesus Christ

I pray to always
Do that which is good and right,
Soul surrendered
Cleansed and precious in thy sight

Morning Song

I awake to my every morning
With a song in my heart,
Since Jesus came in
With his precious promise to never depart

He is the music within swelling up and bursting out
The sweet, sweet melody overflowing from my soul,
He has become my morning song
He has taken the broken pieces and made me whole

He gave me newness of life
Life that all my life I had resisted,
He gave me newness of life
Like I never knew existed

He is my morning song
He is the melody of joy within me,
He is the music of my soul
And praise God he shall forever be

He is the music that bubbles forth
He is the melody of my all day long,
He makes my heart sing
He is my morning song

He is the joyful noise
That joy filled Christians praise and sing,
He is our morning song
And has become our everything

Come on and wake up to a whole new world
Come on and sing along,
Wake up to the joy of Jesus
And make him your morning song

Praise Ye the Lord

There is a poem
That burns within,
Of praises and glory
And honor to him

It is a poem
That's got to come out,
Glory to God
Is what it's about

By him all things were created
Praise ye the Lord,
By him all things exist
Praise ye the Lord

He is the power of powers
Praise the Lord,
He is the Lord of Lords
Praise the Lord

He is the king of kings
Creator of everything,
Praise the Lord, praise the Lord
Praise ye the Lord

All that hath breath
Praise ye the Lord,
Trees and rocks
Praise ye the Lord

We praise you o' Lord
Master, savior, God of creation,
Praise ye the Lord
All ye children of God in every nation

All ye angels in heaven above
All ye creatures here below
Praise ye the Lord

Praise him all your days
Even days without end,
Praise ye o' God of heaven
Praise ye the Lord

Land of the Free

Young men fight our wars
Young men give their lives,
Willing to give their all for our freedom
Leaving behind their children and wives

This nation is free because of them
This nation does not bow down to any,
This nation will use all of it's resourses
To fight terrorism and tyranny

The statue of liberty
Greets those coming to our shore,
To all those looking for a better life
No matter color, creed, nationality, rich or poor

We are a new nation
Compared to many others,
We are one nation under God
And in his eyes we are all sisters and brothers

The land of the free
What a glorious sound,
America
A place of hallowed ground

We have fought many a war
I praise God my country tis of thee,
God bless America
Land of the free

Mark It "Sold"

A 2004 Honda helix
What a beautiful machine,
A gleaming candy apple red powerhouse
Of lean and mean

A shiny red helmet, a black leather jacket,
And the freedom of the open road,
It was love at first sight
As I said: "mark it sold"

It sports graceful lines
250 cc of awesome power,
It gets 70 miles to the gallon
And goes 70 miles per hour

No gears to shift, it's completely automatic
It climbs the toughest hills with ease,
Just turn the throttle
And experience the amazing power that's beneath your seat

This is not just any ordinary scooter
But an extraordinary thing of beauty to behold,
It's lines and curves are perfect
A mechanical marvel worth it's weight in gold

Happiness is blue skys, warm days,
Gentle breezes, an endless road,
And a bright red Honda helix
Marked "Sold"

Less of Me

More of Jesus
Less of me,
More of Jesus
For others to see

It is for his honor that we use the gifts
That he has placed within,
For he is the giver of all good things
All honor and glory be unto him

When you look at me
I pray what you see,
Is more of our Lord
And less of me

We each have a gift
That he has given to us,
We lowly creatures
Of ashes and dust

He is looking down
From heaven above,
To see how we are using
These gifts of love

I pray of my gift
That all may see,
More of him
And less of me

Praise the Lord

Every Day

Every breath that we take
Every morning that we awake,
Every sunrise that we see
And every sunset that he has given to you and me

These are gifts from above
Gifts from the God of love,
In every day that he gives to us
We learn more and more in him to trust

God has made every day special for you and me
Rain or shine, blue or gray,
Rich or poor these gifts are free
Special in God's own given way

We thank you Lord for this day that you have made
In which we breath and walk and have our being,
And for all these beautiful temperal things
Created for the enjoyment of our seeing

We will rejoice and be glad in this day
As we praise you dear God in heaven above,
And we praise you allmighty God for the sacrifice of your son
For us your greatest act of love

Every day that we awake
Every breath that we take,
Every day fresh and new
Dear God in heaven we praise you

Sweet Memories

When someone loses their life mate
The hurting ache goes deep,
You search for answers
As heart and soul continues to weep

Time and caring people are the only things
That will lift you from this valley your in,
It's a whole new world
Reach out and lean on your family and friends

They will pull you through
Life is still worth the living,
You've got a loving heart
Continue your life with loving and giving

As caring people reach out to you
Remember the others that are hurting too,
And remember that the greatest treasures
Are the sweet sweet memories that he gave to all of you

There is no way that we can feel
The pain that you are going through,
But we want you to know that we do care
And we will continue to pray for you

Jesus put it better than I
As his sayings we all strive to keep,
When he said: rejoice with those who do rejoice
And weep with those who weep

Written for Nancy (Barley) Secor
God bless and comfort you Nancy

Heros

Moses, Joshua
And Jesus Christ,
Joseph and his integrity
Concerning Potiphar's wife

David
And Jonathon his closest friend,
Daniel
And the lion's den

Defying King Nebuchadnezzar
Bound and thrown into the firey furnace,
Shadrach, Meshach, and Abednego
Gave the Lord their undying trust

Rahab the harlot
Who hid the spies,,
Elijah and Elisha
And their lives

Sampson and Solomon
And Naomi and Ruth
Our father in heaven
And those who wrote the book of truth

Peter, John
James and Paul,
Matthew, Mark, Luke
And the apostles all

Joni Ericson, Mother Terresa
And Billy Graham,
Corrie Ten boom and millions of others
Of lesser fame

Preachers and teachers
Spreading the gospel of Jesus Christ,
Reaching out to the world
Bringing dead souls to life

Though most of our heros
Are dead and gone,
In our hearts and minds
They will forever live on

But of all there is one who stands above all
The one of which with joy filled hearts we sing,
And that's our savior
Our hero, our friend, our Lord and our King

Pray

Who do you talk too
When your burdens are to heavy to bare?,
Who do you go too
With your every hope and care?

Tell it to Jesus
Is the song that we sing,
Jesus is waiting
For us to trust him with our everything

All of our hopes, all of our dreams
All of the burdens we bare,
All that we are and all that we have
We commit to the Lord's loving care

Do you have a heavy burden
That's more than you can carry?,
Be instant in prayer
Take it to Jesus and do not tarry

Tell him of your heart filled joys
And your troubles all,
Pray, believing
And he will break down every wall

For if you believe and do not doubt
Miracles will come your way,
As you kneel before the king of kings
And humble yourself and pray

Atheist Beware

Atheist beware
If the passion of the Christ comes on T.V.
Turn the channel, do not watch
You may be shocked by what you see

You could be converted
You could be destined for heaven's gates,
You could become a believer
And escape the otherwise hell that awaits

Love, peace, and joy
Could suddenly overflow your soul,
You could have an overwhelming urge
To make converting others your earthly goal

I do not believe in atheists
Now don't laugh,
I do not believe in atheists
And I never have

I do not believe anyone
Can look around and not believe,
The big bang theory is one big lie
Nobody can be that naive

Look at the snowflake and the rainbow
Look at the sun, the moon, and the stars,
These are God's gifts to us
While we live all of this is ours

Now you might say you do not believe
But deep down you desire to know one way or another,
Pick up a bible
And read it from cover to cover

If then you still do not believe
Then there is nothing more to say,
For you will when you open your eyes in death
Become a believer that day

Jack

With finger pointed upward
He rose beyond the sky,
It was Jack's farewell to the world
And to Noreta his sweet goodbye

He was heaven bound
He made his triumphant entry,
He entered the promised land
Soul and spirit set free

Jack is seeing
What every saved soul hopes to see,
That glorious realm that lies beyond
In the endless wonders of eternity

He is seeing his lord face to face
He is rejoicing with the others who have passed on before,
Donnie and Jay and Rodney and countless others
Where pain and suffering are no more

He is singing praises to his maker
No tears are shed up there,
But if they could they would be tears of joy
In this place where there are no more burdens to bare

Jack: We who live in the blessed hope
Are looking forward to that day,
When we shed the old for the new
And point our finger toward heaven and fly away

Some day Jack we're coming home
To rejoice up there with you,
But for now we must earnestly pray and faithfully witness
For others to make it through

Praise the Lord

O' Bright and Morning Star

I have always wondered why god created the earth
And supplied it with jungles, dinosaurs, and swampland,
I always wondered what god had in mind
Before he created man

Now I see more clearly
It was because he had foreseen,
The almost endless supply of energy
That man would ultimately need

Decaying ancient forests over a great period of time,
Would become the coal that we now mine

Dinosaurs, those gigantic beasts of long ago,
Have become the natural gas and the oil
That warms our homes and makes our autos go

He made the stars
And called them the lesser light,
With precision and perfection he placed them in their spaces
To twinkle and sparkle as the bright eyes of the night
He made the moon to mark the seasons
And the sun for light and heat,
He made everything to benefit our lives
To the very food we eat

We praise him for all of his wonderful works
He bestows upon the children of men,
We praise him for his goodness
And for becoming our closest friend

We praise him for the cross
That perfect heavenly plan,
We praise him for the blood
That bridged the gap between God and man

We praise him with all of our being
We praise him with all that we are,
We praise you O' God of heaven
O' Bright and morning star

Where is Heaven?

The rapture of the church
Could happen in our day,
But some say
It just ain't gonna happen that way

They say that their heaven
Is right here on this turf,
They are misrepresenting and miswitnessing Jehovah
The God of heaven and earth

To you I say
You can have this earth,
We'll take what Jesus went to prepare for us
And for all who have experienced the new birth

All who are born again
People from every race in every nation,
Shall be caught up to the third heaven
Paul seen it, as did john who wrote the book of revelation

To be absent from the body
Is to be present with Christ,
He who sets on the right hand of God
In heaven's eternal paradise

When the archangel gives the shout
When the trumpet of God shall sound,
The Saints shall lift from off this earth
O' feet don't let me down

The dead in Christ shall rise first
Then we which are alive shall be caught up to be together with them,
And so shall we meet the Lord in the air
And so shall we be forever with him

A-men

What Then?

You were born
And I said: what then?,
And you said you were going to get an education
And I said: what then?

You said you were going to earn lots of money
And I said: what then?,
And you said you were going to accumulate a lot of perty things
And I said: what then?

And then someday you were going to retire
And I said: what then?,
And you said you were going to travel the world over
And I said: what then?

And you said you were going to grow old in style
And said: what then?,
And you said you were going to enjoy life to the fullest
And I said: what then?

And you said: well I suppose I'll die
And I said: what then?

Yea and a-men

O' For faith that never fails
O' For hope that never faints,
O' For love that's everlasting
O' For the joy of the rejoicing saints

O' For salvation
Full and free,
O' For the blood
That Jesus shed for me

O' To be clothed upon
With heavenly robes of white,
O' To walk those golden streets
In that place of heavenly light

O' To talk to John and James
In that beautiful awesome place,
O' To drink from the river of life
And see my Lord face to face

At the end of our pilgrim journey
When we shed these temples of flesh and bone,
Mortality shall put on immortality
As we are clothed upon with our heavenly home

Rejoice O' Christian soldier
For death is not the end,
For all the promises of God my friend
Are yea and a-men

Hidy Ho

Hidy Hidy Ho
Hidy Hidy Ho,
It's off to school I go
It's off to school I go

Bob's bus is coming
Following the backwater road
Following the backwater road
Turning down W 19 Lane,
Following the backwater road
Through snow and fog and rain

I seen the lights a flash'n
I heard the engine roar,
As the stop sign's arm swung out
And Bob opened up the door

Time was ticking away
And ally knew it wouldn't be long,
As bus # 25 came to a stop
And Bob the bus driver waived her on

Singing Hidy Hidy Ho
Hidy Hidy Ho,
It's off to school I go

Anatomy of a Christian

God did not give us a heart
To fullfill our dark desires,
He did not give us a soul
To be cast into hell's unquenchable fires

He did not give us a brain
To dwell upon evil thoughts,
But rather to contemplate upon the price
For which our freedom was bought

He gave us legs and feet
To go swiftly to help our fellow man,
And arms
To reach out that helping hand

He gave us a voice
To speak out for that which is right,
And eyes
For windows to let in heaven's light

He gave us ears
And the bible as his holy word,
And preachers and teachers
That those words of life may be heard

These are the anatomy of a Christian
These are the anatomy of those born again,
This is the anatomy of those washed in the blood of the lamb
And of all who have given their life to him

One Simple Fact

When you ask Jesus
To come into your life,
When you step out of the darkness
And into his light

All the evil
That ever you've done,
Goes back to the cross
Where those three nails pierced God's son

The Lord of heaven and earth
The great "I am",
Left his home in glory
To become the sacrificial lamb

Are you saved?
Are you sure?,
The blood of the lamb
Is sins only cure

Our father God
Is looking down from above,
With forgiveness and blessings
For all who accept his most precious gift of love

Of all the religions in all the world
There is only one that's tried and true,
Christ is King and Lord of all
Who are you praying to?

If you are looking for the way the truth and the life
Cling to this first John five twelve fact,
"He that hath the son hath life"
It don't get no simpler than that

Unconditional Love

I thank god that when I reached out to him
He reached out to me,
I was bound to the world, trapped in sin
And my God through Jesus set me free

I thank him for all the good things
And all the seemingly bad,
For all things work together for good
He makes my heart so glad

He walks with me
Where ever that I go,
He sets my paths straight
Because he loves me so

He promised to never leave me
Although I've failed him over and over,
He reached down his nail pierced hand
As I sunk lower and lower

His love is unconditional
His love is always there,
O' God how can we neglect so great a love
Of the one who took our sins to bare

Love O' God
Of the one who came to seek and save the lost,
Love O' God
Is what drew my savior to the cross

I love my Lord O' God
More than all else,
I love my Lord O' God
More than life its self

My Lord, my love, my God
Whose love is unconditional,
You took my empty heart and soul
And you filled it to the full

So Much

Thanksgiving is the time to reflect
Upon all that we are thankful for,
Past blessings, now blessings
And all that the future has in store

I am thankful for the cross
The trinity's perfect salvation plan for the human race,
I am thankful for the spirit's call
And the new testament's ushering in of amazing grace

I am so thankful for my five beautiful daughters
And the grandchildren that they have given to me,
I am thankful for my wife, the love of my life
And for being born in the land of the free

So much to be thankful for here and now
So much joy and laughter,
And I'll thank my Lord forever and ever
For the joys that lies hereafter

I thank God for Travis
Who we placed in our father's loving care,
And for all the prayers that went up all across this great land
From the churches everywhere

So much to be thankful for
All of our lives, all of our days,
So much to be thankful for
To God be the glory and to God be the praise

Walking on Water

Now let me tell you
What's dumber than a box of rocks,
Is a man with a mouth full of mousies
Sitting on a square box

Freezing his buns off
On a huge block of frozen water,
Looking down a tiny hole
Praying for the weather to be a little hotter

Frozen fingers and toes
You've got to have what it takes,
To get up before sunrise
And subject your body to uncontrolable shivers and shakes

The thunderous sounds
Of freezing stress cracks rumbling across the lake
Only to end up at your box
And spew ice water in your face

Your first experience of this
Will have you running for your life,
Screaming and swearing
That you will never again step foot on the ice

Ice fisherman
Think they are real smooth,
Wrapped up in so many layers
They can hardly move

They waddle out on the ice
And drill out this small round hole,
And set there shaking
Holding their tiny little pole

"O Holy Night"

Over 2000 years ago an event of astronomical proportions was taking
place
It was the greatest happening since god created the heavens
And the earth,
It happened in a lowly stable in Bethlehem of Judea
For it was there where the Virgin Mary was giving birth

Through the overshadowing of the holy ghost
The word was made flesh and dwelt among us,
And they wrapped him in swaddling clothes and laid him in a manger
And they called him Jesus

Miracles upon miracles were taking place
As angels suddenly appeared in a spectacular display of heavenly light,
Announcing the good news to the shepherds of the fields
That a savior was born to them this " O' Holy night"

A new star appeared in the heavens
To guide the kings of the east to where Jesus lay,
They came bearing precious gifts
Rejoicing on their journey's way

God among us
Lord of Lords, King of Kings,
Creator, maker, and sustainer
Of every inanimate and every living thing

We continue to celebrate a- new
As christmas draws nigh each year,
The time the Christ child was born
The day our God drew near

In God We Trust

We are at thy mercy dear God
In thee do we trust,
We are at thy mercy dear God
In all that whatsoever befalls us

We will not fear
Nor shed narry a tear,
We will cling
To he who is ever so near

God will be God
His will will be done,
We will trust him for the ultimate good
For that whatsoever will come

We pray believing
Knowing in whom we trust,
As we lay our petitions before him
In the holy name of Jesus

We know that no matter what
That from your hand we are receiving,
That you are the God of hope
Who fills us with all joy and peace in believing

We will not be afraid of evil tidings
Our hearts are fixed, our eyes looking up,
All fear is gone, you are our song
You are our full and overflowing cup

O' God of miracles
We know what you can do,
O' God of the heaven of heavens
We lift up our prayers to you

The Promise

So much hope came into the world
Through the birth of Mary's baby boy,
So many miracles surrounded the event
Of this heavenly sent bundle of joy

In a sudden burst of heavenly light
Angels appeared and lit up the night,
Peace on earth, good will toward men
It must of been an earth shaking awesome sight

O' Star of Bethlehem
Hanging low over the manger where Christ lay,
Shining your glory over the Lord of glory
Leading the kings on their journey's way

Honored by shepherds and honored by kings
Born of a virgin was he,
He left his throne, his heavenly home
To die on the cross for you and me

He led a sinless life
It was for our transgressions that he was nailed to Calvary's tree,
He was thirty years old when he began his ministry
And he died at thirty three

But it does not end there
For upon the dawn of that third day,
Mary came to an empty tomb
And she cried out that someone had stolen her Lord away

He had risen from the grave
He ascended to his heavenly throne,
With the promise of the blessed hope
Of one day coming back to take us home

Pray for the Dawn

God is out to accomplish something
Of what I am not sure,
Through this terrible thing that he has put upon Travis
In spite of our prayers he has not sent a cure

I am sure that many, many sincere prayers
Have reached his holy throne,
But his purpose has not yet been accomplished
As for the end of these trials we agonize and groan

God will be God
These trials will continue to exist,
Till his purposes are fullfilled
If only he would reveal that list

In the meantime
Though we don't understand the trials god has sent our way,
We know that God always gives what's best
So we continue to fervently pray

Someday when this is over
We will praise God for all that he has done,
But for now our hearts are hurting
As we go through these seemingly unbearable trials
Upon Tina and Troy and their son

Darkness has fallen upon us
O' God we pray for the dawn to come,
I pray O' God for an end
Of cancer's clutches upon my grandson

Best Friend

In all the world
You only have one best friend,
For over forty years
You've been mine Jim

We've fished and hunted
And party'd hearty together,
We've been through
The good, the best, and the better

We use to play cards
Back when Barb knew all the four letter words,
But since she's come to know Jesus
These are no longer heard

No more do we go to wild new year's partys
Now it's dinner and a show,
Good friends, good conversation, and stone sober
Safely back to our homes we go

You have so much on your hearts and minds
With your granddaughter Awdrey,
You've prayed so hard and long
For her to be set free

Then you got the devastating news
Just after new years it came,
That you have unoperable lung cancer
For all of us life will never again be the same

Jim you are and will always be
My best friend,
And with Jesus by your side
Win or lose, you win

Victory Song

Praise be unto my Lord my God
All glory be unto my King,
My Savior, my Lord, my God
Whom I trust with my everything

When I seek him
When I go to him in prayer,
When I kneel to him day or night
My God is always there

I know that I am not perfect
But my father looks at me through the blood,
He's with me through the fire
And he's with me through the flood

I wouldn't know how to deal
With this world so full of sin,
Nor how to face life's many trials
Without my Lord within

I'm walking the upward journey
Surrendering all to him,
Turning, confessing, and receiving
His full pardon for my sin

There's victory O' Blessed victory
At the end of life's rocky road,
If you walk the straight and narrow
That leads to the streets of gold

Praise, glory, and honor
Be unto my Lord, my God, my King,
Peace, love, and joy unending
Is the victory song I sing

The Empty Tomb

The tomb in which they laid my Lord
The tomb that was guarded and sealed,
The tomb where two soldiers became as dead men
When an angel came down and rolled back the stone
And it's emptyness was revealed

Our Lord and savior, our redeemer and king
Was not where they had lain him,
He had risen as he said he would
Victorious over death-and sin

He paid it all
For all who in faith repent and believe,
He paid it all
For all who reach out to receive

Satan trembled when he saw the angel's of light
Sitting by the folded linen cloths where Jesus no longer lay,
Satan who thought he had won the victory
Faced his greatest defeat on the dawn of that third day

He is a defeated foe
Destined for the lake of fire,
But we through the blood by God's grace
Have escaped this world's muck and mire

Our sights are set on things above
Of bringing others into the fold,
As we walk the muddy streets of life
Yearning for the streets of gold

Good Friday was not a good day
It was covered with darkness and gloom,
But we thank God for the breaking of the dawn of easter morn
And the miracle of the empty tomb

Awesome Power

Jesus loves you
The devil only seeks to destroy,
Jesus died for you
And offers you eternal joy

The devil
Is a murderer and a liar,
And all those who follow him
Will follow him into the lake of fire

Rebuke the devil
And he will flee,
Draw nigh unto God
And he will draw nigh unto thee

Take the path of greatest resistance
Go against the flow,
For the wide path leads to destruction
And that awful place below

Do not be fooled
For the devil can transform himself into an angel of light,
Know your scriptures, keep your heart pure and clean
And your garments spotless and white

The devil was defeated
On the Hill of Calvary,
Where every sin repented of
Was nailed to that cruel tree

That sacrifice is still in effect
And every minute of every hour,
The blood of the lamb
Still works it's awesome power

Again?

My oldest daughter was born
Along about a way back when,
I find it kind of hard to believe
That today she's 39 again

Life is like vintage wine
That just gets better with age,
Don't fret about the years that pass by
Just enjoy to the fullest every stage

Your mom and I have been through many trials
In our long together years,
But every year gets better
As we live it with all of it's joys and tears

Tougher than nails
And sweeter than wine,
Beautiful at any age
Is this eldest daughter of mine

I have one question for you sweet sue
And I think about it every now and then,
How does it feel
To be 39 again?

Written for Sue's 50 th
To be celebbrated Dec. 9, 2006
Dad

Into the Light

When Jesus is in your every thought
Your every heartbeat, and every breath,
Life becomes more beautiful
And there is no fear of death

When he is the light upon your path
When he is the lamp that outshines the rest,
When he is the light that lights up your life
And has cast your sins as far as the east is from the west

When he becomes your everything
When he makes your happy heart sing,
When your heart skips a beat
Every time you hear a church bell ring

When Jesus fills your every being
When the holy spirit becomes your guide,
When you fully grasp that you are the reason
Christ went to the cross and died

When the tears swell up in your eyes
At every song that praises him,
As you think upon that life changing experience
When he called and drew you in

When he is the reason for living,
He who is loving, kind, and forgiving

Shout the victory shout
And all your life do that which is good and right,
And when the death angel comes to call
Go rejoicing into the light

Fathers

Children are earthly treasures
That God has placed into your loving care,
Each one special in their own way
Priceless beyond compare

Nurture them in the admonition of the Lord
Bring them up in the light,
Teach them biblical truths
Teach them about wrong and right

Spend time with your children
Provoke them not to wrath,
Train them up in the way they should go
And when they are old they will not depart from that path

Take them, do not send them, to church
Time with your children is time well spent,
Take them fishing, take them camping
Teach them to bait a hook, teach them to pitch a tent

Be a father
That your child will be proud of,
Spend time with them
And shower them with your love

Introduce them to the Jesus you know
And let them see him in every part of your being,
Let them see him in your words and your deeds
In all your outer action and all your inner feelings

Spend time with your child
For they grow up all to fast,
Spend time with your child
For the time they're a child all to soon is past

Self Righteousness

Our righteousness is but filthy rags
For he is our righteousness who died for us
Self righteousness is a sin that God condemns
In Jesus's shed blood only should we trust

Do not judge another
As the Pharasee did the publican,
For the Pharasee thanked God that he was not like this man
As the Publican sought forgiveness and confessed his sin

Of the two who knelt down to pray
Who do you think was justified?,
I tell you it was not the self righteous one
Caught up in his sinful pride

Do not judge lest ye be judged
Examine your own heart before you cast a stone,
As Jesus said to the accusers of the adulteress
And one by one they left till it was just Jesus and the woman alone

Do not judge another
For it is God who condemns or justifies,
The unrepent self righteous one will burn one day
In the fire'y pool with the father of lies

Husbands love your wives
And tell them so from the heart,
And do not think of yourself better than others
But from self righteousness confess and depart

Jesus is our righteousness
Judge not your fellow man,
And to every soul you meet along life's path
Offer and extend a helping hand

Grace

Jesus paid the price
And offers it to us free,
Jesus gave his all
For the love of you and me

Grace
What a beautiful sound,
There is no sweeter word to my soul
That I have ever found

What is the most beautiful verse in the bible
I can think of only one,
For God so loved the world
He gave us his son

He that believeth upon him
Has everlasting life,
The gift of grace is ours
Because Jesus paid the price

O' How much more beautiful
Is everything that I now see,
Since Jesus came into my heart
And his grace set me free

Grace, grace, o beautiful grace
To my ears, O' How sweet the sound,
That has loosed my soul from eternally lost
To be heaven bound

Though now we see through a glass darkly
Soon it will be face to face,
Thank God, Jesus paid it all
To give us the gift of grace

Gifts

Our gifts vary
But our giver is the same,
Keep your eyes upon the giver
And praise his holy name

All gifts are given
To be used for his glory,
To bring souls into his kingdom
And to spread the gospel story

Look beyond the gifts
To where they're coming from,
Make sure the music, the poems, and the lyrics
Bring honor to God's son

Praise God
From whom all blessings flow,
Praise god for the gifts
He bestows upon us creatures here below

He is the giver of all good things
Given to bring honor and glory to him,
He led captivity captive and ascended on high
And gave gifts unto men

The Class of "55"

Time took wings and passed us by
It's hard to believe it's been fifty years,
Old school chums coming together again
Eyes overflowing with joyful tears

Judy, Noreta, and Donna
All worked hard to get you here,
And we praise their efforts
That brought you from far and near

We looked forward with anxious anticipation
For this special day to arrive,
When once again there would be a reuniting
Of we the class of 55

Jack, Donnie, Jay, and Rodney
Have all passed on to a better place,
And we miss them dearly, but we rejoice
That one day soon we will see them again face to face

From way out Montana way
Sharon came to see her old classmates,
And Charlie came from fountain Colorado
Another one of those far away western states

There's Ed and beautiful Betty,
Jim Freeman, Jim Eberly
And Beverly and Beverly

Ted, Terry, John, and Hal
Dan, Kate, Nancy, and Lorene,
Franny, Jackie, Phil, Harley, and myself
Rounding out this awesome alumni team

As we think back
Upon those good old golden rule days,
May we also share the blessings
Of the last fifty years of God's golden rays

Of children and grandchildren
I'm sure there's many a tale to tell,
And I pray there be many more
Before God tolls that final bell

May we all be blessed of one another
As we mingle and reminisce,
Of days amd memories of old
That causes the eyes to mist

May each take new memories home
Of the joys we share here,
And place those treasures in our hearts
Where they will always be near

Knock, Knock

Are you ready to receive the living waters
That will quench your thirst forever more?,
Are you ready to receive life everlasting?
Are you ready to take up eagle wings and soar?

He is waiting at your heart's door
Waiting for you to invite him in,
He is waiting to cleanse you of all unrighteousness
And wash away your sin

He made his move
When he went to calvary,
It's time for you to make your move
And allow him to set you free

Now!, God says:, go to now!
Do not wait, do not procrastinate,
Now is the day of salvation
Tomorrow may be to late

He stands without patiently waiting
Is he knocking at your heart's door?,
If so, open up and let him in
What are you waiting for?

Come just as you are
And he will give you newness of life,
Come just as you are
To God the son, the son of God, Jesus Christ

Our righteousness is but filthy rags
For our righteousness is he who died to set us free,
For it is by grace through faith that we are saved
Through the blood that was shed on calvary's tree

Wow!

Retirement!
Bobby you're taking an awful risk,
For beware my friend
Of the dreaded honey do list

You will find though
That this liesure time is a great time to be alive,
And it sure beats the tar
Out of working nine to five

Enjoy it Bobby
You've earned this and more,
Keep active, keep healthy
For this is the long awaited day you've been looking for

Spend quality time with the little woman
Tell her you love her every day,
Do things together, buy her flowers
That will blow her mind away

Just enjoy life to the fullest
These are the golden years of your life,
A time to grow closer to God
And time to grow closer to your wife

And as far as the honey do list
No sense doing today what you can do tomorrow,
Just relax and enjoy every part of every day
Every minute of every hour

Two six month vacations a year
You can't beat that no way no how,
You can describe it all in one word forwards and backwards
For no matter how you say It It still comes out "wow!"

Power of Love

Keep your eyes upon the Lord
People will inevitably fail you,
Keep your heart clean and pure
Honor him in all you say and do

Love not the world
Neither the things that are there in,
For the lust of the flesh, the lust of the eyes,
And the pride of life
Are the worlds three deadly sins

Turn not to the right nor to the left
Walk the straight and narrow road,
For the wide path leadeth to destruction
But the narrow to the streets of gold

Take your eyes off the elders
Take your eyes off the preachers,
Take your eyes off the individuals of the congregation
And take your eyes off the teachers

There is one place for your eyes to be fixed
And that's upon the one who is the light of heaven above,
For there is one power that overcomes all others
And that is the power of God's love

Love worketh no ill to his neighbor
By love we continually overcome,
By love the ten commandments
Are reduced down to one

Love is why God sent his son
I scarce can take it in,
Love is what took Jesus to the cross
And paid the price for my sin

Praise God through whom all blessings flow

Forth Coming

We need to go into the darkness
And with joy spread the light,
We need to go while it is yet day
Before the coming of the night

For the night comes when no man can work
The Holy Spirit is now lighting our way,
But one day, oh' terrible dark day
The Holy Spirit will be taken away

The mark of the beast is forth coming
The bottomless pit will be opened and the dragon will be
Released from his lair,
And God help those who procrastinated their salvation
For they will find no mercy from the prince of the power of the air

The mark of the beast will be legal tender for every transaction
This mark is the only ticket by which you can buy or sell,
But no matter what happens, take not that mark
For it is a one way ticket to hell

Pray for loved ones
Witness before it's too late,
Pull them back from the unquenchable fire
Before death or the mark seals forever their fate

There is spiritual warfare all around us
Angels battling the demons of the dark,
Remember the flood
And how few souls was saved by the ark

There may not be a cloud in the sky
But the darkness is forth coming,
And the race is still on
So keep on running

By Faith

Rahab by faith
Hid the spys,
With the promise that all that were hers
Would be spared their lives

A thread of faith
Faith as a mustard seed,
God through rahab's faith
Performed a miraculous deed

Rahab's life literally hung by a thread
Her and her family all,
As Jerico came tumbling down
God spared her and all that abode with her upon the wall
Faith moves mountains
Look at Daniel and the lion's den,
And shadrach, meshach, and abednego
Tales of God's miraculous deliverances over and over again

We are to live by faith
Without faith we could not please him,
It is by faith that we receive our salvation
By faith in the blood that covers our sin

By faith Israel walked upon dry land
In the midst of the red sea,
By faith peter stepped out upon the boisterous waters
Of the sea of Galilee

A chain is only as strong
As it's weakest link,
And when faith falters
Souls sink

Super Glue

Faith is the glue
That is stronger than brick and mortor,
Faith is the substance that bonds souls with one another
Faith is the power over bickering and disorder

Faith brings us together
And unites us as one,
If we disagree with one another
It is Satan's victory that is won

With faith we can win every battle
But all must agree,
For if there is one weak link
We will lose our harmony

If we have any problem of any sort
We must come together and work it out,
God says come and let us reason together
Isn't that what it's all about

A congregation of souls
Must come to agreement with one another,
With every thought and deed in prayer
By every sister and brother

Then if an agreement cannot be reached
Each soul must examine their own heart,
Don't give Satan and inch for he will take a mile
Don't let him tear your church apart

Faith is the super glue
That unites us together as one,
Faith is the victory
By which every battle is won

Quote

He is the God of all creation
He is the God of all that you see,
He is the God of all that exists
Even of all that you do not see

In the most perfect spot in this vast universe
God placed this special spec of dust,
Then he filled it with all good things
And placed it in our trust

He placed the sun where it should be
The moon and the stars he alligned in perfect harmony,
He raised up majestic mountains
And filled the oceans and the sea

He gave the boundaries for the waters after the flood
That they would never again overflow,
Then sealed this promise by his beautiful creation
Of the miracle of the rainbow

He is the God of our mighty nation
He is the God of the land of the free,
He is the God of our salvation
And the God who lives in you and me

Joshua said it better than I
So I'll put this as a quote,
Written down in God's holy word
This is what was wrote

Choose you this day whom you will serve
As for me and mine we choose life,
We must all choose one way or another
To follow self, sin, or Christ

The Devil's Lie

They teach in our schools Darwin's theory
That man evolved from apes,
I thought that God was the sure foundation
Of these united states

Why is atheism even taught
In this supposedly Christian nation?,
Why is the great explosion
Their explanation of creation?

There are many religions but only one God
And only one mediator between God and man,
No man cometh unto the father
Accept through the sacrificial lamb

He is the way, the truth, and the life
His name is Jesus,
He is the miracle of the virgin birth
"Emanuel", God with us

Now I ask you
How can our government be so naive?,
As to see the miracles of creation all around us
And still not believe?

Teach our kids the truth
Put Darwin's theory to shame,
Put prayer back in our schools
And praise Jesus's holy name

God created Adam from a clump of clay
And from Adam's rib he created eve,
Divine creation or the great explosion
Which do you choose to believe?

Refuge and Strength

Wars past, wars present,
And wars yet to come,
Our troops will be there
Until the battles are over and done

We are a nation blessed by God
And we do not enter the battle fields alone,
We will fight evil whereever it exists
And route out our enemys from under every stone

We honor this veteran's day and every day
Those who defend our sacred shores,
Putting their lives on the line
In both foreign and domestic wars

We are a strong and mighty nation
Not to proud to kneel and pray,
We are founded upon Godly principles
And from these I pray we never stray

We are powerful
Not because of the sword,
We are powerful
Because of our Lord

Now here is a quote worth quoting
All gave some, some gave more, and some gave all,
Men and women in uniform we salute you
For answering freedoms call

Praise the Lord

We Thank Him

How many ways can we thank you O' Lord?
How many ways can we show you our love,?
How many ways can we share with others
The joys and blessings you pour out from above?

By faithfully witnessing
And the reading of thy word,
By retaining and the sharing
Of the sermons that are heard

By opening our hearts
And sharing our joys and our sorrows,
By putting him first
In all of our todays and tomorrows

By lifting up others
In our daily prayers,
By showing them the peace that passeth all understanding
That can be miraculously and wonderfully theirs

By living our lives
As a living testimony of his prescence within,
By the tithing and the sharing of all the blessings
That are showered down upon us by him

By putting our feet and our hands to our prayers
By reaching out that helping hand,
By going that extra mile
By doing all that we possibly can

We thank him by giving him the glory
For every blessing that he sends our way,
We thank him by honoring him in all we say and do
Every minute of every hour of every day

The Miracle of Christmas

The greatest miracle since the dawn of creation
To ever grace this planet earth,
Was on that holy night, O' Holy night
When the Virgin Mary gave birth

Through this miraculous event
The invisable God left his heavenly home,
To become flesh, sinew,
Blood and bone

Born in a stable beneath that star so bright
Born of the linage of David the king,
Of this glorious event the heavens opened
And angels appeared and began to sing

They sang glory to God in the highest
Peace on earth, good will toward men,
Shepherds quaked at the sight
When that heavenly light shone round about them

This was the happiest birth date
That God's green earth has ever known,
May our happy birthday's to you dear Lord
Rise as a sweet smelling savour before thy throne

Enemys of the Cross

The atheists in these United States are a minority
We should not bow down to their demands,
Why should this Christian nation
Be degraded and drug down by their unholy hands?

The bible states that the nation that forgets God
Will be turned into hell,
This is a frightening prospect
For our young nation that started out so well

To remove Jesus's name from our schools
To remove his name from the political process,
To remove his name because it offends the few
And to do nothing is a sin we must confess

We must pray for our enemys
We must love them in spite of what they are doing,
And when they sue to get their way
We Christians must do some countersueing

Our voices must be heard
We must stand for that which is right,
We must fight against the powers of darkness
We must stand firm and strong in the light

We must put on the whole armour of God
To withstand the enemys of Jesus Christ,
We must move boldly to the front lines
And proclaim the glory of the benefactor of eternal life

To the enemys of the cross of Jesus Christ
I must tell you that hell is an awful place,
And if you die without Jesus
You have all of it's horrors for eternity to face

Snow Flakes

Hoar frost floating in the air
Sparkling like stars in the silvery moonlight,
Flitting like fireflies
Creating a mystical magic to the night

Then dark clouds move in and slide over the moon
And perfect white patterns begin to form and take shape,
Billions, each differing from the other
Of God's perfect creation called a snowflake

Blanket upon blanket of pure white
Covering everything in sight,
Then the clouds part and the moon shone again
And it becomes like day in the middle of the night

The flakes sparkling like so many tiny lights
Glistening diamonds, each it's own perfect gem,
Reflecting the moonbeams that fall upon them
Shining upward their glory to him

They do honor to their creator
These perfect little patterns of pure white,
Glittering sparks of firey light
Drifting slowly downward in the night

Goo

Love is in the air
Springtime is just a short time away,
Did you purchase that heart shaped card with mushy words of
Goo
For your sweetie pie for valentine's day?

Give her a great big hug and kiss
Tell her you love her more than life,
Let her know that you love her with all your heart
And that you are so happy that she became your wife

She is your valentine
More precious than rubies, diamonds, or gold,
She is your sugar and spice and everything nice
Yours forever to have and to hold

God's greatest gift to mankind
Was the day he created eve,
A helpmate, a soul mate
A companion to share your joys and grief

Bound together in the sight of God
She is not only your lover but also your closest friend,
On your wedding day you two became one
With vows of love with no end

Sweets?, I think not
Buy her flowers or write her a poem,
Let her know that in your house
She's the one that makes it "home sweet home"

Home to Home

She was the youngest of five children
The oldest was eight,
Dorothy "burns" streby on this day
Passed through heaven's gate

Their mother died when she was born
Their father died of a broken heart,
They were orphans at such an early age
A family torn apart

Her brothers and sisters passed on before her
But now all are rejoicing together in a better place,
Reunited in heaven's glory
Shouting halleluahs to Jesus face to face

From a broken home to an orphan's home
To a nursing home to a heavenly home,
O' what wonders lies before them
No more this sin filled world to roam

We sorrow
Because they are no longer with us,
But we rejoice
That they have gone home to be with Jesus

We cannot wish them back
We can only rejoice that one day we will see them again,
Keeping Jesus at the center of all we think, say, and do
Believing and accepting his sacrifice for our sin

Golden Anniversary

Fifty golden years
Ups and downs we've had em,
In fifty golden years
Our love has never grown dim

I know you still love me
And even more so each passing day,
I know I still love you
No matter come what may

We spent our youth together
And we've never mellowed out with age,
For our love for one another
Is a book of fire on every page

A love that endures
Especially for fifty years,
Is filled with many pages
Of blood, sweat, and tears

We never gave up
Life is not always a long stemmed rose,
For a love to last fifty years
You've got to have a love that curls your toes

Our love will endure
Because we still enjoy every hug,
Our love will endure
Because you still give my heart a tug

I love you
I love you more each passing day,
I love you
No matter come what may

Easter Is!

The cross of Christ is the only hope
For a world corrupted in sin,
The empty tomb is the undeniable proof
That the grave is not the end

Jesus is the first fruits
And all the rest at the trumpet's sound,
The rapture of the saints is drawing near
He is coming for all who are heaven bound

Easter sealed our hopes and dreams
The cross was not the end,
For that Sunday following good Friday
The tomb was empty my friend

Jesus's feet lifted from off this earth
As the apostles watched in awe,
He is coming again, we know not when
Whether it be winter, spring, summer, or fall

For he promised that he will return one day
O' what a glorious day that will be,
When the saints both alive and dead
Shall shout the victory

Easter is!
God's promise of life,
Easter is!
Our victory in Christ

Pinnocio

Pinnocio with your nose so long,
What the hey did you do wrong?

Well I lied a lot,
So this is what I got

I wanted something special
But a broom handle for a nose ain't it,
I wanted to become a real live boy
I should have listened to Jimminy cricket

He is my concience you know,
Who follows me everywhere that I go

But you see there was these two shady characters
Who led me astray,
And I failed to see
The error of my ways

Life was all fun and games
I started to become a real donkey,
I even growed a tail and some long ears
And the voice of a mule bellowed out of me

But in the end
I finally saw the light,
And I became a real live boy
And everything turned out all right

Signed: No more sawdust for brains
*   Yours truly*
*   Pinnocio*

Fond Memories

This is the day we celebrate the passing
Of those who have influenced our lives,
Some have lost mothers and fathers
Some have lost husbands and wives

We visit the cemetaries
And decorate the graves,
And ponder upon all the fond memories
Of their earthly days

Memorial day is a day for remembrance
Of all the good times of the past,
Some day we will each be someone's memory
Time flys by all to fast

This is our time to make those memories
For those we leave behind,
Pray that they be good ones
When they bring them to mind

Kneeling before those slabs of stone
As tears flow down your eyes,
May your memories of them be
All golden days and blue skies

Memorial day is just that
Memories of loved ones who have past,
Fond memories
I pray they last and last and last

Cowboys

The cow puncher
Eats trail dust all day long,
Sing'n back in the saddle again
Gene autry's favorite song

Stare'n at cow buns all day long
Eat'n chuck wagon beans al'a cart,
And listen'n to the nightly vigil in the bunk house
Of snore'n and the grand symphony of fart after fart

Bedbugs giv'n em nightly fits
The howl of the coyote beller'n at the moon,
The pungent smell of sweaty cowpokes
And the sun come'n up all too soon

Back in the saddle again
And I'm an old cowpoke,
Songs to ride by
As they roll up a smoke

They say howdy pardner
And yup and nope a lot,
They're proud to be a cowboy, they're miss'n someth'n
But they don't know what

Just like the movies, they leave the girl behind
Kiss'n their horse and ride'n off into the sunset,
You ask them if they like being a cowboy
And they say yup

That long walk from the bunk house to the out house
Knee deep in meadow muffins,
Set'n down at the chuck wagon
Eat'n flap jacks and all the stuff'ns

Cowboys a spout'n their cowboy slang,
Like dad burn it, dern, and dang

Mothers don't buy your sons any western toys,
And definitely don't let them grow up to be cowboys

Lost and Found

Halleluah! I found Jesus!
Now wait arinute for now you see,
Jesus wasn't lost
It was he that found me

O' yes I know
I had to reach out to him,
But he was there all along
Waiting for my heart to win

The world drags souls down
Jesus's hand was reaching out,
He pulled me from the muck and mire
Of worldly fear and doubt

Did I find Jesus
Or did he find me?,
All I know is he came into my heart
And set my soul free

I was lost but now am found
Washed in the blood of the lamb,
Did I find him or did he find me?
In Jesus, for certain, saved is what I am

Pride

Don't get high and mighty
With a better than thou attitude,
Don't fall into that sad, sad category
Of being a self righteous dude

Don't let sinful pride, the world, and the flesh
Lure you into the eternal flame,
Keep always dear and precious
Jesus holy name

Love your neighbor, love your wife
Love not the world or the things therein,
Love God, love family, love your enemys
Love is the commandment with power over sin

Self righteousness will bring you down
Pride will cause you to lose your crown,
No matter what the world offers
In the power of the blood of Jesus hold your ground

There are many factors
That could cause you to backslide,
The lust of the flesh, the lust of the eyes
And the third deadly sin called pride

There is power in the blood
There is power in the word,
There is power in fasting and prayer
And all the God given sermons that are heard

Nothing can cross over the circle of blood
Nothing is more powerful than the cross of Christ,
It is the power of salvation, the power that defeated Satan
It is the pathway of eternal life

Best Friend

Jim and barb have been our friends
For almost fifty years,
Barb has asked me to write something
As Jim's time with us drew near

Barb you didn't have to ask
Jims been on my mind since we learned of the cancer,
And I wanted to write my feelings down
As we all prayed for this cancer's cure

Jim and I worked together for many years
And over that time we became not only good friends,
But best friends

We hunted and fished together
And spent many and most of our new years eves with one another,
We camped, we played cards
Jim was a friend that was closer than a brother

These last two years we planned and took our vacations together
Friendship that lasts that long has got to be true,
Jim you were my best friend
And I'm going to be lost without you

Best friends are hard to come by
And they cannot be measured in years alone,
I know it was so hard for family and friends to let Jim go
As the angels came to take him home

I know for sure, for God has promised
We will see Jim again,
Our love goes with you beyond heaven's gate
So long for now my friend

Written for the best friend I ever had

Awesome Power

Awesome, awesome, is the power
That flows from calvary's cross,
It is the power of nail peirced hands
Reaching out to the lost

It is the cleansing power
That washes away our sin,
It is the saving power
That brings us neigh unto him

It is the power over unclean thoughts
It is the power over unclean acts,
It is the power
That keeps us from falling through the cracks

It is the power
That searches all our inward parts,
It is the power
Over the thoughts and intents of the hearts

Heaven's gates open
Only to those who have been washed in the blood,
Salvation comes only
To those who have been cleansed in the crimson flood

Power, O' yes, awesome power
It is the hedge that Satan cannot cross over to harm us,
This is the power that defeated all the demons of darkness
This is the awesome power of the blood of Jesus

The Good

This is a special time to reflect
Upon all the reasons of thanksgiving,
Of all the good that surrounds us
Of all the wonderful happenings in this life that we're living

Children and children's children
Aunts and uncles and nieces and nephews,
Birthdays, anniversarys, aquaintences and friends
Just to name a few

So much to be thankful for
So many good and wonderful days,
So much gratefulness in our hearts
To God be the glory, the honor, and the praise

Our brothers and sisters
And all of our wonderful kin,
And most of all, Jesus our wonderful savior
Who sacrificed himself for our sin

Our beautiful church family
The music, the testimonies, the uplifting hymns,
The sermons, the singers, the praises and prayers
The inspired poems that flows from the heart to the pen

Beautiful sunrises and sunsets
The moon and the stars, the snow and the rain,
Trees and fall colored leaves
And endless feilds of golden grain

Thank you father for your open hand
In pouring out your goodness upon us,
May we always dwell upon the good
Our lives, our future, our all, we place into your loving trust

Our King

God created a special star
To guide the kings to where the Christ child lay,
The light of heaven was born upon earth
To show the lost the way

Born in a stable
Rags for clothes, straw for a bed,
No room in the inn
No pillow for his head

A multitude of heavenly hosts
Parted the darkness of the night,
And appeared unto the shepherds of the fields
And declared the arrival of heaven's light

Born of a virgin
Honored by shepherds and kings,
God's message of peace on earth, good will towards men
Was carried to earth upon angel's wings

The creator of heaven and earth
And all that is, was, or ever will be,
Came to live among us
And go to the cross and die for the sins of you and me

Don't ever forget the reason for the season
It is why Christians break forth in joy and sing,
It is because we know that we know that we know
That we have life eternal with Jesus our king

We are One

There is no profit to the hearers
In doctrinal dispute,
We must be filled and overflowing
With spiritual fruit

Love, peace, and joy
This is what overcomes the sin and sadness and hate,
Jesus Christ is Lord, king, and savior
Of this there is no debate

Jesus Christ and him crucified
Of this our churchs agree,
It is in petty frivolous things
Of which eye to eye we do not see

Like the gifts of the spirit
Like the length of a person's hair,
Like once saved always saved
Like the very clothes that we wear

If only we could concentrate less
On the so many things that divide,
And unite our hearts together in love
In Christ and him crucified

The Great Physician

How can we face tomorrow
When there's so much heartache and sorrow,
We cling and we cope
Believing that around the corner there's hope

If it wasn't for ministering angels
And the God of joy and peace,
And believing in miracles
All hope would cease

Jesus loves us
I hold fast to this one simple fact,
Jesus has given us many promises
And he will not take any back

Thank God all of his promises are yea and amen
Tried, true, and O' so real,
And through prayer, faith, and trust
We pray our hurts to heal

He is the great physician
Who is only a prayer away,
He has promised to never leave nor forsake us
He is in our hearts to stay

We look to the heavens
From whence our help will come,
We trust in you Lord Jesus
For the victories to be won

You are the great physician
To you in faith we pray,
Dear God and Lord of heaven
Take the pain away

Beyond the Skys

Just like Jesus
Away back when,
We too one day
Shall rise again

O' what a day
What a glorious day that will be,
When we reunite with loved ones
In the endless joys of eternity

To see our Lord face to face
To receive the rewards of our earthly race,
To walk the streets of gold
As all the wonders of heaven before our eyes unfold

Joining the angels in singing his praises
Rejoicing evermore in the land of the free,
All of the heartache and pain behind us
Only beauty and peace as far as the eye can see

Our affliction is but for a moment
It is the Lord's burning away of the dross,
Bringing us ever closer to our savior
Who took our sins to the cross

We endure knowing deep down in our hearts
That we are on a pilgrimage to the promised land,
Our goal is to get from here to there
Letting Jesus lead us by his hand

If we live for him, we will live with him
No more tears shall moisten our eyes,
Only everlasting comfort and joy awaits
With our Lord beyond the skys

The Rock

The bible, the written word of God
Is alive within the folds of it's pages,
Unfailing promises, indelibly inscribed
Tested and proven down thru the ages

It is our guide book for living
It is the most fantastic amazingly true story,
About the creation and the creator
Our most Holy Lord God of glory

The rock
It is the foundation on which we build faith,
It is the map, the guide book that shows us the way
To our savior, Lord God of grace

O' for a thousand tongues
To sing and shout his praises,
O' to be enfolded into his everlasting arms
For all the trials that face us

O' for the faith that moves the mountains
O' for faith as that of a mustard seed,
O' for the faith that the God of grace
Will meet our every need

You have not because you ask not
God says: ask and you shall receive,
All things, God says all things
Are possible to those who believe

He is the rock
On which we've built our faith,
Steady, unmoveable. and unshakeablethe Holy Lord God of grace

Songs of Spring

A symphony of soothing sounds
Of pine trees whispering in the breeze,
And the music of the cottonwoods
As the wind stirs and rustles and rattles their leaves

Then there is the sound of froth covered waves
Breaking gently over a rocky shore,
And the deafening noise of mighty waterfalls
Louder than a lion's roar

The stars add their night songs
Twinkling ever so bright,
And the thunderous explosions in a summer storm
Of every lightning strike

The caw of the crow and the honk of the goose
Morning doves cooing to God for rain,
The pitter patter of raindrops upon a metal roof
And the bellow of a bullfrog trying to sing

The click, click, click of a chipmunk
And the barking of a startled squirrle,
And the cotton from the cottowoods floating in the air
As the wind gives them a merry whirl

Mother nature in full swing
Bursting forth in a symphony of sounds and sights,
With breathtaking sunrises and awesome sunsets
And the mystic dancing flames of the northern lights

Listen to the birds sweet, sweet music
In their joyeous songs that they sing,
With all their beautifull colors in flight
Praising the God of glory for spring

Sweeter Every Hour

Every hour with Jesus
Gets sweeter every day,
As I cling to the special teasures
Of his answers when I pray

Nothing can compare
To our Lord God of heaven above,
For in his nail pierced hands
Are the treasures of joy, peace, and love

Nothing satisfies the soul like Jesus
He alone holds the key,
Let all the world around you
The Jesus in you see

No matter what happens
No matter how bad things look,
Hold fast to the dear and precious promises
That are written in his holy book

The world will fail you
But my God never will,
Trust, obey, praise and pray
For his promises to fullfill

When your desire cometh
It is a tree of life,
We believe and we receive
Because of the indwelling love of Jesus Christ

Sweeter every hour
Is his ever presence with us,
There is nothing more precious to my soul
Than the love of Jesus

Miracle in the Twilight

Oh how it must have broken the father's heart
When he pulled back his hand in refrain,
When his son, the Lord God of heaven and earth
In agony called out his name

O' but the glory
Of God's awesome power and might,
Before the rising of the sun
In that easter morning's twilight

An angel came down from heaven
And took the stone that sealed the tomb and rolled it away,
And glory to the highest
For what they discovered inside that day

Two angels were there
And the linens were neatly folded where Jesus had lain,
The tomb was bare, Jesus had risen
Death could not hold our savior, Lord God, and king

He is alive forever more
Drawing all men unto him,
For as many as believe and repent
His blood upon the cross has washed away their sin

We thank God for the twilight of that easter morning
O' what a glorious day that must have been,
For it is a day that will live forever
As a day of rejoicing without end

My Heart Song

O' how I love the Lord
To wake up to him in the morning,
O' how I love the Lord
O' what a wonderful feeling

My cup runneth over
My heart is bursting with praise,
I'll love my Lord forever and ever
And follow him all my earthly days

He is my sunshine on cloudy days
He lifts me up when I am down,
I rejoice in his holy word
And all the treasures therein that I have found

Praise is upon my lips
Songs of glory keep ringing in my head,
My day is filled with halleluajahs
I pray my every step be spirit led

We can never praise him enough
He fills my heart with sunshine,
I praise the Lord that I am his
And hallelujah he is mine

O' glory be to my Lord on high
Glory honor and praise,
He is my song all day long
As I continue to contemplate upon his ways

Joy, peace, and love
Praise, glory, and honor to the Lord God of hope,
O' Lord you are my heart song
Which no melody more beautiful has ever been wrote

The Greatest of These

You've never experienced real joy
Until you've experienced Jesus joy,
Pick up the holy book and open it's pages
And experience for yourself this amazingly true story

It's all about Jesus and his love
It's about the God of hope,
The God of joy, the God of peace
The greatest story ever wrote

The maker of the stars in the heavens
The creator of the oceans and the seas,
The God of all that exists
The God of you and me

Peace, love, hope, and joy
These are the gifts of Jesus Christ,
These are the glue that holds us together
Throughout all the trials of life.

Our hope lies in his promises
Our peace comes through knowing him,
Our joy is an overflowing joy
Of the love of Jesus within

One word stands above all the rest
Of the ten commandments written in stone,
One word fullfills all the law
And that is love and love alone

The fruit of the spirit
Are gifts from above,
Showers of blessings
Of which the greatest of these is love

Resurrection Day

I remember the crown of thorns
I remember each rusty nail,
I remember the agony of the cross
And his promises that never fail

I remember that dark Friday
When all seemed lost,
And my salvation
And what it cost

I remember that Sunday
About the dawning of day,
And I fall down on my knees
And thank God as I pray

Far and wide all across this great land
The church bells are ringing, what a glorious sound,
Glory hallelujah, praise the Lord
I once was lost but now am found

We serve a risen savior
Worthy of all praise,
Who said he would never leave nor forsake us
All glory to the God of grace

Easter is not a bunny tale
It is resurrection day,
It is not jelly beans and colored eggs
It is resurrection day

It is the day of victory
Victory over sin and death,
As Christians sing out his glory
And praise him with every breath

My Heart Light

Though the world around me is falling apart
And everything is going wrong,
Though it looks like the Lord has forsaken me
He will always be my song

Every day, I pray gets better
And every day gets worse,
I try to keep joy in the poems I write
And put his praises in every verse

But lately my heart is breaking
For all that my wife is going through,
She hugs me and kisses me and crys a lot
As I continue to place my trust in him who is tried and true

Each day becomes harder and harder
My soul is troubled for the trials she has to face,
I pray dear God for your compassion
For you mercy, love, and grace

I pray make each day
Better than the one before,
And we see forward progression
In her body, soul, and spirit, to restore

Our praises we shout to the heavens
Our praises is directed to thy throne,
I pray for her complete recovery
That one day soon I can take her home

I need her dear God
Whole and healthy again,
I love her more than life
More than I can write with ink and pen

She is my helpmate
She is the love of my life,
She is everything to me
She is my heartlight

Silly Sally

Silly sally
Sat upon a sycamore stump,
Right into some sycamore
Yucky, sticky, gooey, oozy gunk

Like super glue it held her there
As it clung to the backside of her lap,
Then suddenly she realized
There was more there than sycamore sap

For silly Sally
When sitting upon that sycamore stump,
Got a sycamore sliver
In her rump

And up silly sally did jump
Up from that old sycamore stump
And pulled that sycamore splinter
From her rump

Sill sally's setter
Was sore,
And upon that sycalmore stump
Silly Sally sat no more

One Drop

One drop is more precious
Than rubys, diamonds, silver, or gold
It is so precious
It cannot be bought or sold

So precious
No treasures on earth can buy,
So precious it had to come
From that heaven beyond the sky

It was placed in the heart
By the one who shed his blood,
One drop more powerful
Than any flood

It reaches from one heart
To another,
It comes from compassion and love
From a Christian sister or brother

It is the perfect crystal
Of one drop of pure love,
Coming from the heart
God's precious gift from above

It is the most precious gift
That anyone could ever give,
The gift of compassion
In this life on earth we live

It comes from the caring heart to the hurting heart
Nothing on earth can make it stop,
That precious gift dear friend
Is a tear drop

Ping Pong

Spin and spike
Slice and slam,
Forehand
And back hand

It's not wether you win or lose
It's about making friends and playing your best,
It's about not losing your cool
It's about putting your patience to the test

You bounce it off the edge
You dribble it across the net,
Looking your opponent in the eye
Trying to make him fret

You shuffle to the left
You shuffel to the right,
Chasing that little white ball
Trying to keep it in sight

Swinging this way and that a-way
Trying your best to be a real go getter,
Sometimes just swinging at air
As paddle and ball just don't seem to come together

Sometimes you run one way
And the ball goes the other,
Sometimes your feet go one way
And your buns go another

Ping pong ain't for wimps
It takes timeing, coordination, and a good eye,
To connect with that plastic round bubble
Before it whishes by

You've got to be agile
You've got to have the right move at the right time,
You've got to watch your opponents moves
And compensate and bring the ball back in line

Watching the eyes usually works best
But not always so,
For I've seen good players look one way
And another way make it go
Ping pong will make you sweat,
It's about as strenuous a workout
As you will ever get

And if you play doubles
It's teamwork that wins the game,
Support your partner, get out of his way
And pray he does the same

Long Ago

Living off the land
In a slower pace of better times,
Remembering the well beaten path to the out house
And setting out trot lines and trap lines

Ice delivered to our ice boxs
Steam engines smoke'n down the track,
Bottles of milk placed on our doorsteps
Wishing those days of long ago were back

Catching up on all the juicy gossip
By listening in on the party line,
And listening to our favorite storys on the radio
Back when you could buy a coke and a candy bar for a dime

Roller skating down the sidewalks
Going to matinees,
O' yes life was o' so wonderful
Back in the good old days

A willow stick for a fish pole
A string for a line,
A bent pin for a hook
In a long ago better time

Hunting squirrels among the shagbarks
And tracking rabbits in the snow,
Gathering mushroons in the spring
And skinny dipp'n down at the old swimm'n hole

Times moved at a slower pace
A way back when,
As fond memories of those long ago times and places
Are reflected back upon every now and then

A Brand New Song

I'm going to a place
Of sweet release.
Where joy is full
In everlasting peace

Where there is no sorrow
And all pain is gone,
Where we will be singing and rejoicing forever
To a brand new song

Where there is no heat nor cold
So I'm told,
Where we will be forever young
No more aches and pains of growing old

We will sing glory to the highest
In the land of uncloudy day,
We will run and not be weary
No more burdens of bodys of clay

We will take up wings as eagles
Rejoicing all the way,
When we leave this land of darkness
And go towards the light of eternal day

We will sing holy, holy, holy
His praises will be on our lips all day long,
He will put within our hearts a melody
Of everflowing joy in a brand new song

Praise, glory, hallelujah, hallelujah, hallelujah
To the lamb of God on high,
We will praise him forever, and ever, and ever
In that land of uncloudy sky

Eleven Fifty Nine

With the voice of the archangel
The Lord himself shall descend from heaven with a shout,
The rapture is close at hand my friend
The catching away is coming about

So many unsaved
So little time,
It is one minute till midnight
I pray don't be left behind

The trump of God
Is about to sound,
The saint's feet
Are about to lift from the ground

First the dead in Christ shall rise
Then we which are alive and remain,
So shall we meet together with the Lord in the air
Praising glory to his holy name

For if we believe that Jesus rose from the dead
And his promise that we too would rise one day,
Then believe this event that is about to take place
When we shall be caught up and carried away

Wherefore comfort one another with these words
Don't ever let your fires go out,
With joy listen for the trump of God
And the archangel's triumphant shout

The seconds are ticking away my friend
This message is for all who have ears to hear
The prophetic clock is winding down
The end of the day of grace is drawing near

Tears of Joy

May the praise that's in my heart overflow
And come out in glorious joyful song,
I pray in my heart to forgive and forget
And make right, ever that I did wrong

I pray to spread the joy
Of knowing the Lord of heaven and earth,
To know forgiveness through his atonement upon the cross
And accept it as his love for what he deemed my soul was worth

To experience that kind of love
Is to make one fall to their knees,
Shedding tears of joy
Desiring forever the Lord to please

Hallelujah glory, glory hallelujah
We cannot praise him enough,
For the new heart and a new start
And cleansing us from all that past self centered stuff

To believe and receive
All the promises written for all who come unto him,
To be washed in the blood of the lamb
Cleansed of every past sin

To confess and forsake
That past way of living,
Soul set free
With a new heart that's loving, kind, and giving

Praise be upon our lips
Praise, honor, and glory to the Lord God of glory,
May our lives be a living testimony to him
A happy joy filled never ending story

Loose as a Goose

Halflytely for colonoscopy
Makes you want to swing and sway,
To potty, wotty, do-do
All the live long day

You drink and you drink
Till you poop like a goose,
Till it comes out clean and perty
Clear and loose

Just so they can ram you in the rear
And take a picture of what's up there,
As you lay there, out like a light
All naked and bare

Now that don't sound
Like a very perty sight,
There's something about this whole thing
That don't seem right

They're looking up there
To see if they can find anything wrong,
As you keep dreaming and singing
That potty, wotty, do-do song

Loose as a goose, clean as a whistle
A picture that's worth a thousand words,
A spick and span uncluttered passageway
Clear and clean of dirty turds

Loose as a goose
Is an expression I've heard many times before,
Now I'm telling you halflytely for colonoscopy
Really opened up my back door

Deafening Silence

Are your heavy burdens
More than you can bare?,
Place them in the Lord's gentle hands
Be ever embraced in his loving care

Is your body racked in pain
Are you lacking sleep?,
Are you so overwhelmed
You want to hide and weep?

Are you falling short
As a caregiver for your loved one?,
Do you feel you are losing the battle
And there is no victory to be won?

Are the endless pill givings
The diareah and vomiting getting you down?,
And the pain your loved one's going through
Breaking your heart with every sobing sound?

The cleaning up of every mess
When accidents occur,
Trying to do your very best
Praying to God for a cure

Clinging to that thread of hope
Praying it will not break,
Day after day carrying on
Losing hope and losing weight

God will not be silent forever
This I believe to be very true,
And out of this dark cloud that has descended upon us
His son will come shining through

Life is Beautiful

*Friends are friends indeed
When they are there in time of need*

*Prayers when prayed in faith
Moves the mighty mountains,
It brings down the living waters
From God's everlasting fountains*

*People coming through
With hearts that are caring and true*

*So much good
Coming out of something that seems so bad,
Our faces should radiate the joy of Jesus
Through the happy times and the sad*

*Love the Lord
Every minute of every hour of every day,
And continually trust him
Come what may*

*God is in control
He sees the end from the begining,
I've read the book
And it's glorious triumphant ending*

*Life is so beautiful
When one is walking in the light,
Living by faith
And not by sight*

Mercy

Is there no end?
Is there no hope in tomorrow?,
Is there no more joy, no more song
Only heartache and sorrow?

We pray without ceasing
My wife's tears are breaking my heart,
O' Lord have mercy
These trials are tearing us apart

Give us a miracle
My wife loves you so much,
All her infirmities
I pray you reach out and touch

Her love dear Lord
Is genuine and true,
In church she breaks down and crys
When the songs are sung praising you

Have mercy O' Lord
Fill our hearts with joy once more,
My wife's hopes and dreams
I pray you fully restore

Reach out O' Lord
And touch the love of my life,
Reach out O' Lord
And restore unto me my loving wife

I pray look into our hearts Lord and know
That our love for you is steadfast and true,
And all our hopes and all our dreams
Rest solely in you

Showers of Blessings

Showers of blessings
What a beautiful song,
A beautiful melody to hum and sing to
All day long

Look to the heaven of heavens
From whence the blessings come,
For God will open those windows
And pour them out until kingdom come

O' how beautiful each new morning
O' how beautiful each new day,
O' what a time for singing God's glory
As he sends his blessings our way

Bless, O' Lord, bless
Each new day as we look to you,
May those showers of blessings you pour out upon us
Refresh us a-new

On the wings of a dove
You send your pure sweet love,
Showers of blessings without measure
Poured out from above

Greater Love

I never knew that I could love my wife
So much deeper and greater than ever before,
Until I almost lost her
We never know what life has in store

When she puts her arm around me
When she hugs and holds me close,
When the dark storm clouds move in
Her smiles and her kisses are my rainbows

God continues to teach us
That he is in control,
And no matter what
He is the master of our soul

He has created within
A greater love than ever I thought could ever be,
When three times my wife was stricken
And each time she became even more dear and precious to me

All praise and glory dear Lord
Rise up to heaven to thee,
For this greater love
That you have created in me

Many gifts
You have poured out freely from above, but O' dear God of all these gifts
The greatest of these is love

Love will win over every trial
Love will melt the coldest heart of stone,
It is love that conquers every fear
And it is love that will take us home

One Heartbeat

One step, one breath, one heartbeat
Every second brings us closer to eternity,
O' Lord God of heaven and earth
May our hearts be totally turned to thee

Convict the wayward O' Lord
Work through us to reach out to the lost,
May our testimony of you touch the world
With conviction to come to the cross

May our lives be a light for you
Like the song "this little light of mine"
O' yes, O' Lord, O' yes
I'm going to let it shine

Jesus is the light of heaven
He is the light at the end of the tunnel,
Crucified at calvary
He died for the sins of one and all

All your and my sins were nailed there
The atonement was full and complete,
You can accept it or reject it
But all will appear before the judgement seat

If God is tugging at your heartstrings
Don't put it off another day,
Jesus is the answer to all of life's questions
There is no other way

One step, one breath, one heartbeat
Brings us closer to eternity,
Find that altar of grace
And the Lord will lift your burdens and set you free

Thank You Lord

I thank God
For my loving, lovely wife,
My five beautiful daughters
And a wonderous wonderful life

I thank him for answering prayer,
And for always being there

I thank God that I was born
In this great land of the free,
I thank him for every breath I take
And for his loving even me

I thank him for the sunrises and the sunsets
That begins and ends each newday,
For the moon and the stars and all of his creation
That continually takes my breath away

I'm thankful that Jesus lives
And that there is a heaven above,
And for his gift of amazing grace
And his infinite endless love

I thank him for this new heart and fresh start
Of being born again,
And for going to the cruel cross of calvary
Taking upon himself the punishment for my sin

Thank you God, thank you
For making my happy heart sing,
Thank you Lord, thank you
Thank you for everything

Blessed Event

God gave us the most precious gift
On that very first Christmas of long ago,
When he sent his son to be a shining light
To all of us creatures here below

He gave us the gift of hope, faith, and love
Joseph and Mary's bundle of joy,
Wrapped in rags, born in a manger
This Christ child baby boy

No greater gift could he have given
Than his only begotten son,
For he so loved the world that he devised a plan
Whereby victory over sin and death could be won

Jesus is the spotless lamb
Whose birth we celebrate Christmas day,
The holy Lord God of heaven
In whose name to God we pray

The gospels that we now read
Tells us of God's most perfect plan,
Mathew, Mark, Luke, and John
Tells of our Lord God who walked this earth as a man

Christmas is a time to beleive, a time of hope
A time of joy and cheer,
A time to remember
The day our Lord God drew near

It's been over two thousand years
Since the miracles that proclaimed and accompanied his birth,
We will continue to celebrate this blessed event
As long as there is a God's green earth

The Faithful Few

Toss a stone into the water
And watch the ripples spread out,
As God's word
Brings his purposes about

As the ripples spread from shore to shore
Think of the faithful few who are sharing the good news,
And those being convicted and converted
Forsaking the don'ts and doing the do's

We are God's messengers to the lost
We are Christ's light in this dark domain,
We must step out and speak up
Of this we must not refrain

The ripples that we create
In our holy savior's name,
Will surely spread from shore to shore
And back again

God's word penetrates to the depths
It will do what it's meant to do,
Now the message that I'm trying to convey
Is the spreading of the gospel is up to me and you

Let the word do it's perfect work
Shine forth his light,
Be faithful in what God has given you to do
And do it with all your might

He is faithful and he is true
And he will bless all you undertake in his holy name to do,
So trouble the waters, create some ripples
And become one with the faithful few

The Blood Applied

Only love can overcome
The darkness that lies within,
Only the blood of Jesus applied
Washes away every stain of sin

The powers that be cannot compare to the powers
By which we overcome,
For none can cross over the hedge
That surrounds those who are washed in the blood of God's son

No effort on our part
Can take away the dark desires,
For it is only by grace through faith by the blood applied
That we escape hell's unquenchable fires

God help us each one
To deal with our demons within,
May we be clothed upon with all the armour
That it takes to evercome the power of sin

Put on the helmet of salvation
Wear the sword of the spirit,
Be shod with the gospel of peace, the word of God
That converts those who read or hear it

Adorn the breastplate of righteousness
And carry before you the shield of faith,
By which we shall quench every fiery dart of the wicked
And having done all to stand, stand firm in God's amazing grace

Those who commit their works into the Lord
Their thoughts shall be established,
Think only upon the good things
And upon the tables of your heart prayerfully ponder upon that
List

"I-Am"

He died for me
That I might live for him,
He rose again
That I might have life without end

He is
He is the great "I-am",
He always was
Of this our finite minds cannot fathom

If he was not
Everything would cease to be,
There would be no moon nor stars
There would be no earth nor sea

He is the way, the only way
He is the truth and the life,
He is the messiah Lord God of heaven
Our savior Jesus Christ

He is the one, true, and only God
Who died and rose again,
The one and only one
Whose blood can wash away your sin

When you kneel before the cross
Beneath that crimson flow,
When you ask the Lord of life to come in
He will cleanse you white as snow

He is
He is the great "I-am",
What can wash away my sin?
Only the blood of Jesus can

Practice his Presence

As I woke up this morning I looked upon the wall
There was a picture of Jesus staring down at me,
This made me realize that no matter what I say or do
"All", my Jesus is ever present to see

We must be fully aware
That he is always there,
He knows our every thought,
Our every need, and our every care

He listens to our prayers
Not always answering like we think he should,
But his answers
Are always for the greater good

No matter where you are
No matter where you go,
Jesus is always at your side
That you must believe and most assuredly know

For the Lord has promised and he cannot lie
To never leave nor forsake you,
So practice his ever presence
In all you think, say, and do

The Last Season

The snow is upon the roof
The fire is going out in the furnace,
The clock is winding down
The winter of life is upon us

The fact that we are growing old
Doesn't hit us until we are there,
It seems that just yesterday we were young
Life just doesn't seem fair

The joints are creaking
The middle age spread continues to spread,
The woman who has stayed close by your side
Has become more beautiful than the day that you wed

Spring, summer, and fall has passed
Winter is upon us,
This is our last season to walk this earth
Before our earthen vessel returns to dust

There is a new springtime coming
Winter will be over before long,
God is about to replace all of our sorrow
With a brand new joy filled song

This last season upon this earth
Is a prelude to the unending season of eternal life,
We must look beyond the sorrows of living
To the endless joys of being in the prescence of Christ

O' for the joys that lie beyond
In that land of eternal day,
O' for that first glimpse of heaven
And our Lord who showed us the way

The Rock

Our feet are planted on a firm foundation
Our roots are in the rock,
We are standing on the promises
Our faith is in Jesus, the unmoveable block

He is the rock of ages
He is the chief cornerstone,
It is faith that has brought us to our Lord and savior
And it is faith that will take us home

Our house is not built
On our own merits and self righteousness,
Our house is built upon Jesus Christ
Nothing more and nothing less

The storms will most assuredly come
But we will weather them all,
Because our house is built upon the rock
We may stumble but we will never fall

So do not fear when the wild winds blow
And the waters come to everflow,
Because our foundation stands firm in Jesus
We will never be caught in the undertow

Blessed be the rock
The cornerstone of our foundation,
He is the reason that this land of the free
Has been blessed as a mighty nation

He is not a stone skipped across the water
He is the same yesterday, today, and forever,
He is the rock that stands firm down through the ages
Throughout all the stormy weather

For Him

To God be the glory
For every written line,
To God be the glory
For every fourth and rhyming line

All that I write
I pray shine forth his glory,
Every poem I pray
Add light to his never ending story

May they bring the eyes of all
To turn upwards towards the skys,
From whence one day our Lord will come
The one in whom our blessed hope lies

I write for your glory
My blessed Lord and king,
I write to bring others to come before you
That on that resurrection day they may rise on joyful wing

I write for you
To touch souls with your love for them,
To bring them to the cross
To be freed from their burden of sin

With pen and ink
I want to declare your prescence to all that walk this earth,
I want to show that no matter what the past
That you went to the cross to pay the price for what you deemed
Their soul worth

There is none so bad
That God will not forgive them,
And there is none so good
That they can cleanse themselves from sin

Worth It All

If I can touch one life with the love of Jesus
Then my life will have been worth live'n,
One life to approach the throne of grace
One precious life to receive the gift of heaven, forgiven

For that soul is more precious
Than all the treasures of earth,
Our Lord on the cross of calvary
Proved what that soul is worth

We are living in a world of lost souls
Many of whom are searching for the answers to life,
I pray for the messages in poems to write
That will direct their paths to the light

O' God I desire not that their eyes be upon me
But that they would turn their eyes upon Jesus,
For some plant and others water
But the increase comes only through Jesus

We are laborers together with God
All glory be unto him,
Our lives should be reflections of our Lord
Examples, for souls his glory to win

Rubys and diamonds are precious indeed
But souls are what we who are saved should seek,
For these are the only treasures that we can take with us
The only treasures that we can lay at Jesus's feet

O' yes, one soul led to Jesus
Makes life worth it all,
A treasure in heaven
Worth more than all the treasures of the big blue marble

Poems of Light

The father of lights
Has given gifts unto men,
I will praise him always
For my special gift from him

Divinely inspired
Are these poems that God has given me to write,
Wonderful words
To shine forth the glory of heaven's light

You don't put a candle under a bushel
But on a candlestick for all to see,
God gave each of us a gift to use for his glory
i thank him continually for this gift that he has given to me

I pray this little light of mine
Will never go out or grow dim,
I pray for ways to use this God given gift
To bring glory to him

Thoughts that are of the written word inspired
Put down on paper with pen,
Verse after verse
With glory filled praises of him

Yes! This little light of mine
I'm going to let it shine,
As these beautiful poems come together
In praised filled line after line

Poems of light
Shining forth his magnificent glory,
Forever praises
Of his never ending story

The Plan

The gospel story of Jesus Christ
Begins with the miracle of the virgin birth, it's about our God incarnate
Descending from heaven to earth

It's about a plan
Devised by the trinity's heavenly host,
The Godhead of all creation
Of father, son, and Holy Ghost

The plan whereby we may overcome
The plan to reconcile us back again,
The plan whereby through God's son
We have grace and forgiveness of sin

The cross was not the end my friend
For there was and is a resurrection day,
Jesus arose triumphant over the grave
In this miracle we celebrate on Easter Sunday

Praise the Lord, this miracle
Opened the gates to our heavenly home,
This miracle is the very heart of the gospel
That melts the coldest hearts of stone

When the Pussy Willows Bloom

The smell of spring is in the air
Pussy willows are in full bloom,
The warming of days and refreshing spring showers
Has brought the land alive with flower and mushroom

The trees are budding to life again
New leaves are begining to take form,
Southerly winds gently blow
As the earth begins to warm

Colorful butterflys have emerged from their cocoons
Jenny wren has returned with a song in her heart,
For the joy of the coming of spring she sings
"O' God, how great thou art"

Life is O' so beautiful
In this season that causes all things to renew,
As the dreary browns become beautiful greens
And the skys become a deeper more beautiful blue

Spring, O' God, to your wonder of creation
Has in all of it's glory and splender arrived,
In this, your most beautiful season of all
The earth, like a flower, blossoms and becomes vibrantly alive

Spring's song is in the air, O' lend an ear, O' can't you hear
This lively little tune?,
The birds are singing "glory to God"
As the pussy willows bloom

The Lazy Days of Summer

The sweet smell of a crackling campfire
The roasting of marshmallows and weiners,
Dragon flys flitting about
Chasing blood seeking skeeters

Turtles lined up on half sunken logs,
The base drum chorus of the big bullfrogs

Getting a tan
And playing kick the can,
Skinny dipp'n down at the ole swimm'n hole
And catch'n bluegills on a old cane pole

Gathering nitecrawlers on a warm rainy night,
And running through the meadow grass in the pale moonlight

Drinking ice cold lemonade
Sitting under a big shade tree,
Enjoying summer fun
Footloose and carfree

Blue herons wading along a shallow shore
Lightning bugs lighting up the night,
Going barefooted, and playing in the rain
Setting out trotlines, and flying a kite

Watching white fluffy clouds float like ships across the sky,
In those lazy days of summer, long ago passed by

Rubys and Golds

Fall has a beauty all it's own
In the miracle that takes place in the trees,
God transforms the world around us
With the creation of rainbow colored leaves

With frost he has painted another masterpiece
In his changing of the seasons,
Autumn's beauty unsurpassed
In our memories he has placed within

Brilliant yellows and fluorescent reds
God's glory of his creation unfolds,
I can see his face in every leaf
In the rubys and the golds

He gives us the changing of the seasons
And promised them as long as the earth remains,
Always changing, always different
Never dull, never the same

God put his brush to the land
And gave us the miracle of fall,
Using the earth as his canvas
He created this most colorful season of them all

Winter's Wonder

God never ceases to amaze us
He created winter as a time of rest,
A time for the earth to sleep
Only to awaken a-new and blest

He created the little snowflake
Each miraculously different from the other,
This season has a beauty that is all it's own
So widely different from another

Blankets of snow covers everything
In a brightness that squints the eyes,
As frost paints beautiful pictures upon the window paynes
And the skeeters and deerflies of summer withers and dies

The air seems clear and fresh
As the snow creaks under your feet,
In this season of beauty and wonder
That makes God's seasons complete

Ice forms on the lakes and ponds
And the freezing of them cracks like thunder in the night,
The snow coverings sparkle like tiny diamonds
Catching the slightest light

Ice storms transform the world
Covering everything in a crystal like glow,
Blazing trees of shining glory
As the sun's rays perform their magic show

There is a breathtaking beauty and wonder
In a world all covered in white,
Wether sparkling in the golden sunshine of day
Or glittering in the silvery moonlight of the night

He Lives

Christ came to seek and save
That which was lost,
His love and forgiveness flows freely
At the foot of calvary's cross

For a world of lost souls
Christ came to earth and died,
He took our sins upon himself
We are cleansed by his blood applied

Faith moves the mountains
With God there is no impregnable wall,
He also moves the mole hills
He meets the needs both large and small

He is the way the only way
All other religions lead to hell,
He is the living waters
That was offered to the woman at Jacob's well

Why are so many people blinded
To the way, the truth, and the life?.
So many comdemned to eternal damnation
Far from the prescence of Jesus Christ

He died and rose again
Victorious over sin and death,
And we who claim his holy name
Will praise him to our last, and forever beyond, dying breath

He lives, our God is alive
No other religion can make that claim,
And we who know him as Lord and savior
Will forever praise his holy name

Peace on Earth

So many divisions
So many diffrent denominations within the fold,
Why cannot we all agree
Why has Christianity become so cold

One God, one faith, one church unified in their beliefs
Would make the world a better place,
If only we could come together in truth
Filled with God's love and grace

If we could just love one another
And search the scriptures daily as the berrians did,
And come to the perfect knowledge of truth
I believe to a pure heart there is nothing hid

O' what unbounding joy
O' what peace we could come to know,
If we could all come to the knowledge of truth
God's pure love in our hearts would flow

A world in perfect peace
Would be like heaven on earth,
Hearts knit together in love
Bonded together in song and myrth

The Millenial Reign

The bible tells of a future time
When the world will take on a beautiful change,
Of peace on earth for a thousand years
In Christ's millenial reign

The earth will be beautifully transformed
Into a world only Adam and eve did know,
The lion will lay down with the lamb
And the weed and the thistle wiil cease to grow

The rocks will cry out for joy
The hills will brake forth and sing,
The shout of halleluahs
Will be heard from every living thing

Peace will sweep over the land
Nations will no longer be at war,
People will live to a very old age
Of nine hundred years or more

The lion will eat straw like an ox
The child shall play in the snake's den,
His rest shall be glorious
And everything that exists shall praise him

High on Life

The days of living off the land are in the past
Of setting a mile stretch of victor traps in muskrat runs,
Of hunting pheasants and quail over a good bird dog
Of owning several old reliable guns

The old trusty 97 Winchester
Was the all around best of the lot,
A 12 gauge with modified choke, slide action, and exposed
hammer
I couldn't begin to account for all the game it's got

Then there's the blot action single shot Winchester
410 model 41,
That's taken more squirrels
Than any other gun

And there is the great times of hunting waterfowl
Over a couple dozen bluebill decoys,
Huddled up in a cattail blind
With a couple other good ole boys

And ice fishing
Setting on an old wooden box,
Spudding a 7" hole
And wearing heavy clothes and 3 pair of soxs

Mushroon'n and frog'n
And dry fly fishing with a fiberglass wonderrod,
Surrounded by virgin woods and open fields
And the uncluttered beauty created by God

This was my boyhood of wonder and excitement
Growing up in a time of living off the land,
We were low on money but high on life
In a time when life was o' so grand

Victory Song

Praise be unto my God
All glory be unto my king,
My savior, my Lord, my God
Whom I trust with my everything

When I seek him
When I go to him in prayer,
When I kneel to him day or night
My God is always there

I know I am not perfect
But my father looks at me through the blood,
He's with me through the fire
And he's with me through the flood

I wouldn't know how to deal
With this world so full of sin,
Nor how to face life's many trials
Without my Lord within

I'm walking the upward journey
Surrendering all to him,
Turning, confessing, and receiving
His full pardon for my sin

There's victory o' blessed victory
At the end of life's rocky road,
If you walk the straight and narrow
That leads to the streets of gold

Praise, glory, and honor
Be unto my Lord, my God, my king,
Peace, love, and joy unending
Is the victory song I sing

God's Glorious Season

I long to see the dogwoods bloom
And the bluegills bed along the shore,
And the spring flowers spread like wildfire
All along the forest's floor

To breath the fresh clean air
Of new mown hay after a rain,
To hear the raindrops gentle patter
Tapping upon the window payne

Mushrooms bursting forth
Pushing their way up through the ground,
God's awakening of the earth to life
Without so much as a sound

The birds returning and weaving their nests
Their music filling the air,
Sweet, sweet, melodys
As they flit about and their colors flare

There is nothing that puts more zest in your step
Like springtime's warming of days,
As the wildflowers carpet the earth
In a spreading colorful blaze

The trees budding back to life
The meadows adorning bright colorful greens,
As all the glory of springtime
Paints amazingly utterly awesome scenes

Birds, butterflys, and dragonflys flit about
As God's vibrant colors take wing,
In this time of awe and wonder
Of God's glorious season of spring

Above and Beyond

My heart yearns for the eternal spring
Of God's glorious heaven above,
In the land of unending wonders
Of peace and joy and love

A place of reuniting
With loved ones who have gone on before,
A place of rejoicing
And of praising the lamb who opened the door

A place where faith becomes reality
A place where the unseen becomes seen,
A place of awesome wonder
A place of eternal spring

Peace that passeth all understanding
Joy unspeakable and full of glory,
The bible's truth unfolded
A new begining to a never ending story

Ivory mansions
In the city of gold,
Filled with the glory of God
Where all the wonders of heaven unfold

O' what a joy it will be there
Beyond this world of sorrow and pain,
In the land of endless wonders
Where we will never shed tears again

Shouting eternal halleluahs to the Lord of life
Casting our crowns before the throne,
Knowing as we are known
Forever praising and thanking God for our heavenly home

Do Something for Jesus

What have you done for Jesus today?
Isn't their some lost soul you can show the way?,
Isn't their someone hurting
For which you can pray?
What have you done for Jesus today?

So many looking for answers
So many looking in all the wrong places,
So many searching souls
With long sad lonely faces

What have you done for Jesus today?
Are you reaching out a helping hand?,
Not a hand out, but a hand up
In Jesus's name do all in this world that you can

The woman who washed Jesus's feet
Jesus said that she done what she could,
What have you done for Jesus?
In his name do something good

A smile, a hug
A word fitly spoken,
When one door closes
Another door opens

Reach out a helping hand
Give someone in need a hug,
Do something for Jesus
Give someone's heart a tug

Read and live by God's holy word
For others daily kneel and pray,
Our father in heaven is asking
What have you done for Jesus today?

Grafted

God has grafted us in
A tiny little limb,
For the greatest thing that we will ever be
Is to be a part of him

Loving God and loving others
Is the greatest commandment of them all.
For love fullfills all other commandments
And breaks down every impregnable wall

Yes! There is nothing greater
Than to be through him set free,
He who willingly paid it all
On the cruel cross of calvary

And forever let there never be
Any failings on our part,
As the love of Jesus
Fills our longing searching heart

He is the tree of life
Come one come all and be gloriously grafted in,
And by the blood of Jesus and the grace of God
Let your victorious life in Jesus begin

Let his love fill you
And may your light never flicker nor grow dim,
Knowing that the greatest thing that you will ever be
Is to be a part of him

A-men

Dreams

We all have dreams
You and I,
Without dreams
We wither and die

We live our lives
Sometimes in hopelessness it seems,
We live our lives
Pursuing to achieve our dreams

Life is full of ups and downs
It is like a yo-yo,
Don't ever give up your dreams
For it is the gold at the end of the rainbow

Hold fast
Never ever let go,
Dreams make life worth the living
It's the greatest medicine that I know

Help someone to achieve their dreams
And just maybe someone will help you achieve yours,
Dreams is for the dulldrums of depression
One of life's greatest cures

I pray for the dark clouds to pass
And for once again those bonny skys of blue,
And for all of our hopes and dreams like sunshine
To come gloriously shining through

Christians Rejoice

Sparkling diamonds
Pressed into the dark velvet of the night,
And the dark orange sphere
Creating erie shadows of pale moon light

God's masterpieces
Created so magnificently,
Glorious creations unbelievably
Made for you and for me

God is so good
He created it all for the enjoyment of mankind,
Endless wonders stretched out all across this land
Greater than any manmade wonder that you will ever find

All of creation is his handiwork
The heavens declare his glory,
Man is his crowning achievement
And Jesus and his sacrifice is God's love to a never ending story

Someday this will all be melted in fervent heat
And all the heavenly bodys will fall from the skys,
And the demons of darkness shall be cast into the lake of fire
Along with that snake of the garden of eden, that abominable
Father of lies

Christians rejoice
For before that day of God's wrath occurs,
We will be transformed and transported
From all that befalls this corruptible earth

A place far more beautiful than all that we see
A place of peace and joy where we shall forever abide,
Because of our trust in the cross of Christ
And the redeeming blood of the crucified

Bethlehem

The star of Bethlehem
Guided the kings of the east from a-far,
To shine it's glory down upon the Lord of glory
The bright and morning star

From heaven to earth he came
Through the miracle of the virgin birth,
Glorious king of kings
Creator of heaven and earth

Born in a manger
A lowly cattle stall,
Name above all names
Creator and maker of all

He came to a dying world
To pay the ultimate cost,
He came
To save the lost

He came, O' yes, he came
And on Christmas day we celebrate his miraculous birth,
As the joy of the season
Spreads it's cheer all across the earth

Songs to be sung, presents to be wrapped
Mistletoe and holly,
Christmas trees, colored lights
And the giving of gifts by golly

Without Christmas there would never have been an Easter
Without the cross we would still be lost in sin,
Praise God for that long ago miracle
That took place in the little town of Bethlehem

Bearcat

It shoots straight
The trigger pull is smooth and light,
The balance is great
And the design is a pure delight

It's the ruger bearcat
A small western style revolver,
You've got to see and try one
Believe me you will fall in love with her

In stainless steel
She's a priceless work of art,
You will love her heft and feel
And the precision of every working part

This is not just another gun
It all comes together with perfection,
Ruger has outdone themselves
And that is without question

They say that it's dead on at 25 yards
I know for a fact at 10 and 15 yards it is,
I fired several shots
With nary a miss

Now let me tell you
For a rabbit or squirrel gun,
Or for just all around plinking
This revolver is the one

Stainless ruger bearcat
Give one a try,
If your looking for a western style revolver
This is the one to buy

Are You Ready?

Are you ready, truly ready
If Jesus were to come today?,
Is your neighbor saved, are your friends?
Are your children ready for that catching away

A new day is coming
A day like no other has ever been,
It is the fullfilling of the blessed hope
When we shall go to be with him

Be ready always
To share the hope that is in you,
Let others see the Jesus
That lives in you

Don't let this world
Like a magnet hold you down,
Listen for the archangel's shout
And the trumpet's triumphant sound

Look up
For your help comes from above,
Wicks trimmed, lanterns full
Holding fast to your first love

Go about the buisness of living
With Jesus at the center of your heart,
Witness of him to the world around you
And to your own household is the place to start

Take up your cross and follow me
This is what Jesus said,
Die to self and live for him
Always spirit led

Beyond the Clouds

Now that you have washed us
And set us truly free,
Help us Lord
To be all that we can be

Touch our hearts
To be tender for others needs,
And may we always walk
Where the spirit leads

Give us the words to speak
From hearts that truly care,
And give us a compassion for souls
Their burdens and griefs to bare

Let our lives in special ways
Touch the world around us,
To prick the hearts of sin lost souls
And tenderly lead them to Jesus

I pray that we make a difference
In this world of corruption and sin,
And that our lives would reflect a saviour
That would draw souls unto him

Bless us father
To do the work yet to be done,
Before that great and wonderful day
Of the second coming of your son

Let us continually sing and shout
Our deep down heartfelt praises,
To our Lord and saviour, God of all
Who one day, beyond the clouds, shall raise us

Ever Upward

Walk the glory road
That straight and narrow way,
All other roads lead below
God says go to now without delay

We are pilgrims
Traveling in a foreign land,
A lifelong journey
That leads upward toward the promised land

Our roots are not in old terra firma
But our sights are on things above,
A place Jesus went to prepare for us
Of ivory palaces, golden streets, and joy, and peace, and love

Pilgrims we are
On a dusty road saved by grace,
Ever upward
Traveling not by sight but by faith

We believe what lies beyond
Because of the words of truth that we've read,
We believe that Jesus died and rose again
As we walk ever upward spirit led

No one can enter heaven's gates
Accept by the blood of the cross,
Many there be drowning in the sea of sin
Waiting for someone a lifeline to them to toss

The promise of heaven is a treasure to precious to hide
We must at all costs reach out,
And share the good news
Of what Jesus and the cross is all about

He Loves Even Me

Hey diddle de-de
The Lord has set me free,
O'what a joy it is
To know that Jesus loves even me

Since Jesus came into my heart
With his promise to never depart,
I'm walking the straight and narrow way
Till I walk it with Jesus in the land of eternal day

O' what a wonderful life
To no more carry sin's burdensome load,
With a song in my heart
I'm walking the glory road

Hey diddle de-de
O'what a saviour who pulled me up from life's stormy sea,
O'what a joy overflowing from my heart
That Jesus loves even me

Though the world around me
Is falling apart,
I have Jesus joy
Deep down in my heart

From the babe in the manger
To the saviour on the cross,
He came from heaven to earth
With compassion for the lost

Hey diddle de-de
It's the Christian life for me,
"Halleluah" what a saviour
Who loves even me

Half a Pair

I've lost a sock
I know not where,
All I know is
I've only half a pair

I've looked high
And I've looked low,
I know not where
My sock did go

I know that when I put on socks
I put on two,
It doesn't make any sense to wear just one
Two's just right and one's to few

I don't go around with one sock on
And one foot bare,
Now what could have happened
To half of my pair?

I've looked in the washer and the dryer
And in my sock drawer too,
I've looked and I've looked
Where it's at I have no clue

Where o' where
Has my little sock gone?,
Hey I think that would make a good title
For a song

I believe on a milk carton
I'll put my sock's picture,
I may have lost my marbles too
Of that, I'm not to sure

Don't Look Back

My son despise not the chastening of the Lord
Neither be weary of his correction,
For whom the Lord loveth he correcteth
And encourages to go on to perfection

Stoke up your faith, renew your first love
Rekindle those dying embers,
You are not alone, God is still on the throne
And his blood still has the power over everything that hinders

Believe
For faith moves mountains from out of their place,
Jesus Christ, the solid rock
Is offering you the gift of grace through faith

Don't ever give up
Don't ever give in,
Turn around, overcome
And don't go back to where you've been

If you have slidden
Get back in the race,
Step out of the pew
And step up to the altar of grace

Jesus is in the forgiving buisness
You need not be shackled to sin,
You can know the peace that passeth all understanding
By repenting and giving your life back to him

Repent, reach out, and go forth
And never look back again,
Jesus is the way, the truth, and the life
And the only doorway to heaven

The Wild Side

Life, like a two wheel iron horse
Is a long beautiful ride,
Till the day you take up wings as eagles
And fly away to the other side

Life is an adventure
To be enjoyed to the very end,
Living and sharing Jesus joy
On the highways and byways and around every bend

Two wheels is the way to see this land
An album of picturesque views on every page,
An unending joy ride
To be undertaken at any age

No watch, no destination in mind
Reach into your wild side,
And pursue that great adventure
Get on that bike and ride

Get a few Christian buddies together
And throw caution to the wind,
And hit the backroads
In an adventure without end

Share Jesus
With all you meet along the way,
Surrounded with all the smells, sights, and sounds
That abounds on life's endless highway

Two wheels and the open road
And a deep desire to ride,
Rev'm up, move'm out
Trip'n on the wild side

Thunder Road

Like thunder
Echoing across the horizon,
On the road at the breaking of day
And riding until the setting of the sun

So much to see
So little time,
A world out there of wonder and awe
A place to rejuvenate and unwind

Straddle the saddle
And take to the open road,
Wrap your fist around the throttle
And watch the world before you unfold

Avoid the thunderstorms
And don't swallow any bugs,
And install a windshield for God's sake
To protect your ugly mug

Look out for wild animals
And avoid the pot holes,
And keeping the shiny side up
Should be among your uppermost goals

And look out for the other guy
Cause most often he won't see you,
May the wind be always at your back
And the canopy overhead be skys of bonnie blue

Nothing revs your motor
Like a two wheeled power house of shiny metal and chrome,
And if you can't find someone to ride with
Take that awesome ride alone

Perfect Love

This is a dying temperal world
Heaven is an Eden beyond compare,
This world may be an awesome place
But it ain't nothing like what's over there

To see the fruits of the seeds that we've sown
To walk the golden streets with Jesus,
Knowing as we are known
With no need that anyone teach us

Seeing loved ones who have gone on before
With all their infirmities gone,
An awesome place of joy, peace, and endless wonder
With happy hearts overflowing with music and song

Beyond the portals of time
A place where awesome never ends,
A place of sweet reunion
With long ago departed friends

A place to raise our praise to the Lord
A place of endless wonders to roam,
A place far from the lake of fire
A place we Christians call home

Wether we live or die
Know that Jesus is always near,
And when we step from time into eternity
His perfect love will cast out all fear

Go towards the light
Heart and soul at peace,
Into the very prescence
Of he whose perfect love shall never cease

Broken Hearts

Both of my grandpas
Succomed to the same fate,
Dying of a broken heart
When they lost their life mate

A love so grand
A love so pure,
That to lose that loved one
Created a hurt with no cure

It is like a dagger in the heart
A raw aching pain,
A loss that can never be replaced
They could never love another like that again

A hurt so deep
A hurt that would not go away,
The sunshine would never rise in their hearts again
The dark clouds overshadowed their day

As God gave Adam Eve
So he gave Alice to me,
And our love for one another
Is an open book for all to see

She is to me
A ray of glorious sunshine,
A marriage blessed by God
To last a lifetime

I pray take the darkness
And turn it into day,
I pray O' Lord God
Don't take my sunshine away

Honor the Gifts

The body of Christ
Consists of various integreal parts,
Each is a gift from God
To touch the cold hard hearts

We each have a gift
To use while upon this earth,
Given to give glory to God
Some through song and myrth

Some he has given the gift of healing
Some teachers,
Some the gift of prophesy
Some preachers

There are prayer warriors
And there are evagelists,
We each have our place
On God's list

If you take away
Any one of these,
It is God
That you displease

The foot is important
As well as the hand,
Do not dismember the parts
For each has a place in God's plan

So wether it's the preacher or teacher
Or those talented in music or gifted in poem,
Honor them and their God given gifts
Till that glorious day that God comes to take you home

Special Angel

Tears flow freely
From a heart so tender and pure,
There is so much beauty
That lies deep within her

When someone on T.V.
Is hurting or dies,
Tears swell up in her eyes
And she unashamedly breaks down and crys

What she went through
Is a terrible crippling thing,
And yet she clings to her savior
And the voice within her continues to sing

She has born this heavy load
With Narry a complaint,
She is as close as I've ever known
Of someone who is a saint

God I love that woman
She is the light of my life,
I don't deserve this beautiful lady
That God gave me for a wife

I'll love her
As long as I live,
To me she is the greatest earthly treasure
That God could ever give

A very special angel
With a heart sweet and pure,
Who loves me
And O' God I love her

To Live Again

I would like to walk in the woods again
When the wild flowers bloom,
And smell the fresh clean air
And search for the tasty morel mushroom

And flip a dry fly
With an old fiberglass Shakespear wonder rod,
To fish calm blue waters
Alone, just me and God

To walk into the woods
At the first breaking of day,
And sit down amongst the shagbarks
And patiently await for a squirrle to come my way

Listening for the gnawing sounds
And the russel of leaves in a tree top,
Clutching a ruger single six
Hoping for a nice clean shot

And tracking rabbits
In the snow,
Just being able to get up
And get out and go

To gather nuts in the fall
And berries in the spring,
And listen for the whipperwills
And their haunting night songs that they sing

To sleep under the stars
And smell the sweet smell of a campfire,
Listening to the night sounds
As the ghostly smoke rises higher and higher

O' To live again
And do all the things I use to do,
My life is in your hands O' God
I entrust it all to you

Faith

Just as rain and snow
Is far from sunny weather,
So faith and doubt
Does not go together

You must believe
To come before God's throne,
Before you can claim him
As your own

Faith is what seperates
The sisters and the brothers,
From the rest of the world
Of unbelieving others

What we see and believe
Is what lies before our face,
What we do not see and yet believe
This is faith

Without faith
It is impossible to please him,
Without faith in the blood of the lamb
We cannot be cleansed from sin

The windows of heaven open to faith
That Godly desires may pass from here to there,
A clean heart asking anything according to God's will
Is answered when presented to the father in Jesus's name through
prayer

Faith in the blood applied
Is salvation for the soul,
Faith takes the broken pieces
And restores and makes one whole

Dust on the Bible

Is the book of the rock of ages
Collecting dust upon the mantle,
Hiding those words of life my friend
Which to your spiritual health is O' so very vital

Take that book down
Dust it off, open it up, and read it again,
And God will bless and reveal unto you
The hidden treasures that are written therein

These are your guide for life
God breathed words to live by,
They will keep you on the straight and narrow
When to the trials of life they are applied

Trust Jesus as your Lord and Savior
And make him your closest dearest friend,
And don't let the dust gather on your bible
Ever, ever again

Words of life
To be read over and over again,
Sin will keep you from this book
This book will keep you from sin

Dust it off, pick it up
And fill your soul with heavenly light,
Write these words upon the tables of your heart
These precious, O' so precious, words of life

Don't let the dust collect
Upon the good book's sacred cover
The book of the one and only true God
Of which there is no other